John R Flippin

Sketches from the Mountains of Mexico

John R Flippin

Sketches from the Mountains of Mexico

ISBN/EAN: 9783337317232

Printed in Europe, USA, Canada, Australia, Japan

Cover: Foto ©Andreas Hilbeck / pixelio.de

More available books at **www.hansebooks.com**

SKETCHES

FROM THE

MOUNTAINS OF MEXICO

BY

J. R. FLIPPIN

CINCINNATI
STANDARD PUBLISHING COMPANY
1889

DEDICATION.

To my beloved wife, MILDRED ADELIA FLIPPIN, the following pages, written in a foreign land, and often in much suffering, are affectionately inscribed. Her patience, devotion, courage and counsels through the long, weary years have been my strength and inspiration. 'T is true a poor tribute to such noble worth; but, such as it is, rich with the wealth of a loving heart.　　　J. R. F.

CONTENTS.

CHAPTER I.

Written from Guadeloupe y Calvo.—Eight thousand feet high.—Freight packed in.—Solitudes. Mt. Murynoira, trout, fleas, dogs, etc.......... 1–6

CHAPTER II.

Agriculture.—Ploughs.—Carts.—Beans.—Tortillas. Fruits.—Woods.—Rattlesnakes, lizards, etc. ... 7–11

CHAPTER III.

Mint output.—Tlacos.—Money.—Merchants.—Style. Women.—Marriage. 12–18

CHAPTER IV.

Examples of Mexican style.—Mexican miner.—Lying.—Cranks 19–25

CHAPTER V.

Indians. — Apaches. — Comanches. — Priests. — Schools.—Penmanship....................... 26–33

CHAPTER VI.

Mexican no conception of value of time.—Hospitality.—" Col. Lo."—Negroes............... 34–40

CONTENTS.

CHAPTER VII.

Mining.—What is required.—Some observation.—
Uncertainty. 41–48

CHAPTER VIII.

Be cautious as to mining investments—Districts.
Balopilas. — Galena.— Cuervo.— Gaudeloupe y
Calvo 49–56

CHAPTER IX.

Dynamite.— Blasting. — Metal stealing.— Receivers.
Perils of miners............................... 57–63

CHAPTER X.

Gambling.—Its results.—How metal is taken from
mines at times.—First experience in going down
ladders. 64–69

CHAPTER XI.

Metal.—Where found.—How extracted.—Failings.
Retorting.................................... 70–73

CHAPTER XII.

Assaying. 74–77

CHAPTER XIII.

Bullion trains. — Comparative safety. — Factions. —
Revolutions. 78–83

CHAPTER XIV.

A revolutionist.—Their mode of operations.—Effect
on capital.— Railroads. — Freights.— Prices of
flour, sugar, etc............................. 84–90

CHAPTER XV.

Mexican Railroad.—Difficulty of making in mountains. —A Georgia railroad.—Telegraphs....... 91–97

CHAPTER XVI.

Postal service.—Experiment to improve it.—Postman's troubles. — Postoffice officials. — Newspapers.. 98–105

CHAPTER XVII.

Navigable streams. —Navy. — Army — Indian depredations. 106-113

CHAPTER XVIII.

Mexican soldiers.—Apaches.—Indian policy.—Yaquis.—Majos.—Home attachment.............114–121

CHAPTER XIX.

Regulators.—Their procedure.—An incident......122–128

CHAPTER XX.

Mexican judges. — Polico. — Carrying pistols. — Knives. 129–136

CHAPTER XXI.

Public order—Texan murdered.— "Accordados."— Mountain lawyer.—Modesty and attainments.137-148

CHAPTER XXII.

Little children.—How they live.—Mortality.—St. John's day.--Dress. 149–157

CHAPTER XXIII.

Peon character. — Lying. — Perfidious. — Labor.— Drunkenness. — Religious life. — Sacred worship..158–169

CHAPTER XXIV.

Miners.—Plan of education.—Incest.—Incident.....170–173

CHAPTER XXV.

A style of dress.—Peonage system............ ...174-179

CHAPTER XXVI.

Creditor Class.—Extortion.—Conscienceless.......180-183

CHAPTER XXVII.

Large landed estates.—Policy as to these.—Transfer of property.—Tax gatherers...................184-189

CHAPTER XXVIII.

Duties.—Smugglers.— Incident.— Imports.— Stamp Duties.—State Taxes.—Municipal Taxation....190-197

CHAPTER XXIX.

Resources.—Population.— Agricultural products.— Mines.—Mexicans as business men.—Security of life and property.—Foreigners mistreated......198-207

CHAPTER XXX.

Difference between our Government and England and Germany as to their subjects abroad.—Incidents.—Traveling in the mountains..........208-212

CHAPTER XXXI.

Ambuscaded by robbers.—Captured.—Tied down.—Robbed.—Escaped.—Observations.............213-224

CHAPTER XXXII.

Murder of an American in the mountains.—Crosses.—Murder of Senator Cooper.—National sympathies.—Immigration desired................225-236

CHAPTER XXXIII.

Reciprocity treaty.—Its aims.—Mexico as a manufacturing country...........................237-244

CHAPTER XXXIV.

Amusements.—Bulltail pulling, etc.—Eggshell performance..................................245-254

CHAPTER XXXV.

Dance.—Dress, etc......................... 255-259

CHAPTER XXXVI.

Bull fight................................. 260-265

CHAPTER XXXVII.

Drinking general.—Evil effects....................266-270

CHAPTER XXXVIII.

Profanity.—Burial customs......................271-276

CHAPTER XXXIX.

Marriages.—How celebrated.—Courting..... 277-284

CHAPTER XL.

Handshaking. — Cutting trees out of the path.—
Cigarette smoking........................ 285-490

CHAPTER XLI.

Rawhides.—Uses.—Wooden pins.—Abode houses.—
Sanitation.—Diseases'..................:..........291-296

CHAPTER XLII.

Yellow fever.—Small-pox.—Mountain Doctor......297-303

CHAPTER XLIII.

Servants.—Gala days.—Population.—Fecundity....304-311

CHAPTER XLIV.

Tournament in South.—Some of our own follies
compared with those of the Mexican..........312-315

CHAPTER XLV.

Scenery.—Rocks.— Mountains.— Flowers.— Atmosphere.—Mountain Torrent.—Rainbow scenes..316-323

CHAPTER XLVI.

Cooking.—"Chile con carne."—"Calabasa" edible. Hogs..324-330

CHAPTER LXVII.

Storms.—Constitution of Mexico.—Important provisions.......................................331-338

CHAPTER XLVIII.

Constitution continued.—International board of arbitration 339-345

CHAPTER XLIX.

Character of the mountaineers.—Missionaries 346-350

CHAPTER L.

How Americans are treated.—Business methods....351-356

CHAPTER LI.

Marrying in the country........................357-364

CHAPTER LII.

Conquest.—Historical facts.—Public debt.—Acquiring real estate..................................365-373

CHAPTER LIII.

Casas grandes.— Legend.— Mexico, land of wonders.—City of Chihuahua.—Cathedral.........374-381

CHAPTER LIV.

Institutions of Chihuahua.—Iron mine of Durango. Education.......................................382-389

CHAPTER LV.

The tramp.—Local attachments.—Packers.—Incidents 390-399

CHAPTER LVI.

Cargadores.—El Burro 400-405

CHAPTER LVII.

Suggestions as to reforms 406-411

CHAPTER LVIII.

General reflections 412-418

CHAPTER LIX.

General reflections—Concluded. 419-427

CHAPTER LX.

Conclusion.—Love of the old flag when seen from a foreign land 428-433

INTRODUCTION.

These pages, in a series of letters, were written from the village of Guadalupe y Calvo, in the southwestern part of the State of Chihauhau, Mexico, in 1877. The village is located in the center of the Sierra Madre range, to cross which one must travel, on foot or mounted, four hundred miles. It is truly to the outside world a "terra incognita." Of the dwellers in these mountains, their habits, customs, laws, industries, modes of business, travel and living, as well as the scenery, products, mining, antiquities, etc., found there, I have undertaken to describe. A residence of nearly five years has given me an opportunity unenjoyed by others to faithfully delineate these things. I trust my readers, while recognizing and indulgent to my faults, may nevertheless find but few pages unentertaining or uninstructive. In passing from subject to subject I have philosophized a little at times, the pertinency of which may be perceived by my readers. With these remarks to the reading public, I introduce these "Sketches from the Mountains of Mexico."   J. R. FLIPPIN.

Memphis, Tenn., May, 1889.

SKETCHES FROM THE MOUNTAINS OF MEXICO

CHAPTER I.

WRITTEN FROM GUADELOUPE Y CALVO.—EIGHT THOUSAND FEET HIGH.—FREIGHT PACKED IN.—SOLITUDES.—MT. MURYNOIRA, TROUT, FLEAS, DOGS, ETC.

I write from these mountains, the heart of the Sierra Madre. This place has an altitude of eight thousand feet, and to the south and west for more than two hundred miles the mountains extend, and to the north for five hundred or more. Parral, a city of some fifteen thousand inhabitants, is distant nearly two hundred miles to the northeast, and Culiacan, the capital of the adjoining State, Sinaloa, containing nearly eighteen thousand people, is two hundred miles to the south. From those two places all freight comes to this and other mountain points, packed on the backs of mules and that other animal called here a *burro*, but which has not been inaptly termed the " mountain schooner." Every class of freight must come in this way, trunks, boxes, barrels, mining machinery. But all machinery must be made sectional, so that no pieces will weigh over three hundred pounds, which is called a "carga," or mule load. Heavy machinery must be bolted together after it reaches its destination in the mountains. In this way they bring in steam engines, boilers and hoisting works. The mules travel from ten to fifteen miles a day. Long trains of these animals may be seen toiling up and down the mountain sides with their heavy cargoes, and thus it has gone on from time immemorial. There are no roads here, nothing but trails, and these only wide enough for one mule to pass along. In many places the mountain sides have been worn for many feet in depth by the hoofs of passing trains. This seems almost incredible, but the continual tramping, as the continual dropping, will wear away stone. Through a long succession of years these things have been going on, and the Mexican muleteer of to-day is the same as his ancestors were hundreds of years ago. The mountaineer is content to " live and move and have his being" undisturbed by the influences of the outside world. He is no progressionist. But as to his characteristics I may more particularly describe them in some subsequent chapter. Writing from this isolated spot I do not undertake to pass Mexico in panorama, but will confine myself chiefly to this section and its people. Books of travel may instruct and entertain their readers with vivid portraitures of Mexican life in its higher phases, but I shall content myself with speaking of these surroundings, and those who dwell in these high solitudes. I repeat solitudes, for those who have never been here can have no conception of these mountains nor of their inhabitants. I am a firm believer in climatic influences. Here you may travel for days without seeing a living creature with probably the exception of some wandering bird, and this seems lost in its lonely flight. The stillness is oppressive. On every hand are the everlasting mountains, one rising on the other, as far as the vision can stretch. At times we feel awed at the contemplation of such vistas and feel our utter insignificance amid these wondrous works of God. Again I have asked myself for what purpose are these in the divine economy? Few and far between are the spots susceptible of culture, but somehow a precarious living is obtained. About twenty miles from this place (Guadaloupe y Calvo) is Mount Murynoira, nearly fourteen thousand feet high. Some years ago I remember passing around its base one March morning, and while the sunshine was beautiful below, its summit was pavillioned in clouds. The scene was awe-inspiring. I could but think of Mount Sinai, its lightnings and thunder, and Moses, the great lawgiver, in conference with God touching the destiny of our race. I could but recall the mountains of sacred history and the scenes they have witnessed in the buried ages of the past. Mountains, like the ocean, broaden our thoughts, deepen our feelings and inspire our reverence to Him who for wise purposes of his own made them all. It is said that the ascent is so gradual in reaching the summit of the Rocky Mountains that one does not know it, but here their sides are almost precipitous, and between them are deep canyons, immense gorges for hundreds of feet below, picturesque but wild in their scenery. In these odorless flowers may be seen wasting their beauty on the air. Bright water and flashing cascades greet the traveler in his torturous wanderings, waking the mountain echoes with their weird psalmody. In these streams are found the mountain trout, for they live in none other than the coldest waters fed by the melting snows. The angling disciples of Isaak Walton might linger here, and sigh for no other earthly paradise. There is no better water in the world, and the temperance advocate with a glass of this in his hand, fresh from its home in the hills, would be invincible. The climate, too, is simply unequaled. Here the thermometer in midsummer reaches about 70, but blankets are indispensable every night in the year. No flies nor mosquitoes to irritate you with their annoying presence, but when one folds the drapery of the couch around him he can "lie down to pleasant dreams." We can not plead exemption from the fleas, those nimble-footed pests which here, as elsewhere, claim such an undue share of female attention. Their presence in such quantities may be in a measure ascribed to the number of dogs thought necessary to complement the life of the average Mexican, for they so abound that no census taker can number them. I am aware that Constantinople has her reputation well established in this particular, but in a world's show of dogs I am sure that Mexico could take both "premium and certificate" for extremes of size, differences of appearance, varieties of breed and general and particular worthlessness. The poorer the *peon* the more numerous his canine retinue. It may be they have found their affinity! *Quien sabe?* Here is the hairless dog, appearing as if he had been wrapped up in a peace of tanned leather. "Blanche, Tray and Sweetheart" are all here, and are living with their "uncles, cousins and aunts."

I have written somewhat at length of this integral feature of Mexican life as it is; were I to omit to do so, I would be an unfaithful chronicler of these times. This is my apology, not to the dogs, but to my readers, for what I have said. I charge this animal with harboring the Mexican flea. This fact alone should put him beyond the pale of human sympathy. The American flea is a gentleman compared wih his Mexican kinsman. The latter is no respecter of age, animal, sex or condition. In the United States, when hotly pursued by day or night, he disports himself from limb to limb and eludes the keenest search in folds or hose, serving simply, in the parenthesis of attention given him, to break the monotony of the moment and excite a good-natured smile upon the part of the luckless hunter. Not so here. This Mexican flea was born hungry and has been underfed all his life. His bite is a sting, and he bites at every opportunity, and everything else, with probably the exception of the cactus plant. He scarcely flees when man pursues, but dies a martyr to his ravenous appetite. The sufferer carries with him for days mementos of his supple foe. I should be glad to dismiss him with a better character, but if I have done him rank injustice then "let other men and other times rise to do him justice." But I have written enough, too much, too, for the present; so good-by. More anon.

CHAPTER II.

AGRICULTURE. — PLOUGHS. — CARTS. — BEANS. — TORTILLAS. — FRUITS. — WOODS. — RATTLESNAKES.—LIZZARDS, ETC.

Agriculture in these mountains is imperfectly understood and badly practiced. Corn is the chief support, and this sells very high. The natives here of all conditions of life grind it between two stones. This improvised mill, rude and simple, is a part of every household. The pack trains carry these stones with them, so that when they stop they can, in a few minutes, set their mill to grinding with no other motive power than human muscle. The same kind of a mill was used, I doubt not, in the patriarchal ages, and the Mexican cares nought for the new-fangled labor-saving machinery of the nineteenth century. In this connection I might mention the fact that he uses still the wooden plough with no handles, but while one holds the upright portion, another drives the yoke of oxen. So you see they believe in the " division of labor," of which political economists write so much. This is, too, the same kind of a plough, if pictorial representations are not at fault, that Abraham told Isaac to bring in out of the weather after having finished the ploughing commanded by Paterfamilias. I like it for its antiquity, but for its serviceableness it will never so tickle the earth as to make it "laugh with a harvest." Some years since I learned some enterprising agricultural implement-maker shipped a lot of ploughs into this country, and some of them were sent out to certain ranches, but what was the surprise of the aforesaid when, going out to see what progress had been made with the ploughs, to find that every handle had been cut off! Scarcely sufficient intelligence to see the adaptation of things. These ploughs are drawn by oxen yoked not with bows to the necks, but with yokes tied immediately behind the horns, so that, in fact, they push the load instead of pulling it. But this is their way, and it is good enough for them, they think, inasmuch as their remotest ancestors did the thing that way, and none other will they have. Here we have no kind of vehicles, as there are no roads; but lower down, where there is some level land, carts are used to a limited extent. These have large wooden wheels, very rude and ungainly in appearance, with no iron tires. As many as six and eight yoke of oxen may be seen dragging these ponderous two-wheeled carts. And in the plains, often, eighteen and twenty mules are hitched to one of these enormous wagons. The mules are small, and what they lack in size they make up in numbers. Nearly all the stage-coaches of the country have mules four abreast. And they go, too, with the speed of Mr. John Gilpin, of dear memory. I have timed them as they flew along the stony road between stations, making nearly ten miles an hour. These coaches have two drivers, one with the reins and the other with the whip and "a pocket full of rocks," the latter to throw and strike the more distant mules. These Mexican teamsters do everything by main strength, mere brute force. The good soul of Berg would die from sheer vexation were he to witness their brutalities for a brief period. But I find I am somewhat digressing, and did not speak of the other agricultural products of these mountains. There is a certain kind of beans raised here which, in fact, is the national dish; the rich and poor eat it, and no dining and no meal is thought to be complete without its presence. It is very nutritious, and it is well it is so, for but few of the poorer classes can afford to purchase meat. The staple commodities of living are corn and beans, from year to year, from generation to generation. From corn is made a thin cake called *tortillas*, and with this he scoops up his beans from some earthen vessel, ignoring knife, fork and spoon, if rich enough to possess them. The way one eats is a pretty good sign how he has been raised. Culture, or the want of it, will manifest itself at the table. Good "table manners" are highly desirable. Fruits abound to some extent. Here I have seen in the month of December, early part, the trees laden with ripe peaches of fine quality. Apples are very idifferent, small and insipid. But we are near enough to the warm country to get many of the tropical fruits. Oranges are plentiful, and I never before saw them from blossom to matured fruit and all intermediate stages on the same tree. Lemons grow wild in the woods. Watermelons grow in the sands along the shores of the rivers. And many other fruits of unpronounceable names, but delicious taste flourish in luxuriance. Cotton, when it grows at all, is no longer an annual, but the same stalks bear a succession of crops. The mountain sides are covered in many places with fine pasturage, which is perennial. In some portions game abounds—deer, bear, coyote, a species of wolf, and the lion. The latter I have never encountered, and shall postpone this introduction to a more convenient season. The mountains are covered with fine pines, in some places with oak, depending upon the altitude. There are many other species of wood, the different names of which I do not now recall. Walnut and cedar also abound. Centipedes and tarantulas are seldom seen in these high localities. The rattlesnakes find a lurking place amid these rocks and clefts, and sometimes betray an intrusiveness and familiarity irreconcilable with personal safety.

Some years since, Prof. Lupton, of Vanderbilt University, in coming over the mountains, spread his blankets upon the ground, as is customary, for the night, but when removing them next morning found a rattlesnake during the night had crawled in and warmly ensconced himself from the chilly mountain air. It is said politics make strange bedfellows; who knows but in this way his snakeship was testifying his approval of the learned professor's views upon our home or foreign policy? Be this as it may, these are sometimes the incidental happenings of the mountain tourist, which leave an experience for the remainder of life, however protracted. Lizzards and scorpions exist in great numbers and endless variety, always obtrusive and always unwelcome.

CHAPTER III.

MINT OUTPUT. — TLACOS. —MONEY.—MERCHANTS. —STYLE.—WOMEN.—MARRIAGE.

In these mountains have been found and worked for long ages the precious metals, gold and silver. Mexico I think, according to well anthenticated statistics has furnished to commerce more than half the silver of the world. Her coinage output since the opening of her mints up to June 30, 1886 was $3,272,452,670.12. Look at these figures again, are they not enormous? And yet digging, delving and coining goes on. Her mountains are furnishing the financial currents to vitalize in no little measure the commerce and industries of the age. These giant mountains then, "rock-ribbed and ancient as the Sun," are not without their mission, in the wisdom of their great Author. Here during the long cycles of the past have remained locked up the treasures of the nations. Abuse Mexico if you will, decry her people and criticise the government, the fact still remains it is the very *home* of the precious metals. This mountain range with its untold mines extends throughout the entire length of

THE MOUNTAINS OF MEXICO. 13

this republic on its western slope, and I think the Andes in South America are but a continuation of the same range with their fabulous history of mineral wealth. Upon bullion there is an export tax of $4.41, but upon coined dollars there is no export duty. The mints of the country are leased to private parties, who for the privilege pay a high compensation. A singular feature of the governmental policy is that private individuals should coin the money of the country, but such is the fact. The origin of the matter, I presume was this, that to meet with ready money the pressing necessities of the government, it resorted to the leasing expedient. In this section there is no paper currency, but silver and copper, gold being rarely seen. The copper pieces were coined for three cent pieces, but these have been debased by public authority fifty per cent. These are called "*tlacos*," (pronounced as if written *claquers*) and it takes sixty-four of them to make a dollar. So you see for a little work one receives big pay. Lycurgus caused iron money to be made of such ponderous size that to take a few pieces of change to the market would require a vehicle of some description. His object was to prevent the love of money from corrupting the virtue of his people. Who knows but that Mexican statesman and financiers may have read up on the old Spartan and are trying the experiment of "hefty money" on their constituents in the Western World? It is a point blank, unmitigated nuisance. There are some banks in the large cities, with large capital which do a fine business, but in these mountains a bank bill is almost as great a curiosity as a college diploma. Some enterprising merchants attempted the introduction of paper money here some months since, but they were looked upon by the rest of the community as most promising candidates for some unerected lunatic asylum. They were about a century or a century and a half in advance of their contemporaries, and the spasmodic effort at the reform of our circulating medium is now numbered with the forgotten nothings of the past. Some similar project may be revived here after the lapse of a few decades when these antiquarians of the granite formation, shall be sleeping beneath the daffodils and daisies.

There is one thing which can be said to the credit of these mountain merchants, they seldom break. Bankruptcy laws are unknown, and the personal credit of the purchasing merchant is more looked to than his actual ability to pay and the compulsory means of payment. They seldom resort to law to enforce collection. His ability to purchase goods, depends upon his faithfulness and punctuality in meeting payments when due. To be protested is almost tantamount to being disgraced.

These merchants, scattered over the Sierras hundreds of miles from Mazatlan, where they make their purchases, I am told after they have left that place with their stocks of goods, may not be heard from for many months, but when their paper becomes due, they almost invariably meet it. They get long credit, and do not trouble themselves much about their indebtness until the maturity of their obligations approaches. The freights being very high, packed in by mules, they sell at figures exceedingly steep. In fact, it is seldom I presume, when they do not make the "Dutchman's one per cent." The merchants look upon themselves as forming the upper crust of society, and hence the ambition of all nearly, is to become merchants. If one is a merchant and in addition owns a side patch of mountain land with a few antiquated adobe huts, then he is "lord of the manor," and after the manner of the autocrat he demeaneth himself. They are very fond of style, and the more and "louder" the style, the more intense is their satisfaction. Gay colors and showy equipages, and particuarly white handled pistols captivate their innermost souls. With them one without style is worse than "poor white trash" in the estimation of our old colored brother in ante bellum times. This love of finery and foolishness, is not limited to one class, but prevades all ranks and conditions. The children imbibe it with their mother's milk and the mother transmits it to the children as their chief heritage. Fine horses, silver mounted saddles, and heavily plated spurs "get away" with all of them. The very children sigh for the speedy coming of the day when they too can ride richly caparisoned steeds, with saddles, and bridles, and spurs, bespangled with silver ornamentations. These things are suggestive of barbaric splendors, and such tastes define pretty well the degree of civilization existing. So then, if you would capture good treatment from the most of them, and the worst of them, give them "good style," and then " stare fate in the face."

The Mexican's object in acquiring money is to live in style, to appear gorgeous before his fellows, and as he goes dashing by on his curveting steed to make the spectators, " poor white folks " commit suicide from superheated envy and thus escape another such vision. While thus passing in review his old friends and neighbors, "he smiles, and smiles and murders while he smiles." Then black-eyed senoritas inspire to deeds of "high emprize" by their encouraging presence these fearless cavaliers. But when did femininity do otherwise? Call her what nationality you please, it matters not in what clime she dwells, in polar snows, or under eqatorial suns, the self-same power she has in the nineteenth century to make man a hero of chivalry, as she had in the twilight of history to convert him into a demigod. The women here are a great deal better than the men—I reckon it is so everywhere. Metaphorically speaking they are made out of a better clay, endure more and last longer. It is well it is so in this land, for the most of them are "hewers of wood and drawers of water." They are practically in a state of serfdom. Their husbands are jealous and tyrannous. Their homes are not homes. There is no such word as home in the language. Domestic felicity is the exception. The fire-side and the hearth are no sacred places over which will linger the sweet memories of the "long ago." Hovels of misery can not be fashioned into homes of happiness. Marriage is said to have been the only institution which survived the fall. But here marriage itself has fallen. This sacred relation is viewed with comparative indifference. The consequences are disastrous to good morals and order. For often the domineering husband becomes the licentious debauchee and ends his life in crime; the poverty-stricken woman with her numerous progeny is abandoned to want and the merciless tempests of the world. This picture is not overdrawn, but simply realistic. I do not say that the average Mexican is not affectionate towards his wife and children, it were unnatural to be otherwise, but this affection with him seems to be a shallow current, with no life long spring for its source. There is a certain philosophy for this state of things, at all events, a theory which may serve as a solution of the matter. Their education and habits of life have much to do with this question. No high moral motives exert their controlling influences upon the Mexican. He has been raised to look upon woman as his inferior, and she has been taught in the same school, and hence plods along in the same beaten track, yielding an unquestioning obedience to her liege lord's unreasonable exactions. To her his word is law, and her disobedience meets with a summary punishment. And here, as in other parts, although abused and beaten by the brute, she unmurmuringly submits, and with a devotion worthy of a better object, she will plead for his relief from a well-merited punishment. Human nature is a unity, and woman's nature is the same at all times and in every place. When he grows weary of her, as a well-worn garment he lays her aside, or if he still retains her, he acquires another new garment of the same pattern, the last completely supplanting the former. She has nothing and can do nothing, and has no spirit to resist the heartless affront. Brought up with these views of the marital relation, she can make no new departures. She neither has heard nor knows of anything better, and thus lives on in sufferance and in suffering to the end. She is the veriest menial and he the supercilious grandee, for whom she toils night and day to minister to his arrogance and grandiloquent style. Illustrations are not wanting to verify this statement, as to the sacrifices made upon the part of the wife to keep up appearances on the part of the husband, so-called.

CHAPTER IV.

EXAMPLES OF MEXICAN STYLE.—MEXICAN MINER.
—LYING.—CRANKS.

I was speaking at the close of my last chapter of the supercilious and ridiculous arrogance of the Mexican and the servility and submission of his wife. Suffer me to begin this with an illustration. There is a couple living a short distance from this village. The man is probably not worth fifty dollars in the world, yet on Sunday evenings he must repair to the village some half a mile distant, to make an exhibition of himself. And however cold or warm the day he arrays himself for the occasion by wearing a white linen coat of the "Seymour pattern," with immense cuffs that reach about midway between wrist and elbows and then with ponderous stick strikes out in advance with his meek wife at a respectful distance in the rear, and she followed in turn at a given distance by a small boy bearing the cheap overcoat of the aforesaid, which in some way or other he has managed to acquire. In this way he makes his triumphal entrance into the village to the manifest delectation of his gazing beholders. But when he returns that *overcoat* is brought into requisition regardless of weather. The transformation scene is completed in act second and he retraces his steps in the same manner to his starting point, which when reached, an air of supreme satisfaction irradiates his countenance, and his vanity is surpressed until the ensuing Sunday.

Some one has said the more he saw of a certain person the better he liked a dog. I do not say this in reference to these people, far from it, but I will say the more I see of them the better I like my own countrymen. National pride is stimulated when I look upon the people of other nationalities, contrast the differences between them in education, morals and everything which goes to make up manhood. Absence only intensifies these home attractions, and no foreign residence can ever wean away the allegiance of a true American. He has breathed all his life the spirit of liberty and law and, whenever he sees a deprivation of the one, and violation of the other, this earnest protest of his nature is awakened. And especially is this so when he sees the natural rights of woman eschewed, and her wrongs unredressed.

It is scarcely within the province of this volume to institute farther comparison between the condition of women here and in our own country. Those, who claim to be higher in caste than the lower order by reason of having more money, or if not having this, then for the fact that some of their ancestors had it, are of but little value in any point of view. "They neither toil nor spin." Work is disgraceful and they would consider themselves as outlawed from the pale of soceity were they to be caught taking home from a shopping excursion the lightest of their purchases, and these are necessarily light from the lightness of their purses. But few mountaineers are wealthy. One may own a few head of stock and a corn patch hidden in some deep canyon or hung upon some mountain side but, all told, will not aggregate more than a few thousand dollars. If he has a mining interest he will talk more flippantly of his expectations, and if you will only listen to him and believe one hundreth part of his statements you may become impressed with his future importance.

But I unhesitatingly affirm that the Mexican miner does not, and probably can not tell the truth about mining matters. I am aware that it is affirmed by metaphysicians that if we take the case of the most notorious liar, that he will speak the truth a dozen times where he tells a falsehood once. That is it is natural to tell the truth and a perversion of nature not to tell it. Those book men never knew a Mexican miner, and wrote at random. Lying with him, as stealing with the

Spartans, is considered a virtue, when not found out. Detection is the disgrace and not the fact, itself. And this is strange too that they will not tell the truth for cash, when they can tell a lie on credit, in reference to mining property. I have known some Mexicans otherwise considered as exemplars in society, models of good breeding, intelligent and kind hearted, yet when approached upon the mining question, went all to pieces and in a few minutes forfeited all their past reputation as good citizens. Now I will not say that this is a characteristic exclusively belonging to the Mexicans. Not so. Americans also betray a marked weakness on the same subject. Right in every thing else, they lie all along the line about their mining claims. There must be something in the subject matter itself, in the atmosphere which surrounds it, that frightens truth away. In moments of introspection I sometimes ask myself the question, old fellow have n't you drifted too just a little from your old moorings and of late veered a little from Truth's reckonings? It is a most fascinating and delusive business, hope ever leading the way and gilding the future with roseate expectations, and golden fruits. The contemplation of such things so long, and the thoughts born of the desire to see their realization so warmly entertained, are calculated to mislead, and betray one into saying and doing things based upon high hope, more than upon fact. May he not unconsciously lie? Lying then to some extent seems to be an inseparable concomitant of the average mining man it matters not whence he hails.

But the veteran miner frequently manifests another striking characteristic, crankiness. I have particularly observed that in this section. Great numbers of Americans and others swarm into these mountains from the States of California, Nevada and from Arizona and New Mexico, all of them broke and nearly all of them with some abnormal development. They have had hard lives and rough experiences; with the dream of earlier life unrealized, they now flock from place to place seeking to recover their fallen fortunes and at some time or other get " back home again." Misfortune and disappointments have soured their dispositions, and the evenings of their existence having grown from bad to worse find them as the veriest of cranks. With them nothing is right, everything is wrong. Without a dollar in their pockets as an evidence of their past good judgments, they will criticize everything and everybody, and immodestly failing to remember that their own lives have been demonstrated failures they will launch their anathemas against the business abilities and management of others. It is an amusement not unmingled with a small modicum of disgust to hear them ventilate their opinions and obtrusively make suggestions of the most gratuitous character. The owners of property costing hundreds of thousand dollars which has been paid for by prudence, economy and sound business tact are the merest simpletons in the estimation of these peripatetic cranks, and know nothing in comparison with themselves, who as employes of the owners, are as a temporary shift, glad to hire for a few dollars, fill up for a few days, and then fly away to some other camping grounds to re-enact the role of their former life. Impudence is one of their shining virtues.

These gentry do not all live in these mountains; their homes are not limited by parallels of latitude or longitude. I have referred to the mining crank for the reason that I suppose he is more gorgeous in his pretensions and unblushing in his conceit than all others. I am continually reminded of a story of some Eastern crank I heard some years since. Some magnificent vessel, costing nearly a million of dollars was being launched when something became disarranged greatly imperilling the vessel for the time. Just then at the critical period, during the suspense, and when silence reigned among the thousands present, a seedy fellow stepped forward trowserless where trowsers should be, a regular tramp crank, and cried out at the top of his voice, "*turn her loose, I will be responsible for her.*" The story ends here, I am sorry to say, leaving the vessel in a state of suspended animation and at the mercy of the crank. Forgive me if I have paid too much deference to this specimen of the genus homo. I have been the victim of so many of his annoyances, I could not well let him pass without some fitting recognition of his multiform virtues. And now with one more thrust of my pen, I consign him to the oblivion he deserves, with the heart-expressed hope he may never in these parts reappear among the living again.

CHAPTER V.

INDIANS.— APACHES. — CAMANCHES. — PRIESTS.— SCHOOLS. — PENMANSHIP.

Heretofore I have failed to mention the fact that near this place live several large tribes of Indians. Many years ago, I had read about the Indians and the Indian legends, until an unusual interest had been excited in their behalf, and for these braves an undue sympathy had been enlisted. I do not doubt I am repeating the feelings and experience of many others. But, at that time, being nothing more than a tender-hearted, sympathetic youth, I had never seen this brave red man of the woods, "this glass of fashion and mould of form." I have seen him now from heel to head, and the vivid imagery of youth must now retire before the naked truth. I have seen much of society, and been to many fashionable gatherings in former days, where belles and beaux, dressed in extremest fashion, reigned; where costliest elegance scarce concealed hidden charms, half-revealed and half-suggested in graceful loops and folds;

yet, in point of dress, I must say, for truth is truth and must be told, these Indians outstrip them all!

To view him well, anatomically and physiologically, he should be divided into three sections—upper, middle and lower. Suppose his average height to be here, five feet ten inches, the upper portion commencing from his "dome of thought and palace of the soul" will extend downwards two feet six inches. The lower portion extends upward two feet and six inches from his noble feet, weather-beaten, I confess, but in their artistic proportions outrivaling the pedal extremities of any model in plaster of Paris vended by itinerating Italians to image lovers. The central section, lying immediately between the upper and lower, and bounded by them upon the north and south respectively, embraces a zone of ten inches in width, clothed with the finest the country affords, a fabric known elsewhere, when new, as white cotton cloth; but here, since long ago discolored with usage, my vocabulary is wanting in terms to give it a proper designation. This band is put in position, wrapped around him several times and fastened, so as not to impede his locomotion, nor to be seen as a banner, "fluttering in the breeze," upon his portly form, as it vanishes through rocks and woods, "o'er the hills and far away." Thus warmly clothed, for his upper and lower sections are guiltless of any covering, he is prepared for the changes of the weather. I remarked he had no other clothing; in this statement I am not borne out by the facts; he has his bow and arrows, and a strip of red cloth, which binds in love-knot his dark, flowing locks. Some claim he is "a man and a brother." The former proposition I admit; as to the latter, I must be permitted the exercise of my own opinion undisturbed. If a brother, then a " big brother," with but little fraternity, and does not act like one of the family. Credit is due him here, however, for his pacific disposition, and for pursuing the peaceful, rather than the warlike walks of life. He is a tender of herds, and tiller of the fields. Herds of cattle, flocks of sheep, and fields of corn engage his attention, rather than the uncertain chances of game. He is democratic in his tastes, and, as before intimated, republican in his simplicity. To compress it in a sentence, these are large, able-bodied, ignorant, inoffensive citizens. If he be a brother, then in this member of the family we can have but little pride, as his morals are low and his intellect as oqaque as the rings of Saturn. He is stolid, cold and uncommunicative. Your persistent inquiries can rarely elicit more than replies in monosyllables. If he is eloquent, as is sometimes said, then it is the eloquence of silence, golden silence. He will never spoil his story by redundant expressions. He is still the child of nature, and unaffected by the artificialities and conventionalisms of modern life.

Many years ago, roving bands of Apaches and Camanches made incursions into these mountains and left in their wake evidences of their cruelty and desolation. These were bad Indians, and now but few of them survive, and none probably now raid this section of the Republic. The marks of their murders and destroying visitations may now often be seen as you journey along wearily over these mountain paths. Here and there may be seen great piles of stones, with a rude cross over them, telling in unmistaken language of some atrocious murder by these predatory bands. Some years since, with a Mexican guide, I was pursuing my solitary way over these mountains, when suddenly I came upon one of these burial places, when I asked its meaning, and my guide understanding the subject of my inquiry, uttered, with a shrug of the shoulders, but one word in response, "Camanche," and that told it all, for here before us slept the victims of his massacre. Some few of these Indians have acquired a little education, but have tasted so sparingly of the "Pierian Spring," that their shallow draughts do not as yet "intoxicate the brain."

These, in religion, are Catholics, and have some churches of rude construction and antique design. The priest visit them from time to time, gathering in his tithes, and ministering to their spiritual wants. I have met the Holy Father on one or two occasions, in making the rounds of his diocese, and he was well attended, and "armed and equipped, too, as the law directs." His trusty rifle and revolvers were in ready position, should the exigency require them, and a well-groomed pack-mule carried an abundance of good provisions and a mysterious looking bottle, fragrant with the breath of "mountain dew." His weapons were carnal, as well as spiritual, and thus panoplied he went forth in the highways and byways, giving invitations to the feast and collecting shekels and sheaves. I should dislike to say that there are here no priests worthy of their profession; but from what I have seen and heard, there are but few whose high vocation is not disgraced by their lives. One died here some years since, whose sinful practices had begotten the most malignant infirmity, leaving to the care of his parish a house full of illegitimate children. And these things are no moral shock to his parishioners, for they say the Father can do no wrong, that he is the vicar of Christ on earth, and that his precepts, rather than his example, should be obeyed.

'Such a firm grasp has priestcraft on this deluded people, that personal independence is ignored, and a blind obedience is demanded and yielded. These Catholics, I am told, are not recognized by the

Roman Pontiff. If this be so, then you can have some idea of the moral standard of these religionists. If they commit murder, they believe the word of the priest can wipe out the blood of the slain. If they steal, his word is all-sufficient to cancel the offence. If they, in their wantonness, violate the sanctity of youth, age and innocence, his word carries a pardoning power, changing vice into virtue and villainy into righteousness. They believe he can bar those gates which "grate harsh thunder," or open those "on golden hinges turning." Such a faith, with such a people, makes them dangerous, devilish and lawless. Believing in the priest's power to forgive, and the ease with which this forgiveness may be obtained, not only weakens all moral restraints, but gives positive encouragement to the indulgence of the meanest passions, and the perpetration of the vilest crimes. He stabs with assassin's hand his fellowmen to-day, and to-morrow, should the law demand his life, the holy confessor, with prayer and crucifix and shrine, sends him on to glory. Future punishment has no terrors for him, for his mediator can change by his transforming power, scarlet sins into innocence and purity.

Do not misunderstand me, I am only speaking of the faith of these people in these mountains, and not elsewhere. Their ignorance is dense, and their superstition indescribable. They seem to have learned nothing in the past, and to be incapable of learning in the future. I now refer to them as a mass, to which, of course, there are some exceptions, "few and far between." There are but few schools, and these of a rudimentary character and not well attended. Ignorance is widespread, and its consequences widefelt, and seen in every department of life.

While the Castilian language is most beautiful, rich and musical, yet it can scarcely be said to be the language of these mountaineers, who speak an idiom peculiarly their own, a hybrid made up from the Mexican, Spanish and Indian. They are as far from speaking pure Spanish, as an Americanized Hottentot from speaking Addisonian English. Their vocabulary is very limited, not embracing, I think, more than a few thousand words. These fall within the sphere of their everyday life, including the most commonplace expressions in daily use. When striving to make them understand some simple something, but without success, it is frequently said by Americans, in a fit of fretful despair, "They do n't understand their own language."

There is one thing they do well, when they can do it at all, and that is, they write beautifully. Their penmanship is almost like copy-plate. They almost unexceptionably write well. Why this is so, I am at a loss to explain, but such is the fact. It may be for the same reason assigned by the dude, when asked by his comrade how it was that he managed to keep his cravat so faultlessly tied, who replied, with an oath, that he gave his *whole attention to it*. But in writing, as in everything else, they take their time. Americans write rapidly, Mexicans slowly. An ordinary business letter an American will finish, fold, seal, stamp and address, before a Mexican will have gotten through with his meaningless formalism and empty terms of endearment. He takes his time, or anybody's else's time, but does it well. My observation has led me to believe that good penmanship runs in families, and what I have seen here, has confirmed this impression.

CHAPTER VI.

MEXICAN NO CONCEPTION OF VALUE OF TIME.—HOSPITALITY.—"COL. LO."—NEGROS.

Heretofore I have indicated that the teachableness of these people is very limited. The common laborers grasp a new idea with much difficulty. You may tell them and show them how to do a thing in a certain way a dozen times, yet a repetition of the act seems to embarrass them, and as soon as you leave them, they lapse into their old ways again, however unwise and costly. They have no conception as to the value of time. They will sit down in front of a ton of rock to break it, and break it as far as they can reach, and then get up and remove any rock unbroken to their seats, instead of moving their seats to the rock. The former will probably take twenty minutes, the latter three seconds. But a greater than Mohammed is he, for the mountain comes to him as it came not to the Mussulman Prophet. In order to remove a pile of metal, probably not six feet, they will fill a leathern bag called a *surron*, with a horn spoon, from the metal pile, and then shoulder and pack it the six feet, where they will dump it, rather than use a shovel lying within two feet of them, and accomplishing the job in one-fourth of the time. They seem to study how not to do it, and in this to take as much time as possible, for this is the cheapest commodity of which they have any knowledge, at least in their estimation. It is hard to run out of the worn grooves of many years; new adjustments require thought and painstaking. To instruct these lower orders and make something out of them, will require the long-suffering patience of the patriarch Job; for in that teacher who instructs them, will patience have had her perfect work.

I will not refer exclusively to unpraiseworthy characteristics, but will give the good and bad as I find them. Among the former I refer to Mexican hospitality. However poor he may be, the Mexican will share with you his last morsel. This is, indeed, a redeeming trait, and eloquently pleads for the brotherhood of man. I shall never forget the hospitable entertainment given me some years since by Mexican strangers. For two days and a night I had been lost, wandering in these pathless mountains, seeking to find my lost way, when, towards nightfall, emerging from an immense canyon, we came upon an obscure path, and following it, we knew not whither, long after night we descried a light, to which we bent our way, and when reached, we found a small Mexican train encamped. Learning our condition, for we were nearly starved and worn out, they came at once to our relief with all they had. That night we slept in their camp and shared their generous stores, and in the morning, receiving their instructions, left on their heads our heart's blessing. The roughest people, and the rudest tribes, I believe, show this noble trait; it is the "one touch of nature which makes the whole world kin," the shining link that binds in sympathetic union the members of our race. Angels have been entertained unawares. And the departing stranger from the place of hospitality, paints over it a bow of peace with loveliest hues, crowned with a double blessing, "on him who gives and him who takes." The curling smoke, when seen from afar by the departing guest for the last time, goes heavenward with his benediction upon the hospitable dwellers below.

Mexicans and Indians, for the most part, make up the population of the mountains, the former in the ascendant. However, the family of Colonel and Mrs. Lo, are no unimportant factors in society here. When heretofore speaking of him, I omitted to advert to his fine physique, magnificent proportions—a living model for a sculptor. In muscular development some of them appear Herculean. The finest specimen of manhood I think I ever saw, was an Indian. I was winding my way down a deep gorge one cold morning, when, but a short distance from me, and above me, appeared in front of his cave a stalwart Indian, unclad, with bow and arrow in hand. The suddenness of the apparition, his apparent warlike preparation, the atmospheric condition, and last, but not least, the uncertainty as to whether " his intentions were honorable," may have magnified his outline against the mountain side; but he then certainly seemed to me a " big Injun heap."

When the biographer of Col. Lo comes to write his life, he should not fail to dwell at some length upon his domestic habits and relations. Here Mrs. Lo can not properly complain of the Colonel for not sharing with her the " burden and heat of the day" in the open corn field. While he sees that she is not neglectful of her open air duties, he is willing to encourage her with his manly *presence* on all proper occasions. This is eminently commendable. While the heads of the household are looking after the family subsistence department, the shiftless little Los must shift for themselves. She careth not for Parisian costumes and drawing-room accomplishments. Ladies' magazines and the light literature of the day, find in her no enthusiastic admirer. They often dwell in caves and under overhanging rocks, seeking no better habitations, and entirely contented with nature's quarters. There they rear their numerous brood, and send them adrift to tread in the path their fathers trod. Some of them live, too, to an extreme age. With shrunken, leathery faces, they remind us somewhat of an exhumed Egyptian mummy. Their physical ailments are few, and when they come, they bear them with an iron fortitude and a stoical philosophy. Dyspepsia and fashionable nervous affections are unknown. No Indian, I presume, ever had the neuralgia—blessed Indian! His "medicine men" know and care nothing for modern therapeutical agents. He is here up with the times in the discoveries of medical science, and the application of remedial agents; but with him the times are unchanged since the conquest of Mexico. It it thus he keeps abreast with a stagnant civilization.

But take him as you find him in his fastnesses of rocks and mountains, living, as he does, I am compelled to say, that for fair dealing and proper demeanor, he is better than his Mexican neighbor of the lower caste. His words and his contracts are better, with less perfidy and treachery. He has less gas and more good-heartedness: does his favors in silence, while the Mexican smears his with a hypocritical politeness, expecting a double reward for a dishonest performance. It is curious and interesting, to note how the Indian mother transports her offspring. No baby buggies have ever reached these altitudes, but with a fastening of cloth she swings him high on her back, and thus snugly tucked in, as if he was in a wicker basket, she trudges along weary leagues behind her brave, who precedes, *burdened* with his bow and arrows. She is the vehicle to move the children and the family supplies, while the Colonel " points the phalanx and directs the way."

There are a few negroes living here also; but "they are strangers in a stranger land." They were not made for the mountains, nor were the mountains made for them. They are exotics, and can not become acclimated and fit their new environments. They learn the language, strange to say, with a noticeable facility. Some few of them intermarry with the *peon* population, and, as it ever is, he soon descends to her level, for the husband seldom lifts up the wife; but the wife drags down the husband to her social scale. The negro is courted by this class of the Mexican population. And by the rest of her associates, fortunate is she considered who can bind in matrimonial chains this sable son of Adam. She is regarded as marrying *up*, and not *down*, as some would suppose. The union is seldom a happy one, for in the course of time, the negro, with more sense, sees his true relations, and finds that in a fatal moment his neck has become entangled in a rawhide noose, from which he would now, upon the slightest provocation, free himself. He realizes, too late, his false step, taken in a moment of semi-delirious enthusiasm, and now, when his head is cool, and his heart is colder, rightly calculates, "that she is not fit for any gentleman of color." These paints do n't mix well, and nature rebels against the blending of such colors. The alliance is unnatural, and therefore unequal. In intelligence, progressiveness and moral status, he is far her superior, and the class to which she belongs. To some of my readers this may appear incredible; but it is nevertheless the truth. He is capable of improvement, and putting himself upon a higher plane of civilization, of better business capacities, and even comprehending the theory of government. Of such things neither she nor her forefathers have ever heard or dreamed; but casemated in her abject stupidity and superstition, she will live and die. But of the *peon* class I will treat more in the future, and now only make these incidental allusions and pass on to other features.

CHAPTER VII.

MINING.—WHAT IS REQUIRED.—SOME OBSERVATIONS.—UNCERTAINTY.

Mining is the principal industry in the mountains; other pursuits are made subsidiary to this. It is seldom you can go into a district without finding a number of mines for sale. It is also seldom you can find any of them of any value. Nearly all of them have a history, which, if believed, would invest them with more than passing interest. Their true history is beclouded with the traditions which have settled upon them, these traditions thickening and growing with the lapse of time. Some of these mines were worked profitably more than a century ago, and in some cases their entrances have been closed by the debris of many long years, and their very locations have been concealed and lost by the displacement of rocks, and the growth of the circumjacent timber. In many of the old churches, in some parts, are records of these mines, their discovery, workings, and output. But to recur: while you are asked to buy by many anxious to sell, were I to give a piece of gratuitous advice, I would say in the matter, "Make haste slowly." The stories you hear may entertain you for the time, by their novelty and word-painting, but, my friend, hold fast your pocket-book until things are proven true. Be convinced yourself before you turn a dollar loose in some hole in the ground with the expectation that it will in a few months place a hundred to your credit in the bank. Experts may be of some service to you; from them you may learn some good ideas; make these ideas your own; incorporate them in your stock of knowledge, and then decide for yourself. Don't relinquish your judgment to any man, much less to any expert, many of whom for a consideration will report favorably for either party, for their information is a marketable commodity. The higher the price, the stronger the report. If there is any business which requires preëminently the exercise of common sense and grave judgment, it is that of mining. It is not a mere speculation, but a business, and should be conducted on business principles. And especially in making investments in such properties should one keep perfectly cool, uninfluenced by the highly-wrought colorings of sharpsters, who are ever on the alert for some "innocent abroad." Hear everything from everybody; compare, digest, and then examine and conclude for yourself. If satisfied at last from the present condition of the property that it has a future and will pay, then the title should be carefully investigated, and leave no cloud hanging over its validity. While here the mining laws are liberal, perhaps the best in the world, yet the owner has only a conditional, defeasible title; can hold it only so long as he complies with the requirements of the mining code. It is imperatively necessary to work so many men so many weeks in the year in order to retain possession, and if there is an interregnum it is subject to the denouncement of other parties, who, hawk-like, are ever on the watch to take in such chances.

Then if satisfied as to character of property and title, its facilities for being worked must be looked into to put it on as economic a basis as possible. The supplies of wood and water are most important items. Pasturage, too, is a matter of much moment, as many animals are needed in the hacienda. Transportation is a live question, and merits a careful consideration. In these parts nearly all the mining supplies come from San Francisco, shipped either by steamer to Mazatlan or to El Paso, Texas, by rail, and from thence down the Mexican Central Railroad to Jimenez, and thence hauled to Parral, from which place it is packed into the mountains. The freight per ton costs from one hundred and twenty to one hundred and forty dollars. Often the freight and duties exceed the prime cost. You will see it requires an excellent producing property to meet these heavy charges.

Again, the character of the mine must be noted, whether easily worked or rebellious. If the metal is difficult of extraction, then what ingredients are necessary, and how shall they be used to facilitate the extraction. The property may be rich, but by no discovered process can it be made to yield up its precious value. In such a combination with other substances is it found that it is practically valueless to its owners. The character of the labor required and the amount obtainable requires careful study. Here nearly all the laborers are Mexicans, with the exception of skilled workmen, who are generally Americans. Mexican machinists are seldom seen. Now and then one can be found who can run an engine or a pump, but machinery is not his forte. Occasionally we may find a passable Mexican carpenter, but in the high branches of mechanics he is not at home. But few of them can be called skilled workmen, or, if so, they do not visit these parts. The Mexican laborer, if no task is given him, works against time. He works for himself, and not for the employer. But to task him is the only way to get the most out of him in the shortest time, for ordinarily he will, ir unwatched, consume more time devising dishonest expedients to defraud you than an honest performance would require. But he prefers the former course, as it harmonizes with his nature and education. These are the men upon whom, for the most part, the investor must rely when he embarks his capital upon the uncertain sea of mining adventure. These are some of the more important facts to which every man should look before he turns a tame dollar loose in search of a wild one. Mining is a legitimate business, and may be conducted on legitimate principles, but mining boards are stock-gambling concerns, entailing wreck and ruin in their operations. While the celebrated Comstock Mines contributed several hundred millions to the wealth of the world, yet the gamblers in her stocks wrought so much ruin, and carried desolation to so many homes, far and near, it is scarcely a question that for the time more evil than good came from its development.

I have read somewhere that the statistics will show that ninety-seven per cent of merchants engaged in business for more than twenty years will at some time become bankrupt. I am not prepared with the statistics of mining men, but suppose with them fortune is equally as fickle. With modern appliances but few mines now remain unexhausted so long a period. For mines, like all earthly things, have their beginnings and their end, contrary to the exploded theory of the old writers who maintained that the deeper you went the better the metal. The beginning and the end of the metal along the line of the vein is limited by non-metaliferous rock. So one, after having made up his mind to go into an enterprise of this kind, must be prepared to take his chances and submit to the decree of fortune.

But a word of caution here: no man ought to put a dollar in a mine unless he can afford to lose it without embarrassment. People who sell their lands, houses and homes to engage in such pursuits are near the border land of idiocy. The husband who would take his wife's money for such a business ought not to be trusted longer unconfined in any well ordered community. The guardian who would thus invest his ward's funds commits a crime, and the court that would sanction such an investment deserves impeachment. Mining is such a fascinating business, with hope ever in the van with her alluring signals, that almost any sweet-lipped, oily-tongued talker, promising extravagant returns on the investment can charm into his pockets the hard-earned dollars from the pockets of others. The old leather purse, tied in the middle with a string, which has been sleeping Rip Van Winkle-like for years must awake, and turn out at the touch of this magician's wand. This persuasive elocutionist may not be deceived himself, but fortunate for the community if the evil effects of his rhetoric are forgotten in years. There is just enough of the lottery in it to popularize it, and make acceptable its extravagant promises.

The fact is there is deep down in the heart of almost every man the love of chance. Did you ever think of it? I believe the principle is almost universal. I know of no nationality where games of chance are not practiced. There seems to be in the human heart a predisposition to such things, and the gratification of this is sought, as we see in a variety of ways, but each having in it that seductive element of chance. Hence we find men in every vocation investing in mining stocks. The lawyer stops in the middle of his brief to turn in his last-earned fee in the " gilt-edged security." The doctor's prescription is left half written, convinced suddenly of the great certainty of mining returns. From the hard hands of honest toil, the dollars to be seen no more slip into the soft, dishonest hands of stock manipulators and mining gamblers. Even farmers, and the sons of farmers, deceived by half truths and whole lies, are at times induced to go into the business for which they are not fitted, either by nature or education, and soon, if there are no homestead exemptions, homsteads, too, must go to meet their indiscreet obligations. These words are the voice of caution and the sounds of warning. If they will only serve to check hasty and ill-advised investments I shall feel that I have been an instrument of good and amply repaid for having written them. It is seldom prudent men will engage in enterprises of which they know nothing; should they do so it must be near home and one with which they can soon familiarize themselves. But men will engage in mining thousands of miles away, and of which they are utterly ignorant. The business must necessarily be in the hands of representatives, and however good these may be, it is not so satisfactory as when under their own immediate supervision.

CHAPTER VIII.

BE CAUTIOUS AS TO MINING INVESTMENTS—DISTRICTS. — BALOPILAS. — GALENA. — CUERVO.— GAUDELOUPE Y CALVO.

I do not wish it inferred from what I have written that I would discourage all mining investments, for it is a legitimate business, as I have before stated, and should be pursued in a legitimate manner and not treated as if it were wholly a lottery. While there are hundreds of worthless mines palmed off upon a too confiding community as good properties, there are, on the other hand, mines of intrinsic value, real worth, and which will be made to yield splendid profits. Nothing scarcely pays like a good mine well managed; the profits are often enormous. But a good mine badly managed, or a bad mine well managed, is a property the sooner you get rid of the better. If you hold it you must incur heavy expenditures without corresponding benefits. But when convinced that a certain mine is a good property upon the most searching investigation, then work it judiciously, looking to the average product and not to the expectations of daily bonanzas, which seldom come and seldom stay. One should not be too sanguine in mining; it will save him from many painful disappointments if he will keep perfectly cool, and remain unexcited in the face of hopeful signs and most promising indications. It is something about which you can not argue. You can neither reason metal into a rock nor out of it. There is an old saying that "all signs fail in dry weather." And particularly is it true in reference to rocks, that frequently all signs of metal are but deceptive illusions. We know that there are certain formations which may carry metal, while we know that there are certain others which do not, and that these simple truths are confirmed by the experience of ages.

In the Sierra Madre I must say that there are some fine mines, some comparatively new, and some old. And right here I would say, if you would invest in mines in this country, be exceedingly cautious about purchasing old mines — those which have been worked and abandoned. The Mexican never leaves anything valuble in sight; so if he has left anything at all worthy of the name it is because of its inaccessibility. This may come from want of adequate machinery in former times, or from now being submerged in water. But never pay the least attention to the word of any Mexican or any of his "able-bodied relations" as to the fine quality of the ore now under water, which you can not see. In this case seeing is far better than faith; faith in an unscrupulous liar. Buy from him nothing unseen; take the water out, if it costs a few hundred dollars, and see the bottom, it may save you many thousands and much misspent time. In such matters a Mexican's word, were he to swear by all the saints in the calendar and cross himself a hundred times, would only emphasize my disbelief in the correctness of his statement. Clouds of witnesses will confirm this observation, some of them having abundant reasons for their opinions. But new mines are always to be preferred, when obtainable, for many reasons. Of this character there are mines in the mountains which will come to light in the future and enrich their owners. Mining districts, as they are called, certain territorial divisions, generally have within their limits the same character of mines. Hence, in examining a certain mine to ascertain its probable character, the question is a most pertinent one, What is the character of the other mines in the said district? If they are deep or shallow, then this one is most likely to be the same. This is a good starting point in the examination. Certain districts produce native silver, as in the Batopilas district, some six days journey from here; in others native silver is not seen.

And here I may remark that the latter, rather

than the former, is to be preferred, as it is much more probable to continue. In mines producing native silver it is a "feast or a famine," a bonanza or nothing. When these bonanzas are struck the output is very large while they last, but when exhausted you may work on for a year or so, and get nothing until you develop another.

Not so with the other class of mines. Where the metal is well distributed the profits are regular and uniform, which is much more satisfactory. In some mines gold without silver is found, but this is seldom here the case. Often in going down the gold gives out, but is then succeeded by the silver, the gold being the later formation. Often the silver is found without the gold, or but a perceptible trace of it. But frequently the gold and silver coexist and are in value in nearly the same proportions. These metals live very harmoniously together. Since the great depreciation of silver of late years gold-bearing mines are more eagerly sought and highly appreciated. Again, mines yielding gold exclusively, in its reduction its expenses are comparatively light, the processes fewer, and the machinery much the cheaper. In consequence of this fact gold mines of much lower grade than silver can be profitably worked. But, as the grade goes down, the capacity of the mill must be increased, so as to put through and make up in increased quantity. In some portions of the United

States there are mills of one hundred stamps capacity, crushing from two hundred to two hundred and fifty tons daily.

The largest mill known to me in this section has only forty stamps, some two days from this place, within the borders of the State of Sinaloa. It is a good property and is owned by an English Company, and has been shipping monthly about fifty thousand dollars. This is an old mine with a new company, which has expended upon it, I learn, nearly two millions of dollars. They have made extensive and costly improvements. The ore carries no gold and is very rebellious, and its successful treatment requires great skill. Near it are several good properties, which are being worked with more or less profit. To the south of this place some twenty-five miles are the Galena and Cuervo mines, now operated by a Texas organization. The latter named was brought somewhat prominently before the public some years since by reason of Tennessee's State Treasurer having been connected with it. These are believed to be good properties and promise well in the future. They are old mines with fine records.

The mine at this place was discovered in 1835. Was for many years leased to an English company, which from well authenticated sources took out many millions of dollars. Upon the expiration of the English lease referred to it was worked by the

Mexican owners for many years with much profit, until, it is said, such a depth was reached that the machinery then employed was inadequate to clear it of water. So after being submerged for many years it passed into the hands of the company now working it, a Tennessee organization. After making the utmost allowance for the extravagant statement concerning the yield of this property in former years, enough yet remains undisputed to say that a great many million dollars were extracted. From the best data I can gather from different sources, probaby more than thirty millions. It is an immense fissure vein with the boldest croppings I have ever seen. It carries a high percentage of gold, as often the bullion is more valuable in gold than silver. The gold continues to the lowest depths reached, indicating at least the continuance of the silver to a still greater depth. Such was the immense yield here and the product of the neighboring mines that many years ago it necessitated the erection of a mint at this place. The building, with its portholes for defense, still stands, the finest in this section of the country, costing probably more than one hundred thousand dollars. The mint machinery was costly, and many of its pieces were very heavy, requiring a great number of men to pack them over the mountains. There are some pieces of machinery which can not be so sectionized as to reduce their weight to the packing capacity of these small mountain mules. To these men hitch on in great numbers, and with levers and fastenings transport them to the desired point. The Chinese are said to move the heaviest iron safes, by means of their great numbers, the burden in some ingenious way being so distributed that each one aids in the undertaking. The Mexicans rally numbers to the task, and in the same way, too, accomplish their object, but apparently in the most awkward manner. As an illustration of their way, I will here mention the fact, if they wish to move a log, they do not do so by putting the handspike under it and thus lifting it, but they put it on top, and then tie it to the log before they proceed to lift it at all.

But I see I am digressing somewhat from the mine, and return to make some additional remarks concerning the same, and the mode of mining generally practiced in the county. This may be a matter of interest to some readers. The apology I offer for particular reference to this property is that it is historic, and also with it I am better acquainted than with others. Many years ago the village is said to have had a population of ten thousand people subsisting in one way or the other upon the mine. After it ceased to be worked for a great many years its reduced population is said to have lived upon working over and over its dump pile. The excavation along the line of the ledge is nearly two thousand feet, its width varying from six feet to sixty, and its depth in the deepest shaft nearly five hundred feet. It is quartz formation, very hard, with encasing walls of porphyry. It is said to have furnished sufficient metal for sixteen large haciendas, the ruins of which are now seen for many miles below the village.

CHAPTER IX.

DYNAMITE.—BLASTING.—METAL STEALING.—RECEIVERS.—PERILS OF MINERS.

The art of mining, like that of war, was revolutionized by the invention of gunpowder. I am told that in some eastern countries, and in Japan, tunnels may be found driven for hundreds of feet without the use of powder. They kindled fires in the face of the drift, and when sufficiently hot, they cast upon it water, and in this way, by peacemeal, broke their way forwards, after so long a time. Dynamite was a great improvement upon the common black powder, which, in mining, has now almost gone into disuse. But the introduction of this powerful agent is, comparatively speaking, of but recent date. It is harmless in appearance, resembling sawdust, and may with impunity be cast into the fire without any expolsion; but strike it with a hard substance, or give it a sudden concussion, and then "the trouble begins." It is said to expend its force principally downwards, and hence, lay a charge of it on a rock unconfined, and its discharge will shiver to atoms the rock beneath it. Holes are drilled with steel bars into the metal-bearing rock from one to five feet, charged with dynamite, or giant powder, as it is called, and then exploded by firing a fuse, at the lower end of which is a cap, containing a fulminating substance that has been previously inserted in the charge of powder. When a number of these are to be fired at the same time in the same working, it is attended with much danger, and sometimes loss of life. For after the fuse is lighted, it is necessary for the person doing so "to go at once, and not stand upon the order of his going"—up a ladder, anywhere to some secure retreat, for giant powder, like time and tide, wait for no man. If there is a premature discharge, or a failure for some reason to "go off," then the probabilities are somebody will get hurt. If there is a failure to "go off," then the effort to dig out that shot, or make it effective, must be made with the greatest caution. Being a prudent man, and not wishing to intermeddle with the business of others, especially where that is of such a delicate nature, I retire until the "trouble is over." The shots are now fired in many mines by an electric battery, at times separately, at others simultaneously, and with greater effectiveness under certain conditions.

There is great art displayed in this branch of mining, requiring intelligence, careful observation, and much experience. The fact is, intelligent labor is much better in every department of life; will accomplish more, with less cost and in less time. There is a head man who directs the ordinary Mexican miner how, and where, to place his shots. He is paid for what he drills, and not otherwise, and if he were not directed, he would drill in the softest place, and the least time possible, caring for naught else than his contract money. Generally, the miners divide themselves in pairs—one holds and turns the drill, while the other strikes it, and from time to time exchange places. Frequently, at the foot of the shaft, or in front of the tunnel, are found a crucifix and burning candle, where they hold their services ere the labor of the day begins. I will not say this does not mean anything, but only this, and nothing more, that it is no safeguard against their stealing any choice piece of metal which they may find during that day. With the Psalmist they say, " the earth is the Lord's, and the fullness thereof," and especially the mines, and the fullness thereof, are His, and not man's, and whose claims to which he practically and persistently ignores on every possible occasion. At many mines ante-rooms are provided for the miners, where they exchange their clothing for a working habit, which consists of a piece of cotton cloth tied around their bodies, and upon coming out after their work is finished, they are subjected to a search, to see if they have stolen anything. Yet, notwithstanding these precautions, they manage to steal a great deal. They resort to the most novel and ingenious devices to conceal stolen metal, hiding it in their hair, in their mouths, and other parts of their bodies, often to the great peril of their lives. Between the bottoms of their feet and the pieces of sole leather underneath, called guaraches (pronounced wayrach-ies), they carry it in considerable quantities. The fewest number, when an opportunity is presented, can resist the temptation. Moral principle has but little to do in the direction of their conduct at this point. With them, as with the old Spartans, as already stated the crime consists not so much in the stealing, as in its being found out. They can always readily dispose of their ill-gotten gains, to those willing and anxious to buy at a reduced valuation. In fact, they are encouraged to steal by these receivers of stolen goods, against whom the law is a dead letter. I will venture the assertion, that there are more receivers of stolen goods to the square mile adjacent to the mining camps in Mexico, than in any other portion of the habitable globe. There seems to be no punishment for this class of offenders, or if one is promulged by the law, it is a mere empty paper bull, and, in fact, without vitality. And, strange to say, many so-called *respectable merchants* will purchase from these thieves, with full knowledge of the facts, and if an effort is made to reclaim your property, will laugh in your face for your intermeddling. Here I have never known one to be punished as a receiver of stolen goods. Often the owner is compelled to buy his own property back, when stolen, from the thief. Of course, this stimulates a repetition of the offense; but there are times and situations when certain articles are stolen that it is absolutely indispensable to recover them in almost any way, or stop your business at a very heavy loss. It is a dose of humiliating medicine for which we do not cry to take, as vermifuge venders report the children as doing for their worm-expelling nostrums. The authorities render you but little assistance in such cases; but as to the character and efficiency of these, I will take occasion hereafter to speak.

The life of a miner is one of peril. Hundreds of feet deep down in the earth, he is working with his dim light, and with hundreds of feet above him of overhanging walls. These incline at certain angles, giving to them the appearance as if in the act of falling, when viewed upwards, and the vein matter between them having been taken out from top to bottom, he is at the mercy of falling substances, the lightest of which may jeopard his life. These walls, especially in rainy seasons, often give way, and with a mighty crash go thundering below, to the entombment of the living. It is a marvel if one escapes from the heartrending catastrophe.

Their wives and children come to the spot, they can go no further, their lamentations fill the upper air, while the seal of the sepulchre is upon their buried ones below. Suffocating gases kill many. Accidents are many from falling rocks and timbers, from broken ladders and breaking machinery, from carelessness in many ways, from missteps in ascending or descending ladders hundreds of feet, with dim lights and heavy burdens. While the law throws every guard around them for their protection, and exacts the most rigid observance of its rules for their preservation, yet such is the nature of the business, its perils so frequent, that many lives are sacrificed notwithstanding the precautions required and observed. Again, a familiarity with danger begets indifference and carelessness, causing many deaths. The law requires here, that if an accident occurs in a mine, whether trivial or serious, that it should be immediately reported to the chief political authority of the place. The purpose of this is, that an investigation may be made, and subject the delinquent owners to some punishment commensurate with the gravity of the offense. Miners, like mariners, by reason of their habits of life, are the especial pets of the law, and around whom it throws its peculiar guardianship. And that it is so, is well, for there does not exist a more reckless and improvident class than these. He works just enough to get the actual necessaries of life, and this from day to day. He does not see a month ahead of him, and does n't care to look into the future so far. He may be happy in that he does not anticipate trouble, never crossing the bridge before he reaches it. He works some six or seven hours in the twenty-four, in which he can generally make from one dollar to one dollar and a half. During the same time an American miner would make nearly twice as much. But when this is made, the Mexican suspends operations for that day. Whether he has many or few in his household to provide for, it is all the same to him, his task, at least, is done, and he can trust to the future to supply the future's wants. With him it is not an exhibition of faith in the providence of God; but on his part purely an exhibition of reckless improvidence. Some few of them may be impelled by different motives. When the Hon. Hannibal Hamlin was Minister to Spain, some years since, observing that an excellent shoemaker there only worked a small portion of his time, he inquired of him why, with his capacity for making money, he did not work more and lay up something for to-morrow. To this the knight of the last, in justifying his course, replied interrogatively, for the Spanish race, "Ah, senor, who has promised us to-morrow?" Thus he manifested his realization of the fact, that no future moment is given until the present is taken away.

CHAPTER X.

GAMBLING.—ITS RESULTS.—HOW METAL IS TAKEN FROM MINES AT TIMES.—FIRST EXPERIENCE IN GOING DOWN LADDERS.

For gambling they have an intense passion, and will bet their last cent upon the turn of a *tlaco*, a small copper coin. Men with large families, unprovided with two meals, will sit down on the roadside, on their way home, and gamble away their week's earnings in a few moments. Young and old indulge in this vicious sport. With some it almost seems a species of insanity. They will play anywhere, everywhere, with anybody, everybody, to gratify this mad passion. No reverence of person, or sacredness of place deters them for a minute; all things else are engulfed in this all-absorbing passion. These gamblers would not hesitate to gamble for the privilege of tabling their games upon the tomb-stones of their wives and children, did they possess them, so dead have they become to the nobler virtues, and lost to the holier impulses of the heart. The little children in the streets, taught by the pernicious example of older ones, perchance their fathers, have already become embyro gamblers, and unrebuked by any, give rich promise of poor, wasted lives. The children are the children of the State; but the official guardians turn them loose unrestrainedly, to riot in profligacy, and through such excesses to rush on to ruin. This vicious policy betrays bad morals and bad statesmanship, and will, in the end, react upon the welfare of the commonwealth.

Those considered the most respectable — the high-toned — probably gamble the more, as they have greater opportunities for doing so. But few are exempt from the pernicious practice. And they will gamble with anything, and for anything. Parents and children, men and women, crowding to the same places, night and day, and betting against each other all they have, not even excepting the clothing worn by them at the time. And on some festal occasions, I am told, Governors will *grace* them with their presence, and will dignify their high office by playing with the rabble a few games of chance. With such examples for imitation and encouragement, the common people may be judged the more charitably, for failing to find in the practice any iniquity. But never before, as here, to me has its evil effects been so apparent. It robs women and children, clothes them in rags, sends them hungry to comfortless beds, to arise in the morning hungrier still. The morning birds worship with songs in the groves, "God's first temples," but then these poor, unfed ones, the victims of this vice, send on high, from saddened hearts and cheerless homes, no thanksgiving songs. Say what you will, emptiness of stomach is unfavorable to holiness of heart. Christ fed the hungry multitude with the loaves and fishes, when he was feeding them with the bread of life. Habitual hunger tends to discontentedness, and this drifts into impiety. I paint the picture from scenes of life around me. They are too sadly real to ask the aid of imagination for coloring.

But the poorer classes are the greater sufferers from this vice. In mining districts the common laborers reap more largely the consequences of this vile habit; those men who dig in the mines and lift out its rock; those, who underneath the earth for many fathoms, toil night and day, without sun and stars, with sledge and steel to release the imprisoned metals from "adamantine chains." The fruit of the labors of those whose duty it is to take the metal, when broken within, to the surface without, goes in the same way. That such is the case, to describe their labors may make you the more readily realize the iniquity. The miners blast the rock and leave it where broken; after this it is removed by others, packed on their backs, either to an underground car, which runs to the shaft, to be hoisted to the surface, and thence to the mill, or the metal is packed by them up many flights of ladders, to the outside, where it is for the time deposited. These ladders—to be called such is a mis-nomer—are nothing more than long pine poles, from six to eight inches in diameter, with notches cut in the same, for steps, at regular intervals. They are similar in appearance, though somewhat larger, than the notched poles in an old-fashioned country hen-house. Upon these ladders will the "burden-bearer" go, with one hundred and fifty to two hundred pounds of rock in a leathern bag, with a light in one hand, and the other resting on the ladder, as a security against accident.

The broad, leather strap, fastened to the bag, comes over the top of his head, which bears up the burden, while it is retained in position at bottom by resting on his back. This is the way he makes his living, and earns it just as honestly as any fugitive cashier or railroad wrecker. You may think it is a hard way to "raise the wind," and it is, but he "blows it in" all the same. We are told that the limbs of the human body most exercised will be most developed, and as an illustration, see the arms of the blacksmith. That will account, I presume, for the little brains and immense necks some of these fellows have. The former have been compressed by the leather strap weighted with heavy burdens, while the muscles of the neck have been, from long usage, enlarged and strengthened. This they have practiced since they were small boys, and now, when grown, can carry incredible loads. But in no other way do they exhibit their strength, as one good-sized laboring American, under a log, will lift more than two or three of them. But from long training he can carry the most surprising loads up those long flights of steps; practice has given such muscular development. But should he make a misstep, or lose his balance while ascending, the rock and the Mexican will be found below—the rock unhurt, but a few pieces of clothing, and a scattered Mexican, will be the remains for an impromptu funeral procession. Now, the pay of these men is generally from seventy-five cents to one dollar, and if it were three times as much, it would all go in the same way; no forethought, no idea of economy; but what remains after getting the scantiest necessaries of life, he gambles and drinks away. His is truly an unhealthy and perilous life, exposed to ever-present danger, to noxious gases, and thoroughly wet from day to day from dripping rock.

One's first experience in going up and down these mining ladders is not soon forgotten. He may forget the hickory entertainments of his beloved school-master, the domestic chastenings for failing to lift more rapidly the dasher of the family churn, even the faces of his creditors may change beyond a street recognition, but he will never forget the time, the first time, he attempted to go down the succession of poles several hundred feet below. However great he may have felt a few minutes before, outside, now, when within, and on the down grade, that greatness he feels is dwarfed into utter helplessness in the presence of a paralyzing fear. Coolness, steady nerves, and strong resolutions, are necessary if you would become a success as a mid-air performer. While I have become familiar with these aerial voyages, yet I have never cultivated such a fondness for them as to give them the preference over many other modes of travel, for example, "a Pullman palace sleeper." These notched pine poles were introduced, I think, by the Spaniards, used by the Mexicans and Indians, and now sometimes adopted by the Americans. They must be used at the bottom of the shaft, when being sunk, as the other kinds would soon be broken by the blasting rocks.

CHAPTER XI.

METAL.—WHERE FOUND.—HOW EXTRACTED.—FAILINGS.—RETORTING.

As it may be instructive to some of my readers, I will tell how the metal is taken from the rock, for at last that is the end of the whole business. The gold, the silver, is in one sense the product, the end of labor, its very quintessence. Nights and days of labor, with all the necessary cares and troubles, end here at last, compressed in a few shining pieces of metal, the representatives of value. But how much toil, headaches, and heartaches are expressed by these little pieces of metal! And they are small to be the representatives of so much value, value in time, physical and mental exertion. Think of it, one ton of silver, Troy measure, is worth $37,709 50, and one cubic foot of the same, $12,355 20. One ton of gold, same measure, is worth $602,927 36; while one cubic foot of the same, weighing a little more than 1,200 lbs., runs up to $361, 808 64. Did nature not put up her precious values in small packages, then we might the more frequently hear of men as being the

THE MOUNTAINS OF MEXICO. 71

owners, not of so many herds and lands, stocks and bonds, but of so many cubic feet of gold?

The metal is found diffused through the rocks, sometimes visible and sometimes not. This rock may be quartz, sandstone, limestone, or some other formation. It is taken from the mine to the mill to be crushed into a powder. It first passes through a machine called a rockbreaker, reducing its size to that of walnuts or hickory nuts. After this it passes to the battery which consists of heavy iron stamps weighing each, generally, about seven hundred and fifty pounds. These have a fall of about seven inches, and drop ninety times to the minute, crushing the rock to the finest powder, and which is then conveyed to tanks. After this it is taken from the tanks into which it has gone from the battery, and placed in large pans of one and two tons capacity, where it is kept in constant agitation from three to eight hours by the application of steam to swiftly revolving mechanical appliances. The pulp, or powder, in the pans has been mixed with warm water, and certain chemical agents have been introduced to break down the refractory nature of the ore, and make it susceptible to the action of the quicksilver in the pans, which, possessing a strong affinity for the gold and silver, acts upon, and amalgamates them. By this is meant, that the quicksilver takes up the metalic particles by its chemical attraction for these substances. A good battery, with new stamps, will crush about twenty tons of rock in twenty-four hours. This, however, will depend much upon the character of the rock, whether hard or soft, and the fineness of the screen through which it must pass. From the pans it is drawn off into large settlers, where it is kept in constant motion for hours, after which it is conveyed in sluice boxes to the tailings pit. That which goes out of the settler is called tailings, and their value consists in the metal remaining in them, which escaped amalgation. These tailings are often worked over after the lapse of time, during which time they have lain in a pile, undergoing chemical changes, when subjected to the action of the sunlight and air.

The amalgam is made up of quicksilver and the gold and silver in combination. This, then, is placed in a retort, communicating with which, is an open, iron tube, at the farther end enclosed in a water jacket, at the extremity of which, is a vessel for catching the quicksilver, coming, when condensed, from the retort, under which has been kindled a good fire. The fire soon vaporizes the quicksilver, which passes into the water-enclosed tube, and is condensed and runs down to the place of deposits, from which it is taken and again used as before. In this way the quicksilver is separated from the metal, leaving this as the residuum. Now the metal is melted and run into bars, for shipment to the mints. After melting, the bars are essayed, to ascertain their value in gold and silver, if mixed. A certain quantity is weighed, say ten grains, cupelled in a muffle, then reweighed, to ascertain loss, by which its fineness is learned. The button, after cupellation, is subjected to the action of nitric acid, when the silver is taken up in solution, leaving the gold precipitated. The gold is thus dried, after the silver solution has been poured off, and weighed, and in this mode is ascertained the gold and silver value of the bar. The most sensitive scales are required to reach accurate results.

Such, in brief outline, is the process by which the ingenuity of man extracts the metal from the unwilling rocks.

CHAPTER XII.

ASSAYING.

Now, in passing along, I will tell you how the value of the rock is ascertained. Its proper treatment, as well as its value, is learned from repeated assays, by changing the chemicals, diminishing or stopping some of them, or putting in other ingredients and effecting new combinations. The methods for doing this have been greatly improved within the last half a century. Results from old processes formerly were not obtainable for many days, now by the application of improved machinery and the science of chemistry the same results may be realized in a few hours. The process described is called "pan amalgamation," necessitating the use of quicksilver. But there are other processes, called respectively smelting and lixiviation. The nature of the ore, its ingredients, and the combination will determine the nature of treatment. In amalgamation roasting may not be necessary, in lixiviation it is indispensable, and in smelting the rock is placed in furnaces with proper fluxes and melted, the precious metals falling to the bottom by their greater specific gravity, leaving the slag above, which is tapped and drawn off through lateral openings. Each process has its advantages dependent upon certain conditions, and the amount treated in a given period upon the capacity of the plant. Mills of less than five stamps are rarely seen, except when used by the prospector, but some possess as many as one hundred and twenty, these crushing from two hundred and fifty to three hundred tons daily. Many devices have been invented of late years to supersede the use of stamps, and go under the name of "rolls," "crushers," and "pulverizers," but up to this time the merits of none have been so marked as to induce general commendation. The fact is, I think, that in consequence of their cost and their short lives they have been much more successful in pulverizing their stockholders than the ore. I knew a company once that brought a certain pulverizer, so called, from San Francisco here, some years since, after so long a time "turned her loose," and within thirty days it wore itself completely out from top to bottom, from "stem to stern." As the injudicious experiment cost much time and several thousand dollars, there is not a stockholder in the concern but that will vote himself thoroughly "pulverized." And I venture if these gentlemen were asked again to reinvest in any machinery sailing under such a designation, the Recorder's Court next morning would have for trial a high-toned case of assault and battery. This is not the place for the introduction of new-fangled notions, but only for those which have been tried, and after many years approved by the most practical men. It is too far from a base of supplies, transportation is too difficult and expensive to indulge in experiment. I say this much for the benefit of those who may hereafter contemplate working mining properties in these mountains.

A simple assay is made by taking, say two hundred and forty grains of the powdered rock, mixing this with fluxes, say lead, litharge, borax, soda, in given quantities, and then melting the whole in a crucible or scorifying it in a muffle. When melted well pour same in button-shaped mould, the lead, the gold and silver in union being the heavier, will go to the bottom, leaving the slag above, which, with one lick of the hammer, flies off. You then take the lead button and cupel it in a bonedust cupel with a strong heat. The porousness of the cupel will absorb the foreign substances and the heat will vaporize the lead, leaving at the conclusion a small round button composed exclusively of gold and silver, where only these elements exist in the metal. You then take and weigh the button, and by referring to the standard table of value learn its worth. The gold is separated from the silver in the mode hereinbefore indicated.

This, in simple language, is a summary of the process ordinarily used. But to be a good assayer requires much study and long experience; in fact, one should be a good chemist and have a good laboratory at his command. But with a little practice almost any one can know "coarse" assaying, to employ an expressive term used by my friend John E. Randle, of Memphis, Tennessee, in reference to a knowledge of law; he said he knew *coarse law* as well as anybody; but as to *fine* law he confessed himself at sea. So a faithful and efficient assayer is a valuable adjunct to any hacienda, for upon the accuracy of his knowledge, and his watchfulness thousands are made or lost.

CHAPTER XIII.

BULLION TRAINS.—COMPARATIVE SAFETY.—FACTIONS.—REVOLUTIONS.

From the mountains all bullion is packed to Culiacan or to Parral, from which latter point it is taken by stage to Jiminez, and from thence by the Mexico Central Railroad to the mint in Chihuahua. The bullion in bars is securely fastened upon the backs of mules, placed in charge of some trusty man, who takes with him well-armed guards sufficient in numbers to repel any assaulting party. Sometimes with only two or three men he will carry out ten or fifteen thousand dollars, and return with the same escort, bringing in from five to ten thousand dollars in coin. Strange to say, it is very rare, indeed, that these trains are ever molested. Robbers of bullion, if immediately pursued, could hardly escape on account of its weight, and to avoid capture must abandon it in their flight. While *Conductas* have gone from these parts for many years, yet the oldest inhabitant can not tell you of one which has been captured and robbed. This may be thought a singular fact, and it is such, but it is an undisputed fact, however. How long do you suppose such a train would be unmolested, its direction and time of departure being well known, were it to start from any of our cities in any direction for such a distance? Probably it would not travel half a day before the whole outfit would be "gobbled up." If, then, express cars are rifled and hundreds of passengers made to stand and deliver by the persuasive revolver in the hands of desperate men, how long, I again ask, would a pack train such as described, go undisturbed? The question provokes a smile, and the answer is known ere it is spoken. But in making the contrast the question will not down, "Is civilization a failure?" I think not. Then there are a great many more people there than here, from which we may reasonably conclude that there are many more lawless persons. There, if the robbers are captured, punishment is neither swift nor certain. An ignorant jury, the law's delays, technical trivialities, furnish obstructions to the speedy coming of justice. Here, if on the highway a robber makes an assault and is captured, the law compels the officer living nearest to the place where the offense was committed to try him, and, if proven guilty, to have him executed within twelve days. And the same rule obtains as to railroad wreckers and those who cut the telegraph lines used by the railroads. These miscreants have no "jury of their peers," but some official from the vicinage, who "sits down" on them, and when he gets up they stay down. This sudden and swift retribution strikes terror to the lawless element, and is one of the strongest safeguards to society. Again, in this country, as nearly every one is more or less, directly or indirectly, interested in mining, it is to their interest to run down and destroy any train robbers. These are some of the reasons, I have thought, why bullion trains traverse these mountains in comparative safety. But where bullion is stolen for any length of time before its loss is discovered, the chances are many to one against its recovery. It will soon be cut up and remelted, thus destroying all evidences of its identity. Again, the facility with which it can be sold and bought, by men knowing it to have been stolen, baffles the owner in its pursuit to recapture. In these parts, and I say it to their shame, there are but few merchants who will not buy the stolen property and encourage the thief to double his stealings. A low standard of morality, I confess, but one they have made for themselves, and to which they have conformed from time immemorial. Complaints to the officials, by their inactivity and indifference, only provoke a spirit of desperation. And you settle down at last in the conviction that no one man, nor set of men, can change the habits, customs and morality of a people case-hardened in the mould of centuries. The undertaking may be praiseworthy and prosecuted in the spirit of a missionary, but the effort will be as futile as the attempt to dart straws through an armor of brass.

I do not wish it understood from what has been written that these mountains are exempt from the presence of robbers. Such an inference would be at variance with the truth. There are so many hiding-places and secure retreats to which they may flee and elude capture, it would be strange did they not abound in considerable numbers. But now they are less numerous than formerly, as law is becoming in other sections more firmly established, and order being gradually restored, thus lessening the number of malefactors, and consequently the number of outlawed refugees to the mountains from these parts.

In former years the country was affected with periodic revolutions. Some ambitious man, aspiring to power, would get up a disturbance, issue a pronunciamento, gather around him a gang of desperadoes, and endeavor to unseat some rival in position. Sometimes fortune and sometimes misfortune attended his expedition, but sooner or later one of the contending factions met with disaster, and those not killed in the conflicts were scattered, and fled to the mountains as outlaws, henceforth from necessity to live by plunder. Happily for the country, the era of pronunciamentos seems to have passed, and authority is not so easily overthrown as in other times. Those petty chieftains, the leaders of gangs from twenty-five to three hundred in number, would descend upon some mining camp, take what was in sight, cause the employés to join their standard, and be off to other fields to conquer. At times acting with an utter recklessness as to the rights of others, and then again for what was seized passing their receipts with a knightly courtesy, payable, I presume, "after a ratification of a treaty of peace." As this referred not to the peace of death, which soon followed the one or the other leader, but to the peace of the living, those paper tokens are still extant in the land with all the vigor of "Confederate States Scrip" to be enforced by the tribunals of the future. The higher officials acted upon the motto, "Once in office, always in office," and notwithstanding their terms may have expired and been defeated in their candidacy for re-election, yet they did not voluntarily retire, but fortified themselves, and, with their sturdy retainers, resisted the change in the administration. But it was immaterial whether they should or should not have given place to their rival, a conflict would almost invariably ensue before the incumbent could retain his place or be deposed. Of course, resignations were unknown, and death, except by violence, infrequent.

From this country and from those times may have been imported the aphorism that "officials never resign." However this may be, they have much official vitality. With them office meant enlarged opportunities for making money, and money gave them grandeur and "style," without which life was but an empty pageant. The governor's office was a rich prize, around which these conflicts centered. With a prodigality of promises, partisans were easily obtained, and the country was kept in a state of violent agitation to the detriment of every material interest. A change, when it came, was too frequently but a change in name, leaving abuses unreformed and the public welfare secondary to personal aggrandizement. While this is too often the case elsewhere, yet such was strikingly so in this country in the past. But as time at last sets all things even, so these things, too, have been changed from bad to better, and now one of these improvised revolutions is seldom heard of, as fewer men now care to risk their "life's fortunes and sacred honors" against the powers that be. The fate of the vanquished is left in no uncertainty. Such at least was not the case in Mazatlan some years since, when the lifeless body of the insurgent was exposed in the public plaza for days to the curious gaze of friends and foes. Of recent years I have heard of but one of these mountain chiefs who has eluded capture and death.

CHAPTER XIV.

A REVOLUTIONIST. — THEIR MODE OF OPERATIONS.—EFFECT ON CAPITAL.—RAILROADS.—FREIGHTS.—PRICE OF FLOUR, SUGAR, ETC.

A Mexican gentleman, the manager of a mine in the section where he was operating, told me of having been interviewed by one of these rebel chiefs at his place of business. He had collected about three hundred well armed men, desperate like himself, and had organized them into different departments of his army. He had his commissariat and ordnance department each properly officered. The most rigid discipline was maintained by him throughout his army, a disobedience of orders being punishable with death. He had his scouts and spies, to note the movements of the government forces who were after him, and to report to him where designated, the marches and the countermarches, the number and disposition of the opposing troops. He had, too, his sharpshooters, the practice of whom he was permitted to see, and which he describes as having been remarkably accurate. The chief sent word to my informant that he would be at his place on a certain morning, and at a certain hour, and told him not to leave there. To have left, would have been an abandonment of all that he had, and thinking the matter over, he resolved to await and abide his fate. So, sure enough, at the designated hour, there came in sight a herd of cattle, driven by men approaching his place of business. The men proved to be the herders in the subsistence department, and soon commenced slaughtering for the troops, which were but a little distance behind. The chief came up also, in due time, made his house his headquarters, placed a guard around his premises, took nothing, and remained with him a couple of days, in the meantime telling him his history, recounting his grievances against the government, for a redress of which he was now on the warpath, and rehearsing the history of his war exploits. He was a young man, probably not more than twenty-five years of age, of fine address, moderate education, unflinching courage, indomitable will, and unquenchable ambition. He possessed fine military capacity, with the eye of an engineer saw at a glance defensible and indefensible positions, and being as cool as he was brave, with his troops moulded to his sovereign will, in the dangerous emergencies of action would throw them here and there to meet the varying phases of the fight. For several years he has kept up the unequal contest unsubdued, and still survives the fortunes of war. These leaders would march into a village, place guards in the streets, that none might escape, arrest the monied men of the place, levy forced contributions upon the citizens, and with a rude equity, apportion to each a payment corresponding to his supposed financial ability. Useless were the demurrers of the "tax-payers," for the "tax-gathers" held the execution then in their hands, and a levy was made by a swinging to the nearest tree, unless the money was forthcoming upon demand. Thousands would sometimes be exacted, to the impoverishment and ruin of the robbed, who was dismissed with the consoling assurance that he was fortunate in not having been hung.

In this way the depleted exchequers of the gangs were often replenished, the rich made poorer, and the poor made richer. For these reasons many Mexicans, who had accumulated money, sent it away to the United States, principally to California, to avoid such depredation. Especially was this the case in the States of Sinaloa and Sonora. And many of this class, with their families, followed their treasures, and are now living abroad. Capital is always sensitive; but no capital could stand, for an indefinite time, these lawless raids, first by one party and then by the other; but, to protect itself, sought safety in flight. When

THE MOUNTAINS OF MEXICO. 87

capital involuntarily expatriates itself, then home rule is home ruin.

As before intimated, the followers of these revolutionary leaders were inspired by no worthy motives, no patriotic principles. They were a set of madcap adventurers, going out with the hope that in the change sought something might turn up to their advantage, as they had nothing to lose, either in reputation or estate—a gang of reckless daredevils, willing to risk their bodies for the sake of adventure and the chances of plunder. The instances were rare, I apprehend, where these revotions could be justified; but doubtless there were some exceptions, when not to have fought would have been dishonor and cowardice. I know almost any government is better than no government, for when anarchy comes, society is free from political restraint, its members fall back upon their natural rights, and might becomes right. The wildest excesses follow where crime and ruin strike hands, stalk though the land, kindling fires and shedding blood. In some instances the governing powers had become so notoriously profligate, corrupt and oppressive, that revolution, anything, was right to bring about change in the existing order of things. 'T was then some brave spirit came to the front, and other brave spirits came with him; the oppressor was overthrown, order restored, and right and law again asserted their supremacy. The righteous purpose justified these revolutions. But enough has been said to give at least some insight into the condition of things which prevailed from time to time in portions of this country. These local disturbances, however serious and formidable, must expend themselves in their own districts, unsuppressed by the federal government, the seat of which was at a great distance, and with scarcely any means of communicating with its remote provinces.

But of late years great progress has been made by the Mexican Government in railroad building, and in extending telegraphic communications. The government has manifested a very liberal policy toward railroad companies in grant of subsidies, extravagant, in view of the impoverished condition of its treasury. These have been foreign companies, with foreign capital, which have infused new life into the old land. In a few years the principal cities of the republic will be connected by these iron ways. As yet, the neighing of the iron steed has never been heard in the Sierra Madre. I am aware that intelligence, energy and money, can accomplish almost anything, and may, hereafter, as they have heretofore, accomplish apparent impossibilities. The steam engines, harnessed to the rushing train, may yet bring the valleys nearer to the mountains, and the mountains nearer to the sea. Distance shrivels, and remote sections become friendly neighbors, with an interchange of thoughts, and feelings and products. It is four hundred miles across the mountains. Nine times, from this point, have I crossed them, going east and west. With their geography, topography and trails, I am now pretty familiar. At first view they seem to have been thrown up and left as an everlasting barrier against the presumptuous enterprise of man, saying to him and to his daring schemes, "thus far shalt thou go, and no farther." Their abruptness, more than their extreme height, will be the obstacle to the engineer and roadbuilder. The defiles are such, that it would not require three hundred men to make of each of them a Thermopylæ. Yet such have been the triumphs of engineering skill, that a dozen years may not elapse before that transcontinental trains, laden with people and products, may, with their thunders, wake up the echoes of the Sierra Madre canyons. Timber and minerals must comprise the outgoing freight. Agriculture could send nothing abroad. In fact, breadstuffs are now brought in to supply the failure of home production, upon which are paid high tariffs and freights. Flour now costs ten cents a pound, and other articles of food, when imported, correspondingly high prices. Sugar is worth twenty-five cents, grown in this country, and rice same price. Bacon is not purchaseable at any figure, but has been known to sell for fifty cents a pound, of course, as a special accommodation upon the part of the seller, to some hungry friend! Beef is more moderate in price, and more muscular than elsewhere, as the exertion required to climb the mountains in search of daily subsistence develops the muscles, and toughens the beef amazingly. Irish potatoes grow to the size of partridge eggs, and should be eaten as "spoon victuals." I refer to these things to show that the railroads could not rely upon the production of this section other than that mentioned for outward bound freight, as they do not raise enough to supply themselves. And to bring these articles in any considerable quantities, so as to earn freight, would hardly be profitable, as the poverty of the purchasers would preclude them from buying large amounts.

CHAPTER XV.

MEXICAN RAILROAD.—DIFFICULTY OF MAKING IN MOUNTAINS. — A GEORGIA RAILROAD. — TELEGRAPHS.

If railroads ever come here the Mexicans will never build them; at all events, if I may indulge in a reasonable prophecy, for a century or so. They started to build a branch road from Jimenez on the Mexican Central to the city of Parral, some sixty miles distant. It was to be "exclusively a Mexican enterprise," spent a good deal of money, and it has proven "exclusively a Mexican failure." Judging from the serpentine course of the roadbed one might infer that the engineer did all his surveying in the mornings, while still staggering under the effects of the night's drunken carousals. Now, I do not assert such was the fact, but as it was an "exclusively Mexican enterprise," it might have been; and I am always willing to give credit to whom credit is due, be he Mexican "or any other man." From my observation here, it is as much as the average Mexican can do to engineer the average mountain burro, and in this he has acquired a proficiency from long acquaintance with that animal. But to build and operate a railroad is higher than his highest thoughts, and greater than his capacities. But foreign capital, directed by other people, may penetrate and traverse the mountains and go down to the Pacific Coast, and there connect with the fleets of commerce for distant shores. Then over these iron highways the treasures from the far-off East may come, and by the interchange make glad the mountains and valleys of the Western Hemisphere.

Some years ago the government granted a large concession to a railroad company to build a road from a place called Tobolovampo, on the Gulf of California, to some point on the Rio Grande, probably Eagle Pass. Some surveys were made and other preliminary work was done, but up to this time, practically speaking, it remains a paper railroad. Its route over the mountains, I think, yet remains undetermined. It is claimed that such a road will shorten the distance from New York to the East Indies seven hundred miles; that its Pacific terminus has a fine harbor, where fleets and vessels of the heaviest tonnage may ride in safety. As to the truthfulness of these statements I am not prepared to say, but modestly suggest their acceptance only after corroboration. The railroads here, too, have had a hard time of it, though fostered by the government. Business depression here, as elsewhere, has been so wide and deep that no class has been exempt from its blighting influence. In fact, the promised subsidies of the government, upon the faith of which many roads were built, could not be paid, but were for the time suspended in consequence of its financial distress. The government, in the readjustment of its own debt with its foreign creditors, was compelled to modify its railroad grants, for a time at least, for its own salvation. I do not question its integrity of purpose in doing so, and believe the sequel will prove its policy judicious and far-seeing. But be this as it may, the roads from these or other causes have not, so far, reaped the golden grain of their fine anticipations. The truth is, their projections were miscalculated somewhat. They thought magic hamlets, villages and cities would spring up along their line as they penetrated the interior, and that the pulsations of commerce would wake up the sleepers and enliven trade and travel along these thoroughfares. It was too sudden for the Mexican, and he stood rather stupefied than awakened, as cars went rushing by him and his burro train. That was some years ago. He is now rubbing his eyes, selling his pack mules and gradually retiring his nimble-footed burros from competition with the national lines of transportation. He deplores the day of their advent, but yields to the inevitable with a characteristic grace. In a few years, if prosperity should generally abound, this republic, too, will have its system of railroads penetrating every accessible region, and everywhere imparting health, vigor and life. One thing can be said of those which have been so far built, they are good roads and make good time—unlike one in the South during the war, in the State of Georgia, on which over the rear platform of the car was a large warning placard which read, "Passengers are positively forbidden to stand upon the platform and pick blackberries while the train is in motion." These are well constructed and well equipped, and while "in motion" the wayside berries will remain unpicked, and such printed cautions to passengers are only "love's labor lost." But ascending these high grades I do not expect railroad engines for years to come. I would almost as soon expect to see aerial steamers coursing the upper deep, laden with drummers and merchandise, landing the one and discharging the other at the mountain peak way stations. But whatever may be the increased facilities for transportation from aboard, it is to be hoped that the character of the importations will be of a better class than heretofore. In this respect Mexico has been much imposed upon. Stocks of every description, which could not elsewhere be disposed of, have been bundled, hurried and dumped into this country, until it has become the veritable "waste-basket of the nations." Honesty is not only the best policy, but the best principle, and a departure from this sound business maxim will react upon its authors. I thought it not improper, even in this connection, to make the foregoing observation, as it may be of benefit to some living without, as well as within, this country.

We have telegraphic communication with all the outer world. While the modesty of the lightning rod man has prevented his visage from being seen in these parts, the telegraph people came nearly two years ago, and now we are connected with the seaboard and the far east. Between here and the coast, more than two hundred miles, there are but three offices. From Mazatlan, nearly four hundred and fifty miles from this point, there is communication by wire with the city of Durengo, and on to the city of Mexico, and from thence by land and cable to all parts of the world. Should I desire to send a message from here to San Francisco, it must go by the city of Mexico, for the reason, I have heard, that it is to the interest of certain parties living in the capital that all messages should go on certain lines, however circuitous the route taken. This may be a slander upon the living; if so, no wonder, for even the dead do not escape the vile tongue of the traducer. This service has been much improved since its establishment. I remember a gentleman sent a message to the city of Chihuahua, less than five hundred miles, making inquiries concerning his mother, who was, at his last accounts, in an extremely critical state, and the message was received only *twelve days* after its transmission! It would now probably reach there in twenty-four hours if the lines were uninterrupted. Dispatches coming from the States were scarcely decipherable—looked as if they were in the last stage of confluent smallpox, having been translated and re-translated in their passage by unscholarly operators, until the identity of the original was lost in the "base counterfeit presentment." They were then delivered, a jargon of English and Spanish, misspelt at that, no less humbling the pride than exciting the wrath of the receiver. It mattered not how urgent and important the matter, if he acted at all upon the receipt of the message, he did so with many misgivings as to the correctness of his interpretation. But now the operators have become so proficient that they send and receive messages in English, and with the exception of some misspelt words, they are correctly given. But the tariff of charges is very high, which is regulated by the government, being the owner of most of the lines. Strange to say a dispatch may be sent to the United States, two thousand miles, cheaper than a few hundred miles in this country. From this point to Parral a message of ten words will cost four dollars or more. The same, if sent by the city of Mexico to the

THE MOUNTAINS OF MEXICO.

United States, will cost probably not more than two dollars and fifty cents.* You ask why is this? I can't tell you. It is hidden in the wisdom of the official powers. It is, to use a common-place expression, "what no feller can find out." The telegraph lines are sources of considerable revenue to the government, on which a great deal is expended in their maintenance, traversing as they do long stretches over mountains and plains, through sparsely settled districts, necessitating much time and expense in repairs of damages from mountain streams, falling trees and other causes. Here but few people avail themselves of this public convenience, but as they become more familiar with its workings they will gradually come to adopt it. Even now some of them are not yet reconciled to the mail system, for when they wish to communicate with some distant place to which the mail goes, instead of sending the letter in that way, they employ a private messenger for that purpose. This is very common, and if the matter is of great importance probably the better course to pursue, because of the uncertainty of the mails.

---

*Now since this was written greatly reduced.

CHAPTER XVI.

POSTAL SERVICE.—EXPERIMENT TO IMPROVE IT. —POSTMAN'S TROUBLES. — POSTOFFICE OFFICIALS.—NEWSPAPERS.

Some words as to the postal system in this section may not be uninteresting. In other localities, doubtless, the service is better, but here it has many annoying imperfections. These shortcomings are to be ascribed not so much to the local officials as to the postoffice department itself. Until within the last few years, before the influx of Americans, the correspondence was comparatively nothing, and the efficiency of the mail service reduced to a minimum. But increased correspondence necessitated increased efficiency, and how to obtain this from the department has been a problem of difficult solution. For the numerous efforts made, and the time consumed in them before the least change could be effected, it would appear that the department in the city of Mexico had forgotten the existence of these mountaineers, much more their convenience and business interests. Probably a recital of the facts may enable my readers to appreciate the more the blessings of their own system, unsurpassed by any other. Nominally there was one mail a week, but frequently at certain seasons this did not get in once a month. This was very detrimental to the different mining companies whose correspondence was with the United States for machinery and supplies. Without knowledge of the arrival of freights they would remain awaiting shipment for weeks at points to which they had been consigned, as to which there were letters sent but none received. So grievous had things become that the different mining companies resolved to remedy the matter, and accordingly employed two postmen to take the mail to the city of Parral, after repeated efforts to obtain an improvement had been ineffectual. The letters were stamped properly and the men paid by the companies for their services, so that the government lost nothing. The letters were mailed in Parral for distant points and received there for the companies. These men made but one or two trips when they were seized and imprisoned at the instance of government officials, and those setting on foot the new system threatened with prosecution. These hostile measures killed the effort for increased mail facilities for the time. However, a petition was then drawn up and forwarded to the postmaster-general, reciting with particularity the inconveniencies and positive damages to the people and to the mining community resulting from a want of an efficient postal service. This was not honored with a reply for many months, after the lapse of which it was returned with the statement that the revenue stamps on the same were not sufficient in law, and therefore it could not be entertained. And this from a government to its people seeking redress of their grievances! The paper was then "sufficiently stamped" and returned. After the lapse of many months, when it gave no sign of life, other efforts were made in the same direction, and when all seemed unavailing, the head of the department suddenly turned over and ordered two mails a week instead of but one, but by the same route, crossing snow-clad mountains in the winter and swollen streams in the summer, the same insufferable obstacles which we had sought to avoid. In the winter, at times, the mountains have three feet of snow, and in the summer, after the rainy season has commenced, the latter part of June, the streams become torrents, and they are impassable for many days. Snowbound in the mountains is unwelcome news to those who are thirsting for news from business correspondents, family and friends. It means all communication shut off from the outside world for an indefinite time, and that you may settle down and compose yourself with the exclamation of the well-remembered song, " How tedious and tasteless the hours."

Footmen carry the mails, and these are often Indians. They can make forty or fifty miles a day, and pack from thirty to fifty pounds of mail matter. No horse or mule can begin to keep up with them; in a kind of a "dog trot" pace they go for hours and hours without intermission. Up one mountain and down another, on and on they go, these carriers of the government, from early morn until night overtakes them, when they sink to rest. When day breaks in the east they are off again, and so they go until their journey is ended and their charge delivered. Their pay is about one dollar per day. Their provisions they take with them, coarse and scant. Into the streams they plunge and cross at all seasons, unless dangerously swollen, for over them are neither bridge nor boats, not even a foot log spans these madly rushing waters, nor is there a light canoe to ferry him over while doing this government service. This servant of the government is treated like a neglected orphan. And at times when he fails from some cause to deliver the mail at the designated hour, they reward him with imprisonment, this trusted employé of the State! When he reaches an unfordable stream, he sits on the bank until it runs down; if not too long, adjourns to some neighboring ranch, or returns, leaving his mail, it is said, in some hollow tree, or under some rock until he retuns. In this way, and for the causes stated, these postmen fail to make connections, to the great disappointment of the public—or, at least, the letter-writing and letter-sending portion of it. The mail bags have only recently been introduced. Before these the carrier placed the correspondence in a convenient bundle, protected from the rains by a waterproof cloth tied up with strings and secured in no other way. They were an accommodating set of public servants, too, very unlike those in "Uncle Sam's" service. Here you might meet one of them in the road, and ask him if he had anything for you. Inquiring your name, he would stop, examine the package, or rather let you do it, as but few of them can read, and if you were fortunate enough in finding a letter, you could take it there and then, giving him a receipt for the same, which he delivered at the designated office. A little "free and easy," you will say; yes, nothing "stuck up" about him! He carries valuable packages of several pounds weight; registered letters, also, but none of them, I think, contain money, as nothing but coin circulates here. In some of the cities the "general delivery" letters are thrown down on a table and one may go and help himself. A letter may be intercepted by the party addressed at any point before it reaches its destination.

I have found the postoffice officials courteous and obliging, and from want of familiarity with American names they often ask the parties to look for themselves. In the villages the offices are genererally kept in some little store, and the letters either thrown promiscuously together in a box or stuck in between goods on the shelves. Now I know as well as you that this doesn't look very well, "sorter" careless like, an undignified looseness, but we must remember that this is their way, and if we don't like it we have the privilege of retiring, as they sometimes say. The postage is according to weight; ordinary letters within the State or republic, ten cents; same class for the United States, five cents. Mexico belongs to the postal union. Some of her leading men advocate the reduction of interior postage to five cents, believing that in a short time the increased correspondence will make up the loss. Upon the whole the department has within the last few years greatly increased its efficiency. And to the credit of these moutain carriers it may be said they seldom lose a letter; it may linger for weeks behind, no one knows where, but comes in at last soiled and disfigured, "but still in the ring." I have known letters returned nearly destroyed by fire. Their guardian had doubtless slept at his post. I have known them to be on the road for more than twelve months, but came smiling in at last, not very fresh, but with unbroken contents, all the same. With this department promptitude seems an inferior consideration to ultimate certainty. Expostulations are simply a waste of precious breath, and to expect a radical change, as well might you expect to change the revolving seasons.

As I have now spoken of railroads and telegraphs I will make a brief reference to the newspaper, that other medium for disseminating intelligence. In these mountain wilds there are none published. However, a few come here published elsewhere, the majority, I think, from the city of Mexico. In that city there are some papers of enterprise and ability, with their foreign correspodents and daily press dispatches from different parts of the world. Their columns are unmarked by the rude billingsgate that often disgraces the American papers, and towards their confreres of the press they almost invariably speak in terms of courtesy. Their editorials exhibit intelligence, strength and culture. But I believe outside of the more important centers they are but poorly patronized. Here newspapers do not spring up at every crossroad and railroad junction, for there is not such a reading public to sustain them. Parral, with a population of many thousand people, has no newspaper, so the news must be gathered by the ear and not by the eye. Culiacan, with a population of many thousands, has one or two thumbpaper sheets, meagre in size and more so in information. The city of Chihuahua, with a population of eighteen thousand, has the veriest apology of a newspaper under Mexican management, but as it happens to be the official orgal of the government, the public patronage gives it a sickly vitality. Mazatlan, with a population of fifteen thousand, has also one or two newspaper adventures, which, with, a passable enterprise, catch and record the current events. A few of the numbers of their journals are seen and read up here by a few of these people, for but comparatively few have mastered the alphabet, and beyond this to "baker" is to them a "terra incognita." Upon newpaper pabulum they do not feed; their modest thirst for knowledge is quenched by other waters; in fine, so ignorant as almost to believe "the visual line which girts them round, the world's extreme."

In this village are type and office materials for a newspaper, but unused, except to strike off invitations to a ball or funeral by the solitary typo resident here, who is "non-union" of necessity, and like Sothern's bird, "flocks by hisself." So the masses are deprived in the main of their great educators, newspapers, and will remain so as long as they evince neither taste nor ability to sustain them. So far as this generation is concerned, to hope otherwise is to hope in vain. Upon its intellectual advancement night has settled.

CHAPTER XVII.

NAVIGABLE STREAMS.—NAVY.—ARMY.—INDIAN DEPREDATIONS.

There are no navigable rivers in the interior of the republic, and hence no steamboats with their traffic and travel, and explosions. Before the era of railroads, wagon and pack trains did the transportation of the country. Their immense wagons would often have hitched to them eighteen and twenty "light weight" mules, and would haul goods more than a thousand miles. The roads were generally good, with gravelly foundation, and running through undulating plains, so that immense loads could be wagoned. But the railroads came and the wagons went, another illustration of the "survival of the fittest." While the Mexicans have some ocean vessels, and some of them make good sailors, yet, like the negroes, they can not properly be called a sea-faring people. They like a house and land better than a ship and water. The navy of the nation is neither formidable in number nor armament. Its vessels, like those of its northern neighbor, any fourth rate power might almost "rout them, and scout them, nor lose a single man." The difference is this, the United States, with an overflowing treasury, has no navy. Mexico, with an empty treasury, has none, and for the present century can build none. Both, when the hour of peril comes, seem to rely upon their land forces to gain their ocean victories. Or it may be that what has been misconstrued as supineness upon the part of the United States has really been only an anticipation, upon their part, of the millennial era, "when the sword shall be turned into the ploughshare, the spear into the pruning hook, and the nations learn war no more." Often a preparedness for war is the surest guaranty of peace, and a defenseless condition an invitation to merciless aggression.

Hence, in view of men and nations as they are, and not as they should be, there is much wisdom in the aphorism, "in the time of peace prepare for war." It is a fortunate circumstance that the aforesaid navies belong to neighboring republics, and nothing but bad taste and the grossest impropriety could induce the one to criticize and make mouths at the fleets of the other. Could there be an alliance between these nations, some league offensive and defensive, then their present navies conjoined under some puissant admiral with good wind and time, might sweep the seas successfully *before any pursuing power,* "and leave not a wreck behind." But rightly considered national safety is a subject of too much gravity to be treated in a vein of irony, and I recommit the question to the enlightened statesmanship of the "Sister Republics." The fraternity of nations, the universal brotherhood of man, is a beautiful ideal, and in the providence of the Almighty it will come in the distant future, " when the lion and the lamb shall lie down together and a little child shall lead them," but at present the outlines of that coming period are but dimly seen. Selfishness, ambition, greed, the conflicts of human passions and human interests are yet too strong to be sunk in sweet submission to the higher, purer and holier rules of life which must obtain, ere "righteousness covers the earth as the waters the face of the great deep." I am not pessimistic. I feel thoroughly convinced that the world is growing better. History tells me so, as I scan the pages befouled with nameless crimes, and bespattered with purest blood from earliest periods when men commenced to make it. Aliens once were enemies, but just as the barriers of non-intercourse were broken down and intercommuncation began, acquaintance ripened into friendship, and friendship grew into associated unions, thus widening and deepening the channels of human fraternity. With nations as with individuals, when they come to know each other better, partialities may be strengthened, prejudices dissipated, enmities forgotten. Steamships and steam cars, rapid transit in a word, is a most potent civilizing influence bringing about a swift interchange of thoughts, feelings and commodities, and thus, in no other way, introducing the nations of the earth to each other. But while man is better than he was, and nations are gradually growing from year to year into a higher intellectual and moral development, yet at present the thought is premature that governments may rely upon the integrity and good dispositions of other governments, and not upon themselves as a guarantee of their rights, and a redress for their wrongs. Such being the case, practical, rather than sentimental, statesmanship says, seek peace at all events; if need be, through ample preparations for war. Wishing things were otherwise will not make them so, and to meet them as we find them is the part and duty of enlightened legislators.

Closely allied to the navy is the army of the country, and as I have spoken of the former I will now make a few remarks as to the latter. It consists of about forty thousand men. In such a body there must be some good officers and good men, but as an army organization it will not favorably compare with that of any first-class power in any respect. It is said that often amnesties are granted to the most highhanded lawbreakers, criminals of every description, if they will join the army. The morals of an army, formed in a great measure from such recruits, are necessarily bad. Such a leaven so widely diffused spoils the whole camp. Association is contaminating, and the regular soldiers too often come to be regarded as fit associates for their unworthy companions. A soldier ought to be a gentleman, an officer never should be otherwise, but the practice resorted to here to fill up the ranks lowers the tone of the army, and weakens its better influence. These soldiers I have seen at different times and places leave upon me, generally, the same impression. They do not heed the maxim of Napoleon, that great master of the art of war: first feed, then clothe, then arm your soldiers. A hungry man won't fight unless it is for something to eat, nor will a naked man unless it is for something to wear. He has no spirit, no pride, no courage. The appeals of patriotism are poor arguments to him while hunger gnaws and cold shivers his emaciated frame. To arm him before he is fed and clothed is to reverse the natural order of things. Put something in his mouth, something on his back, then arms in his hands, and he becomes at once a nation's defender. From what I have seen and heard, these soldiers are neither well fed, well clothed nor well paid. He receives only a few cents a day for his services. His endurance is remarkable, making long and rapid marches in short periods of time, his baggage and subsistence being light. The well-fed American soldier would have as much contempt for his rations as the English officer had for the sweet potatoes of Gen. Francis Marion. A few corn cakes and a few beans make up his perpetual bill of fare. Now an ordinary man could stand this *menu* for forty or fifty times, but to make a regular thing of it, it becomes monotonous, and the stomach cries out, paraphrasing the words of Richard, "A change, a change, my kingdom for a change!" The bean is his meat, and its nutritive property must be great to sustain him as it does in the bivouac and march. But to see men dressed in linen and sandals while the snow is on the ground and the waters are frozen, does not magnify the importance of these "heroes in the strife." I know some who regard soldiers as mere pieces on the chess board, to be pushed here and there, as judgment or caprice may dictate, mere machines to do the bidding of superior wills. But there is such a thing as a soldierly spirit, without which he is a mere figure, but with it he is a controlling power. The majority of the rank and file here lack this element, indispensable no less to soldierly bearing than to leadership. The conditions calculated to inspire this martial spirit may be wanting, as he sees nothing hopeful beyond his term of enlistment. It is said they fight well. Judging from the texture of their uniform, linen—pardon the pleasantry—they ought to keep cool in battle, and coolness truly is a prerequisite to efficient soldiership. For many years they have been much occupied with the Indians. These have given this govenment a great deal of trouble, destroyed many lives and much proporty. To prevent their incursions from the United States along the border, and to overtake and punish those who make them, necessitate a considerable force along the frontier and an expenditure of much money. These Indians came from the United States reservations for the most part, from which points they would sally, after having been fed and pampered for a good while, and make their way into Mexico, leaving blood and smouldering ruin in their course. Once in these mountains it was with the utmost difficulty they could be found, or when found, dislodged. When their thirst for blood had become somewhat assuaged, and if pressed by pursuing troops, then they were magnanimously permitted to surrender to the United States forces, which, obeying orders from the Interior Department, punished them most condignly by placing them again on the deserted reservations! And then they were warned if they ever again abused the hospitality of the United States, by breaking away from bread, bed and board, and playing such unkind pranks upon our Mexican neighbors, they would be caught again and placed once more upon the aforesaid hated reservations! In fact they would keep on putting them there so long as the government furnished red blankets and rations and a frontier Mexican survived their practical jokes. Such has been the policy of our government for years, until within a short period, greatly to the detriment of this country, its people, and treasure. The unvarnished fact is, that the United States should maintain its reservation so near the border when its horde of savages would at will break loose, steal and slay in a neighboring friendly nation, and thus keep up along the line perpetual apprehensions, if not a state of terror, were nothing more nor less than an inexcusable outrage.

CHAPTER XVIII.

MEXICAN SOLDIERS.—APACHES.—INDIAN POLICY.
—YAQUIS.—MAJOS.—HOME ATTACHMENT.

The Mexican government has a right to ask indemnity and security against the border reservation system of the United States. Shall no one be answerable for the acts of blood and violence of these petted wards of the nation, these blood-soaked villians who riot in the very wantonness of cruelty, and who feast their souls upon the expiring agonies of their victims? Innocent, helpless women and children perished piecemeal under their terrible tortures, and the *murderer's reward is the settler's home on the Reservation!* No wonder the Mexican soldier, in fighting such fiends, gave and asked no quarter. He raised the flag of extermination and taught the savages that war meant to fight, and to fight meant to kill. Rewards, too, were offered for the heads of Apaches, and these doubtless stimulated the vigilance and courage of the Mexican troops, who often made the conflicts "short, sharp and decisive." In these engagements the Mexican soldier sufficiently illustrated his endurance and prowess.

THE MOUNTAINS OF MEXICO.

The picture of an Apache once seen, will long hang upon the walls of memory, the dust and cobwebs of years will never efface the impression. In the city of Chihuahua, some years since, I saw quite a number of Apache women and children in the public prison, recently captured by the State forces. I noted a conspicuous absence of the Apache braves among the prisoners, but remembering the "Indian policy" of the country, there was a solution of the enigma. The brave had crossed "over the river," and gone to other hunting grounds, where no bow and arrows hang in the armory, moccasins never tread and ponies never feed. But the mistaken policy of the United States in locating these Indians upon the frontier reservation was cruelty to its own citizens, hundreds of whom upon an outbreak fell victims to their atrocities. But forgiveness, shelter, safety, and provisions followed pursuits and capture, and thus it went on through a series of years, the Indians murdering and flourishing, white people on both sides of the border victims of the bloodiest tragedies, dying the cruelest deaths.

Coming down to the bottom facts, to speak plainly, out of such Indians you can't make gentlemen. Sooner will the Ethiopian change his skin, and the leopard his spots than gentle blood flow through such veins. Such bad blood can only be washed out after the lapse of generations by the continual infusion of new life currents.

Text-books, tracts, and sermons won't do it, when he has murder in his heart, the torch, knife and rifle in his hand. As well might we believe the wildest fictions of mythology as such an improbability. This is my conviction, but a sickly sentimentalist may reach other conclusions as to these border murderers, and in prose and rhyme rehearse the Iliad of their woes. In the lives of peoples and tribes, as well as individuals, after a long existence of horrible enormities, when the cup of their iniquity is full, it is the exemplification of righteousness that the sword of justice should descend in the hands of an angel of doom, and suddenly number them among the nations of the past. Reread the history of Canaanitish tribes. Such a fate well befits the monsters of whom we now speak, who have trampled under foot all law, human and divine. So when the facts are fully known, I am not prepared to disapprove the Indian policy of this country as carried into practice and enforced through the instrumentality of the army. Men are not susceptible to moral precepts with arms in their hands. Rebels make bad disciples. First arrest the ear by the voice of authority, then the arm by the might of power, and after this it may be the heart, by the inculcation of moral doctrines. Exact obedience to the civil power, by peaceably or forcibly inspiring respect for it, or in a word, law, government, order, first, and then religion. In my humble judgment, to reverse this order, to make savages into citizens, is a mere chimera of the brain, an Utopian dream. The Apache could no more be made a law-abiding subject of the government than you could convert a hyena into a lamb. When he does, then the wild cat will become a symbol of innocence, but not till then.

But to pass on to the neighboring State of Sonora. The Mexicans here had much trouble and hard fighting of late years with two powerful tribes called the Yaquis and Majos. They number many thousands, and one of their chiefs is a man of education and great force of character. They occupy a large fertile tract of country, lying a portion of it on the Majo River, and were engaged in peaceful pursuits—agriculture and cattle raising. They are said to be industrious, fine workers, and when unmolested, inoffensive citizens. But when their peace is disturbed, or their rights threatened, then the animal is unchained. The land occupied by them, they have claimed and lived upon a great number of years. Between them and the general government a dispute arose as to this land, and I learn an effort was made to dispossess them, which was resisted. This led to some negotiations, but they failed of their purpose, and then by resort to arms, it was sought to compel what negotiation had failed to accomplish. For years collisions occurred between the contending forces generally, resulting in the discomfiture of the government troops. Upon the extensive tracts of lands held by these Indians are said to be some fine mines, but they will neither permit Mexicans nor Americans to invade and settle upon their territory. They fear the permission of such a privilege may prove a Trojan horse. You may pass through their country journeying from one place to another, and you will be unmolested, but with them short stops make long friends. If they do not adopt the former phrase, they do the latter of the Scotch maxim, which runs, "Welcome the coming, and speed the parting guest." This they will do with an unmistakable emphasis should you linger, for in no section are delays so dangerous. I was told of some mining men who went over their line and commenced working some mining property, and thought they had struck a good thing, but the chief sent a delegation to invite them to his quarters, and the invitation was so urgent that they repaired thither immediately. The interview was brief, his command of language was superb, for he indulged in no Delphic oracle utterance; he told them to go, and not to stand upon the order of their going, but to go at once. Too courteous to disregard such a well meant injunction, under a special escort furnished for the occasion, they left instanter for other prospecting fields, well pleased with the country, but ill pleased with its people, and shaking the dust from their feet as a testimony forever against that nation.

The experience of that party is that of many others. I am not sure that the land question has yet been settled between them and the Mexican Government. For his land he will fight to the last. For this has for him an attraction which nothing else possesses. He knows nothing of the divisions of property spoken of in learned law treatises as being real, personal and mixed. Like one of old, "he careth for none of these things." But he does care for his land, his flocks, his hunting grounds, the graves of his wives and children. There are strong local attachments which nothing can break save a superior physical power, and this he will resist to the last extremity. But when was it an Indian of any tribe would, without a struggle, give up his land? He knows this, and for it will make his stand, and in it will make his grave. And at this we need not wonder when we reflect that dirt, land, in a word, and women have caused more strife than any other two things in the world. I am not blaming her. She can not help it. Too often she leads when she was made to follow. She reigns where she was made a subject. She bears not the olive branch of peace, but the apple of discord. All the Helens in all the Troys are not yet dead. I do not mean to be ungallant, much less untruthful, when I repeat that dirt and women, probably more than other things, have engendered strifes and maddened men. But territorial extensions have ever been a fruitful source of misunderstandings and conflicts among men and nations. What is taken by one party must be taken from the other. New acquisitions for the service of more extended dominion, a wider sovereignty to fill up ambitious desire. Territorial slices for war indemnities. But I tread tenderly here while a guest in the home of my friends, as I do not wish to awaken any historic memories. But so universal is this desire for land, for more land, and this desire to keep it, and to keep it at all hazards, that it seems an instinct of our nature, and that our affections become rooted to the soil, as are the shrubs and vines and forest, resisting the elemental strife. That the Indian has this feeling, too, of which we have spoken, need not surprise us. It appears a sentiment deeply imbedded in the constitution of our nature. To desire land acquisition is natural, to have it not so much in common, but separately for one's self, is the idea entertained, the desire sought to be gratified. Feeling thus the Indian naturally resists all efforts at expulsion and at its mention, on comes the war paint and the war dance, and off he goes on the war path. This land grabbing, land stealing, and land annexation business are the sources of unnumbered strifes, collisions, and wars. The Indian problem here, as in the United States, is not free from difficulty. State craft has found its solution beset with so many exasperating embarrassments that some high in civil and military authority have declared that the best Indians are the *dead* Indians. The humanitarian would object to such a sweep in classification, and have exempted from such a fate those who will cease to be savages and learn to be civilized men. And I agree with him, while some of these can, some can not, I believe, be reclaimed from their barbarism and nomadic modes of life. Some of the most distinguished Mexicans of whom history speaks have been native Indians. President Juarez is said to have been a full-blooded Indian, who inaugurated reforms which will leave their impress upon the country for all time. He died poor, which speaks volumes for his integrity, as contrasted with that of others who have filled the same exalted positions.

CHAPTER XIX.

REGULATORS.—THEIR PROCEDURE.—AN INCIDENT.

The public order of a country excites the inquiry of every thoughtful man. We have seen in times past, in some sections, how men would rise up and overthrow the established order of things. How some warred against the existing authorities and managed to maintain a regular army organization for an indefinite time against the supreme authority of the State, a kind of "imperium in imperio," with an autonomy of its own. These anomalies indicated the weakness of the government. Happily now the public tranquility is less frequently disturbed by this species of disorder. The State has more strength and its forces can be made effective the sooner to quell any insurrectionary movements. Generally speaking, outside of the mountain districts, throughout the country, a higher respect has been cultivated and is observed for law and order. And in some of these mountain cantons, when things become desperately bad, some bold men come to the front, and feeling that self-preservation is the first law of nature become a law unto themselves, and in the shortest possible time execute the greatest possible number of malefactors. Here leniency to the guilty would be further cruelty to the innocent. And in justice to these regulators, if I may so call them, their motives are good, and while their excutions are not in due course of law, they are in due course of justice. A righftul conviction rightfully reached is the cry of the criminal's eloquent advocate ere he expiates his crime. But here these self-constituted judges rightfully convict, but may wrongfully proceed, reaching a rightful end, but by an irregular route. Crime is punished, order restored, substantial justice attained, and while one of the ends of punishment can not be secured, the reform of the offender, for he passes beyond its power, the other may be obtained, deterring others from the perpetration of similar offenses. In such organized communities, such swift administration of law, or of justice, if you please, is often the most wholesome practice, and the surest safeguard for the public peace. Often in such places the officials are the veriest weaklings with neither knowledge of law nor strength of will, and are soon despised and over-ridden by the evil-doers of the land. 'T is then, in order to protect their life and property, these leaders arise, and having courts of their own, administer a law without the law's delays, and mete out to the culprit a swift and certain punishment commensurate with his misdeeds. As much as we may deprecate such a procedure in a bettter regulated society, yet here justice administered without law is better than when neither law nor justice is administered. In some cases the innocent may be punished, most rarely, however, but the guilty seldom escape. The accused and his witnesses are heard, the testimony concluded, the decision rendered, the sentence pronounced, and the execution follows. There are no misdirections of courts and misbehavior of juries to vitiate the verdicts; no continuances, no new trials or motions in arrest of judgments granted. No penitentiaries and workhouses to receive him, and no governor to pardon. He is absolutely naked, defenseless and hopeless in the presence of the grave to which he is speedily consigned. A swift retribution has followed him for his crimes, and will await others of like kind at the hands of these forest tribunals. I believe it is seldom they commit an error, for it is only upon the fullest investigation they inflict the severest punishment. When these men go after a miscreant his sudden flight and no return is his best security, for if caught, trial, conviction and death follow in rapid succession.

Such are some of the features of these irresponsible tribunals, but there are others acting within the purview of law which have ways of their own in administering it. The judge, attended by an escort, goes from point to point to where the accused may be imprisoned. He looks into their cases, some of whom he will discharge, and others he will direct to be placed in the charge of certain men, with instructions to take them to a given point. The given point they never reach in this life, but somewhere or somehow they *are lost on the way*, and such in spirit at least is the compliance with the judicial instructions. You may call it a rude way of doing such things, but these people look more to the satisfactory results than questions of taste and sentiment in such matters. Some time since an officer with a guard was moving some prisoners to this place, when he says they attempted to escape on the way. He shot them down at once, but failing to kill one of them instantaneously, only wounding him severely, he shot him again, as he said, to relieve him from his sufferings! His humanity was so painfully sensitive, that only in killing the sufferer his tender-heartedness could find repose. After relieving himself from the care of his prisoners on the road in the manner stated he came on and in a business manner reported his "acts and doings in the premises" to the proper authorities. As he asked for an investigation of the matter this was willingly accorded him. And taking some parties out where he started his new burying ground, they found the bodies where he had told them, and they promptly concluded that an official capable of so much truth must be incapable of any wrong. Their report not only relieved him from all imputation of blame, but complimented him for his meritorious conduct and superior marksmanship. When officials, as here, receive but little compensation for their services, that is, legitimate compensation, surely honor should not be withheld, honor to an active public servant, to whom honor is due. The caged criminals tremble upon the approach of these circuit judges, for they feel that time is brief before the disposition of their cases. It is the certainty and celerity of punishment, which strike terror to offenders more than its severity. But the manner of administering the law, here more than elsewhere, seems to depend more upon the official incumbent than the letter of the law itself. Hence in some cantons it is applied with unnecessary severity, in others it is a dead letter, and has no enforcement. I have heard it stated that some years ago one of the mountain Jeffreys had a miner shot for having stolen a candle! It is further stated that for a long time after this candles "went. a begging," to be stolen, but no one wished to humor them by taking their lights. Positive law with fixed limitations, and not caprice or arbitrary power should determine the measure of punishment. Judges are but men, and men too often weak, corrupt, or tyrants.

There is no doubt, however, but that some of

these circuit judges perform most valuable services in their sentences of extermination. No one unfamiliar with the matter has any adequate conception of the condition of things, which absolutely necesitates the enforcement of such vigorous measures. Lawlessness in the ascendant means terror and anarchy below. And here in many places these bad elements would get and keep the mastery unless speedily crushed by the arm of authority. Desperate diseases require desperate remedies, and desperate men the swift infliction of the severest penalties. Society must protect itself in one way or another, if not for some good reason according to the forms of law, then outside of those forms it must vindicate its right to live by the death of its assailants. I am aware of the ground upon which I am treading and that the views expressed may savor of the mobocratic. These remarks are now designed to apply to some of the localities where the better elements of society are compelled to do something in self-protection, for the law itself has no more strength than a rope of sand. It is the assertion and maintenance of natural rights against this invasion by gangs, organized and unorganized, of ¦cut-throats and robbers. When the law lives and the courts are open no one would be farther than myself from countenancing such irregular proceedings. A change of condition and circumstances necessitates a different treatment, and looking to the temperament of the patient and the history of his infirmity, as wise advisers, we must, at the proper time and place, apply the particular remedy best adapted to heal the ailment. And this is all there is of it when we go to the foundation of the matter. Mexico is not in the United States, nor are these mountains the better portion of Mexico. Law, to be effective, must accommodate itself to the genius of the people, backed by a popular sentiment. But when there is no popular voice to sustain it, as in many parts of these mountains, then it is only remembered to be despised. And could you see some of these judicial officials, muffled to the eyes, with a blanket thrown around them for the judicial ermine, I am sure ever aftewards you would have greater respect for the opinion of Mr. Justice Dogberry. They hold their office by appointment, and as kissing goes by favor, upon no other reasonable hypothesis can we account for the fact that such creatures fill such places. Young ladies who have rejected many good offers are sometimes warned by interested parties that one may go through a forest and then pick up a crooked stick, so it would appear here, that the sorriest judicial timber in the whole forest has been taken, out of which to make judges. They can not rightfully assert as the pompous Texan justice claimed, as to his baldness, that it came from "a vast knowledge of the law."

CHAPTER XX.

MEXICAN JUDGES.—POLICO—CARRYING PISTOLS.
—KNIVES.

Sir Isaac Newton replied to one who was congratulating him upon his wonderful attainments, that he had only picked up a few pebbles of truth upon the shore of the great ocean of knowledge. The Mexican judges have never yet taken a pebble, nor heard of such an ocean of information. They can scarcely read and write. I do not know the fact, but think it not unlikely some of them can do neither. Upon the principle that what has been done can be done again, I see no reason why their opinions, if well edited, ought not to *sell*, for many of them have been *sold* once. Without reference to age or qualification, these men are selected to fill the position of honor and trust. I now call to mind one who for years was a hanger-on at the jail; now he dischages the judicial functions in a manner satisfactory to the public. And the public like him too, for, as *quasi-judex*, he entertains some of its best citizens in a manner long to be remembered. If by some international arrangement the burlesque

"Arkansaw Justice" and the Sierra Madre Judge could for a season interchange ridings, just to clear up old cases on the docket "you know," it might be advantageous by the diffusion of more light in the nebulous regions of the two republics. Ignorance may be excused in such places, but corruption never. It is notorious that their wares are as marketable as sheep in the shambles. The heaviest purse gets the heaviest verdict. Justice is represented as blind, but here take the bandage off her eyes and the condition is unchanged. She is yet blind to justice. They incline the scale when you put something in the scale to incline it. They must see where "Jeems comes in." "Jeems" was the given name of a celebrated Tennessee legislator, and was approached on divers occasions, opportune and inopportune, by a clergyman who was much interested in getting some reform legislation, and relied upon "Jeems" to put it through who had approved it heartily. But when "Jeems" moved slowly in the matter, the cleryman asked him why it was. He said he approved the measure, thought it would be a great blessing to the country, and yet had not taken a step toward its passage. "Jeems," feeling himself somewhat cornered, replied in the slang of legislative parlance, " Brother ——, I repeat all I have said as to the merits of the bill ; it has my unqualified indorsement, but you have not yet told me or showed me *where Jeems comes in."* And so it is with some of the judges, they can see nothing until they see something first. I presume a more corrupt set of "Jeemses" do not anywhere exist. Were they more so their very meanness would extinguish vitality. The executive and legislative departments may be corrupt, yet if the judiciary stands in its incorruptible integrity, it may preserve the rights and liberties of the people. A judiciary "unawed by power, and unbribed by gain," is the best bulwark of constitutional liberty. It allays the popular clamor, arrests the wild frenzy of the hour, and fixes impregnably upon their pedestals that imperishable trinity, right, truth and justice. It is a source of much satisfaction to know that the suits of all, rich and poor, will receive at least, and at last an honest determination by an impartial tribunal. Even suspicions to the contrary weaken the administration of law, for probably more than all others the judge should be like Cæsar would have had his wife above suspicion. But superadded to ignorance and corruption we find them often supercilious, overbearing and browbeating in their demeanor. For ignorance we can exercise charity, for corruption loathing, and for haughtiness, deep if unexpressed contempt.

In my meditative moods I have thought that there was a long distance between one of these officials and a life statue of Lord Mansfield. Marshall, Kent and Story, of whom they never heard, were the merest tyros in legal erudition to these men, in their own estimation. How true it is that generally all over the world modesty and merit go hand in hand, that humility and worth are firmest friends. I do not mean to say that greatness is invariably dissociated from vanity, for the reverse is sometimes true, but then it is greatness in spite of vanity, and beyond it. Instances of this kind I now remember, and can but think that the character would shine the more and be the more lovely were these blemishes wanting. From such courts you know not what conclusions will be reached, for no one can reasonably anticipate a decision even in the plainest case, when that decision may be reached without a reason. A benefit conferred, a favor expected, a few pennies in the pocket are worth more than pounds of arguments. The former he sees and accepts, the latter he neither sees, nor hears, nor feels. As before intimated, the dispensation of laws depends here almost entirely upon the character of the official, calling to mind the saying of some English judge in reference to equity, that it might depend upon the measure of the foot of the chancellor! What I mean is that the same offenses in different localities receive different punishment, or no punishment at all. For instance, I am told that near the southwestern part of the State there is a district where the penalty for stealing property worth fifty dollars is death, and less than that sum fifty lashes under an uplifted shirt. Both remedies have their advocates, and both are said to be remarkably efficacious in the suppression of theft, so much so that valuable things may be left "lying around loose" anywhere, and they will remain undisturbed while this common law of the country remains in force. But in other sections the same offenses would scarcely be noted as worthy of investigation, or only a few days' imprisonment at most. There is a want of symmetry in the system, of uniformity in its application. In some of the cities the police department is well conducted. Take, for instance, the cities of Chihuahua, Paral, Culiacan, Mazatlan. In them the police force are well organized and disciplined, and are efficient bodies of men. In fact, you will find the police force as well kept there as almost anywhere. They have a singular custom, for policemen go around at night with lanterns in their hands to find the person sought. At this an American policeman may smile, and it does seem very ridiculous. But while in the cities crime is very well suppressed, in the mountains the reverse in the main is lamentably true. The weakness comes from the imbecility and worthlessness of the officials charged with this duty. They seem to be either indifferent about the matter, or terrorized by the worse portion of the community. For the most part worthless themselves, they can not lift themselves out of, and above themselves. I am told, for instance, that there is a law against the practice of carrying weapons, and yet the practice is universal. An American witness who had been robbed informed me when he went into the prison with the judge to identify the robber they both went in armed for that purpose, and this at the instance of the judge. I have seen boys not ten years old with butcher knives in their sheaths upon their persons, ten inches long. Training them up, you see, in the way they should go, so that when they get old they will not depart from it. Pistols, you may be sure, are worn by everybody—pistols little and big, of every style and description and pattern. I am not aware, however, they change them to suit the probable requirements of the occasion, as has been reported to have been done by a Tennessee bad boy, in which State the law is very severe against carrying weapons. His brother was the witness, and when asked if he knew any one guilty of that bad practice answered like a little man, "Yes, sir, Brother Bill has two pistols." And when pressed for an explanation of the necessity of having two, he said the larger one he wore when he went to muster—elections, barbecues, and "sich like"—the smaller one he took with him when he went to preaching and prayer-meetings! These fellows never see the fitness of things, and to suit the occasion vary the size of their ordnance. But where the practice is so general, there must be a harvest of violence. The habitual wearing of weapons, familiarity with their use, somehow seems to create a desire to use them upon the most inadequate provocation, and in spasms of passion. Hence the wisdom of the law against such an evil practice, to protect its members against both hasty and deliberate acts of violence. The cold-blooded villain uses them for the purpose of intimidation and business, that is to say his kind of business, which is to steal, rob, and if need be, murder. The hot-headed young man, upon some bare suspicion, some misreport or fancied grievance, employs them to wash his honor clean in the blood of another, and then throw himself upon a jury of the country, which, after having been well fed and filled during the progress of the trial, charitably sees an uncontrollable impulse or momentary insanity in the act, and in their verdict tenderly bid him depart, amid the "God bless you's" and "close call, old fellow," of sympathizing friends, free from dungeon and death, free once more as the unimprisoned bird! But here, practically speaking, carrying weapons is only a theoretical violation of law, a mere obstruction of which the court takes no cognizance, entertains no jurisdiction. It is a matter judicially considered here as of the most trifling importance, yet fraught with the most baneful consequences to the good order and well-being of society. I venture the assertion that no place can be found where human life is cheaper than when surrounded by a gang of drinking and drunken Mexicans, and each one armed either with a pistol or knife. The peace officers, in the presence of such a mob, are as powerless as the arms of a puling infant. They take the town and "paint it red," those not using the brush carry the paint buckets. The authorities for the time retire into their shells, and only emerge when the danger is passed.

If, in a word, public order exists, it is by the sufferance of the rabble, and not in the effective excution of the law. One never having seen such a condition of things must of them have an inadequate conception. Here authority without power is a mere mockery. Here it seems to be a disintegration of things, a general loosening of important parts, a lack of cohesive power to keep in proper play the machinery of society.

CHAPTER XXI.

PUBLIC ORDER.—TEXAN MURDERED.—"ACCORDADOS."— MOUNTAIN LAWYER. -- MODESTY AND ATTAINMENTS.

I begin this with an example of Mexican justice. In a village containing only a few hundred inhabitants, within the last three years, I believe more than twenty men have been killed outright, and many more than this number wounded in personal altercations, and yet not one of the offenders has been executed, and no punishment inflicted beyond a mere temporary imprisonment. Many fled for the time, but some of them returned to the scenes of their butcheries after a while, and in a brief period it was made all right with them, and now the blackhearted murderer is the welcomed fellow-citizen! Officials now clasp him warmly by the hand, and he, in the magnanimity of his spirit, forgives them for the temporary interference with his personal liberty. And they are so glad to be forgiven by such an *honorable man*, after having explained away the harshness of their treatment, the reconciliation is as sweet as that which comes to lovers after the war of words. There are numbers living in that place who have not only "killed their man," but two or three of them. Why, murderers play the part of soldiers, and guard in the streets to to the jail those unfortunates who have fallen under the influence of too much drink. Think of it, a murderer taking a drunken man to prison! The clerk of the court, or who has acted in that capacity, has been convicted and sentenced to a long imprisonment for several murders, and yet the sentence is unexecuted. The most cold-blooded assassin walk the streets with impunity, fearing no harm from any official quarter. If they have any apprehensions of evil to themselves it is from the kindred of those whom they have murdered, and not from the ministers of the law. To one unaccustomed to such a state of society it would be alarming, but daily familiarity with such scenes makes it less horrifying. Many of these criminals are never even arrested. They go out by "easy stages" from the village, and the pursuers either faint upon the way or soon grow weary and stop the pursuit, and report, "non est inventus." Thus the consciousness of duty discharged soothes the official mind, and about such a common matter there is is no popular indignation ever afterwards to disturb his mental equpoise. Thieves, notorious thieves, receive the recognition and friendly greetings of the best men in the village, having stolen long enough an enough in quantity and quality to give them passports of respectability. How true the couplet:

> " 'T is petty thieving to rob a henroost of a hen,
> But stealing largely makes us gentlemen."

The law is good enough, but there is no one good enough to enforce it. Near that village in December, 1883, one of the most outrageous murders was perpetrated by two Mexicans upon a young Texan for purposes of robbery. It appears from the best data obtainable he was traveling, was taken ill, went into an old house out of a snow storm about nightfall. Some time after this the two Mexicans came along, went to the same house; he gave them some oranges to eat, lay down for the night, and while asleep they took a large stone and crushed in his skull, stripped him of his watch, valuables and clothing and then dragged the body some distance from the cabin and concealed it behind a fallen tree, where it was discovered only after several weeks and after the snow had melted. The young man not appearing, his business partner, an American, growing uneasy, instituted search and recovered the body, offered a reward for the murderers, and eventually succeeded in having them arrested. The mother of the murderers, at some gathering, was seen wearing in her hair some pieces of the stolen watch or ornaments, and this led to investigation and arrest of her sons. They made a confession, and from this most of the facts are learned in reference to the manner in which he was killed. It is also stated that after his skull had been shattered by the incarnate fiends, he raised himself up halfway, and with glaring eyes fixed upon them in the agony of death, sank back into eternity. These men were tried in 1884 upon confession and other overwhelming evidence, and yet to-day they live—no fouler murderers in the annals of time. Some months ago both broke jail, but they were recaptured, and they now linger in jail, their crime almost forgotten. If such crimes as this go unpunished you can readily infer what disposition will be made of less conspicuous offenses. Of course the assassination sent a thrill of horror through the American residents, yet this and all things else failed to move the decrepit judge to do his simple duty. I might refer to other notorious instances, but with the same view the uncertainty and cheapness of life, the non-administration of law and the worthlessness of its ministers. The desirableness of a habitation in such a locality is not enhanced by such an announcement as made, but my purpose is only a truthful narrative of the facts as they exist. I strive to paint them as I find them, as Cromwell would have had his painter "to paint him, nose and all." It seems that other artists, from flattery or other cause, had failed before to throw aright on canvas that great Puritan proboscis, and hence the command to paint him true to nature.

The foregoing remarks as to the mal-administration of the law do not, as before stated, generally apply to these sections, for I would not have you to believe that such a condition of things generally exists. It is bad enough, and I would not desire to exaggerate its evil condition.

The Mountain Judges have no fixed compensation, I learn, and their legal pickings are very light, and as a consequence the best citizens will seldom fill such positions. And so it is the world over, talent always commands a premium. For the services of intelligence and integrity a fit compensation must be paid, and, it matters not in what vocation of life, asked and rendered. But these officials must live either upon the bounty furnished by the State or upon that drawn from the pockets of the suitors in court. Judges, more than all others, by liberal salaries, should be made to feel independent, unswerved by any improper influences in any guise coming at any time from any quarter. Unless such is the case inefficiency and corruption creep in and the State hastens to its fall. I hope these reflections will not be considered ill-timed.

There is yet another mode by which the notoriously bad are disposed of, and of which I have not spoken. Organized bodies of men called "accordados" start from opposite points and meet by understanding at some intermediate place, cleaning up all the villains as they go. Sometimes certain settlements become so desperately bad that as a *dernier ressort* the "accordados" take the matter in hand and conquer peace. This movement requires much secrecy and swiftness to be made effective, for if known, or slowly made, the game escape and are not entrapped within the enclosing lines. These vigilantes have the sanction of the proper authorities to wage this war of extermination. And nothing short of this will answer the purpose, give adequate protection to society. There are times when blood must be taken to prevent its effusion, and life, too, must be taken to save the State. Napoleon well understood this when he directed his cannoneers to fire upon the mob in the streets of Paris, as he said, "to prevent the effusion of blood."

From what has been written you now have the modes in which the public order is maintained, and how the law enforces its sanctions. Closely connected with the courts are its officials, known as lawyers. The Sierra Madre mountains should not be permitted to pass until the lawyer passes in review before my readers. His modesty is less robust here than in any other section I have ever visited. His air and style immediately provoke the classic inquiry, "On what meat doth this our Cæsar feed that he hath grown so great?" His pretensions are as great as his ignorance of law, and this no man can fathom. Were he less immodest he would be more endurable, for we somehow or other will associate modesty with merit and immodesty with the want of it. Cynical and hypercritical persons charge this as a drawback on the profession, and I must confess, not without some reason, if the entire profession is to be judged by some of its members. But notwithstanding this blemish, he is upon better acquaintance generally a good-humored kind of companion, and almost disturbs you with his attentions in order that you may pass a good time. Disposed to be convivial and to indulge in those pastimes of the profession too often indulged in, drinking and gambling. I doubt if there is a lawyer in the mountains exempt from these excesses, and this is not paying them a flattering compliment. But there is a greater defect than the practice referred to—one that goes to and destroys the foundation of character and usefulness. I now refer to his want of proper integrity, for such is his character in this respect. There is always a suspicion of unfaithfulness, and that for a better consideration his treachery is purchasable. But the fewest number of these will hesitate to take money from you as their client, and from your adversary, from both sides, "and take it little and take it long." That he is unscrupulous is proverbial, and the extent to which he will go is only limited by the ability and willingness of the party upon whom he levies his exactions. He feels *his* conscience void of offense, and is more than willing to take to the uttermost farthing, and that from the nearest available source. He has no professional sense worthy of his high calling, but elsewhere in the profession among its honorable members would be regarded as a veritable *shyster*. Fit associate of those who daily visit the purlieus of crime and social ruin and fatten on their offal. A kind of petty crime scavenger that lingers for favors in the ante-chambers of jails and criminal court-rooms, and makes the very welkin ring in recorders and police court tribunals to the delight of gaping rogues, and roughs, and shabby gentility. He smelleth bad meat from afar, and with carrion talons hasteth to the feast. As to professional ethics, of these he has never heard; his game is, grab his client's victims, his life a standing fraud, a continuing libel upon the profession which he disgraces. Mexico has many eminent lawyers, men of great natural abilities, profound erudition and great professional attainments, but they do not live in these mountain ranges. In the city of Mexico and other large cities are men of high standing and of great reputation, an honor to their profession and to the republic. Side by side they might sit without any disparagement with those worthies who adorn the historic galleries of other countries. But to these men of eminence these parts are a "terra incognita," an unvisited far away land. With such courts and such lawyers you may readily imagine how the law remains unadministered, while justice sleeps, the right is stabbed and the wrong triumphs. The thing would be farcical in the extreme were not the consequences so momentous to liberty, property and life. Charitably speaking, there is a probability it may not be worse here than in similar sections in other parts of the world, but as to this I am not sufficiently advised to speak affirmatively. In certain classes the suits are conducted when the law is strictly pursued with much dispatch, but in others the "laws delays" are fully recognized, fully appreciated and fully adhered to. There are regular counterparts of the celebrated Jarndyce vs. Jarndyce which have a beginning, but like a ring without an end. If in these any considerable amount is involved before the end of the suit it has "grown small by degrees and beautifully less," until the parties in interest are glad to escape by leaving the "remainder interest" to the wrangling lawyers. And then these fellows fight on like Kilkenny cats till nothing is left, neither hair nor hide, and death curtains the scene. To this class to entrust the collection of money will be to say, "buenos noches" (good night), and for you the song of the money will be, "farewell, vain world,

I'm going home." Lawyers collect more money than all other agents, and this without bonds, and yet to their credit be it said, there are fewer defalcations among them than any other class of officials. I now, of course, speak of the worthy members of the profession, whose integrity is their bond, whose past life is the surest guarantee for the future, and not the professional sharps and scapegraces, who daily dishonor themselves and bring reproach upon the profession. These pettifoggers have not the remotest conception of law as a science, as a philosophy, but as thousands do, have gone into it with some collateral object, as a stepping-stone to something beyond. These are unworthy motives, and those who are prompted by them will never pass beyond mediocre positions on the highway to professional eminence. Truly has it been said by a great master, the law is a "jealous mistress" and to her you must give your time and talent, your toils through the long years, if you would fill a conspicuous niche in her temple. Hence she will have no half-hearted consecration to her service, but her requirements are the best you have of time, talent and energy. Her members, in ancient and modern times throughout the world, have graced and strengthened every position in government, been foremost in peace and in war, been leaders in camps and in courts. They have given to senates and cabinets the wealth of their fame, and crowned the higher judiciaries of the nations with the luster of their imperishable names.

But I find I am pursuing the theme further than the proprieties of the occasion demand, and now this unworthy mountain professional I will turn over to the tender meditations of my indulgent readers. But I forget, there is one other characteristic which he possesses that should not go unnoticed. In his efforts to collect money he is cold-blooded, conscienceless, and as remorseless as fate. To do this, ingeniously fruitful in resources, vexatiously annoying in expedients, in season and out of season, unmindful of age, sex or condition, he presses forward to the accomplishment of his purpose regardless of the wrecks left behind. It is said that a Tennessee lawyer caused an execution to be levied for debt upon the plank, called a "cooling board," on which the dead body of the debtor but a short time before had been laid preparatory to interment, and this in the presence of his agonized family. This I have regarded as an exaggerated story, but some of these men of whom I am now writing are capable of greater heartlessness. They would even strip the body of its scanty burial vestments and send it out of the world as naked as it came into it, a selfish meanness that shocks even the savage breast.

And now for having spoken so much of the mountain shyster I make apology, and leave him in the pillory of his own creation, on the summit of his "bad eminence."

CHAPTER XXII.

LITTLE CHILDREN.—HOW THEY LIVE.—MORTALITY.—ST. JOHN'S DAY.—DRESS.

It is always interesting to note the early manifestations of character, " the baby figures of giant things to come at large," and to follow developments through intermediate stages into maturity, to see the spring flowers, sweet prophecies of the summer and autumnal fruit. The fond mother watches with an undiminished interest her child, as in the volume of life are turned the pages from infancy to childhood, from childhood to maturity and age. And so have I here watched the unfoldings of character, seen at first as through a glass darkly, but when oftener seen, the salient features come out in relief and bespeak the "true inwardness" of their possessor. The study of character including its analysis, has not only an attractiveness but a fascination. And thus have I broken the weary tedium of the hours by taking to pieces different Mexican characters, examining their constituents in relation to each other and searching out the motives and main-springs of conduct. There is much truth in the paradox, "the child is father to the man." For example, the poor children exhibit the traits of their parents; they can not rise higher, and hardly sink lower. And to note these in the habits, aptitudes, mental and moral manifestations is an interesting study. I have had opportunities to see them in different phases of life, under different conditions, but in the main presenting the same stereotyped characteristics. With one sentence they may be almost photographed; mental weakness and moral obliquities distinguish them from all the children I ever knew. Doubtless much of this is an ancestral heritage. Physical deformities and their repulsive ailments, coming through vitiated blood for generations, are seen on every hand. There is not that light-heartedness of childhood we are accustomed to see where sunshine fills the homes and hearts. If now and then sunshine comes, it seems to come through rifted clouds, and shadows soon succeed, and leave their spirits sad. Childhood has no joys for them. I have thought they did not play nor sing, nor shout as others did, but for some reason there was wanting that zest so necessary to make the enjoyment complete. They play and sing but little, and with merriment seldom boisterous. How unlike childhood in happy homes, where happy parents are made the happier by shouts and songs of happy children; where the little girl, in sweet mimicry, plays with "Dolly," life's pursuits, until weary with her joys she sleeps in mother's arms; when boys signal their departure and herald their return with noise and make the household feel there is life within and life without. It is a great thing to be a boy; we can only be boys once, with their hopes and aspirations and energies, sound sleep and wakeful hours.

It is a great thing to be a school-boy, with books and fun and frolic, to play as well as study, and on holidays with dog and gun to hunt the nimble squirrel, or chase the hare through woods and briars, or with angling rod and worms in shallow streams to take the silver minnows, and then to close the rounds of the day's delight and take a *forbidden bath*. It is great to go to town, to go to the mill, to see the clown, to take the forbidden fruit, as others did, to wear store clothes and first cravats, to be father's pride and mother's joy—and then to be a man! Sweet memories come from childhood's hours to smooth the wrinkles of old age. These are thoughts that come from far-off home, and not from scenes around me. These little ones with pinched and unwashed faces tell of want and of some one's neglect. With scantiest clothing and shoeless feet, from cold they seek the sunny sides, and find in the sun a friend who shines for all. It is a curious fact that in villages of many hundreds of people you may not find a half-dozen fire-places outside of the quarter used for cooking purposes. And this, too, in places where the snow at times falls to the depths of several feet. Here blankets are necessary to sleep comfortably every night in the year—ice in May, and yet no fireplaces in the houses. The people say that fires are unhealthy. The little children may be seen in the streets on the frozen ground in midwinter barefooted and nearly naked. While but few present a really healthy appearance, it indicates to what hardships one may become inured. Were these things to take place in the United States, those having charge would be taken into custody by the officials of the "Society for the Prevention of Cruelty to Children." But here these little ones are overlooked by the philanthropist, and it is, turn them loose, do as you please, "root pig or die." They seldom taste meat, but subsist on tortillas and beans, and by way of a change invert the order and eat beans and tortillas. Now one can stand the same bill of fare for seventy-five or a hundred consecutive times, especially if it only comprises two articles of diet, but to make a regular thing of it, impairs the digestive apparatus. With fireless houses, sameness and insufficiency of food the little children have a tough time of it. The percentage of mortality is necessarily high—the statistics I do not know, as none are kept—for while human nature is very accommodating it can't stand everything.

Many of them have a sad expression before the activities of life have commenced—a look as if some hidden something was beclouding and burdening their young lives. It is sad to see the face of childhood with tearless eyes and penciled with lines as of premature care. Better far to see the falling tears swiftly followed by the rippling laughter. The faces of these little ones are washed but seldom, and in the course of time there is such an accumulation of dirt as to be suggestive of a "boom" in real estate. The truth is, they are not encouraged either by example or precept to indulge in such ablutions. They appear to have a natural aversion to such a practice, and all kinds of excuses are framed not to do it. Seeing a little fellow once with an unusually dirty face, I asked him why he did n't wash his face. He gave me some evasive answer. After the lapse of several days, seeing he had not done so, I again asked him why he did n't wash it, when he aswered, "Well, *Senor, manana,*" to-morrow. This reply illustrates two traits of Mexican character, his indisposition to wash his face, and the habit of procrastination. They reverse in practice the wise maxim, never put off till to-morrow what can be done to-day, by never doing to-day what may be done to-morrow. I asked a Mexican gentleman in the morning, who had remained with me during the night, if he would wash his face, and he replied in the negative, saying the *water was very cold.* There is one day in the year, however, when it is said all of them go to the little stream and indulge in a bath. I think it is St. John's Day in June. It is possible that this may be something of a religious observance, and enjoined upon them. I believe, on this occasion, the little children also go in and make the acquaintance of fresh water. Better once than never. You may imagine well how they look with patches of grease and dirt on their faces as large as the map of Cuba. Long black streaks are sometimes seen in the foreground like strips of adhesive plaster binding the severed parts together. The circle around the neck begins where the clothes cease to protect, and is as visible as the high water-mark around the trees after the subsidence of a freshet in the lowlands. Infrequently the comb visits the hair, which remains matted and tangled in skeins, or if you please, poetically *disheveled,* and with hair uncombed as a consequence, its numerous denizens would continue undisturbed, did not intrusive finger nails for the time break off the riotous feast. If cleanliness be next to godliness, then the inference is, the unclean and the ungodly are neighbors.

Observation every day teaches the lesson, that so much neglect and filth are unfavorable to moral growth and a pure life. These children, although having fathers and mothers, appear like orphans in the world, floating pieces of drift wood in the stream of time. "Just as the twig is bent the tree is inclined," and these tender twigs are rudely bent, and furnish bad materials out of which to build a State. The State is as are its citizens, and its citizens are its children full grown. But of this class the fewest number know even the rudiments of an education. So ignorance and vice go hand in hand to the final subversion of good morals and good government. The little fellows, children of penury, so poorly clad and fed, do not, by any means, lead lives of uninterrupted ease. I have seen them when certainly not more than six years of age following burros, goaded by others, to urge these patient animals forward to their destination. And to get up a "star route" for a burro and "expedite" him is no child's play, but business of extraordinary character. The male children are clothed in pants, to use the language of Wilkins Micawber, ere they have ceased to draw from the "maternal font." The natural inconvenience resulting from such a style of dress, it would appear, would induce a change in the fashion plates, but while the seasons change this style "goes on forever." "Little kids" in pants before the appearing of the first tooth, when the mother cries in rapture, "I found it first," are as ridiculous as "puss in boots." The little girls wear dresses reaching nearly to the ground and appear like little old women of the Lilliputian race. Every female, children included, wears "rebosas," a kind of veil or wrap, artfully thrown around their necks and heads, concealing very much of the face on all occasions and in all seasons. The richest are undressed without, and the poor are dressed with it. They will persist in wearing it, notwithstanding its inconvenience and uselessness, even when occupied in many household pursuits. The little boys, in place of jackets, wear a wrap, generally woolen, thrown around them, called a "zarape," which is their covering by day and by night. With thin shirt and pants and zarape, and no shoes, he seems born to be the "legal tender" of the burro train, and grows to manhood following over the mountains these slow-paced animals. The Arab children are said to sleep unharmed in the tent of the high-mettled steed, but here the boys of the mountains take to the burro with an unsurpassed enthusiasm, as if he were their "long-lost brother." Have you never noticed that sometimes there seems to be a similitude between some animals and their owners! It may be a mere fancy, and the principle of asssociation may suggest the resemblance, but so it is, the remark is often made, whether founded on fact or imagination. Now the boy and the burro are on such intimate terms that the one seems a complement of the other, and the boy without the burro or the burro without the boy gives rise to the apprehension that a link is lost and that the family circle is broken. The boy cuffs him and beats him as boys will do, yet if not on the dry mountain sides, down in the heart of the urchin is an Eden of pasture for the musical friend of his youth, the caliope donkey. But at this time I do not propose further comments upon this animal, reserving these for some future occasion, when under discussion may pass his merits and demerits, his uses and abuses.

CHAPTER XXIII.

PEON CHARACTER. — LYING. — PERFIDIOUS. — LABOR. — DRUNKENNESS. — RELIGIOUS LIFE. — SACRED WORSHIP.

In time the full-fledged peon boy becomes the full-grown peon man, and to this individual I will now direct your attention, for he is worthy of consideration. In the make-up of Mexican life he has his place, and his place can never be filled by proxy. The truth is, in the social economy he stands, like a drinking friend of mine once said in reference to whisky, that *this* " stood like Adam's recollection before the fall, *alone.*" The pen can not paint him as the eye sees him, or as the ear hears him, or as the mind perceives him. A faithful delineation can hardly be made, for he escapes the coloring of the mere pen artist. The instantaneous photographic process may catch him as he is, as it takes the race-horse in its flight, but I am sure nothing short of this will, in faithful portraiture, transfer to canvas this unique type of man. I can only present some of his more salient features, a rough outline, but the picture must be disappointing to those who see him as he is, a "McGregor on his native heath." In physique I should say rather under than over the medium size, of swarthy complexion, and generally dark hair and eyes. In his blood is a large admixture of Indian, but this element has rather improved than debased him. One of Mexico's greatest and best men is said to have been a full-blooded Indian. I now refer to President Juarez. The history of the Republic would be incomplete were the public measures inaugurated by him during his administration left untold. But the Spanish and Indian, when mixed, have fused into them the evil traits of both, and present to the world, I think, an anomalous character. At least in my wanderings, upon careful analysis, I have never found his counterpart. I am a great believer in blood—in blooded stock, blooded men and women —and hence I refer to the peon blood. And is there not much truth in the saying, "blood will tell"? Little buzzards are never found in the nests with eaglets. Giants do not spring from pigmies, nor do gentlemen from base-born slaves and boors. Culture may do much to weaken the taint, but now and then, after the lapse of a generation, it may be, it will reappear in some distant scion of the bad-blooded progenitor. Surely to the third and fourth generations it descends, exhibiting ever and anon its vicious manifestations.

In the first place, his life is a daily violation of

the eighth commandment, "Thou shalt not steal." Judging from the proficiency which he has acquired in this business, of necessity taking much time, one can almost imagine that he was born stealing. I am sure had he been consulted, and could he have exercised his preference, he would have *stolen into the world*. What he won't steal must be either invisible, inaccessible, imponderable, or in some way inappreciable. There is nothing susceptible of human handling, either too hot or cool, too wet or too dry which I have ever seen, that can escape his stealthy touch. He appears to steal first for the pure, or impure, love of the thing, "to keep his hand in," and to gratify an inborn desire to get hold of that which belongs to another. And this desire "grows by what it feeds upon," and he is careful to give it plenty of food when opportunity presents itself, and clothing, too, for that matter. Many things in this way he will appropriate which he does n't need, nor can he make them serviceable in any possible way; yet take them he will, obeying an instinct of his nature and the education of his life. He is expected to steal, and he never disappoints expectations; in fact, even among those who are accustomed to his "ways that are dark and tricks that are vain," the novelty and dexterity of his thefts are a succession of surprises. But this only shows what well-directed efforts can accomplish. It may take time, much time, if the conditions are unfavorable, and there is no natural aptitude for the business, but persistency of effort will ultimately achieve the coveted prize. But reverse the order of things, and with an inherited proclivity to do certain things, these then can be done almost without any apparent effort. This may furnish a key to the wonderful performances of the peon, in the line of which we are now treating. The juggling feats of some of the Eastern men are said to be most marvelous—putting your money in their pockets, unseen by you, and then in the same way returning it to you. These peons can beat these tricks, for by a species of legerdemain they can take it out of your pocket and *never return it!* Had he happened with Judas Iscariot in his hour of contrition, he might have relieved his conscience by relieving him of the thirty pieces of silver, with which he would have bought Palestine whisky, and never invested it in a "field of blood." I do not say he will permit the fox to eat out his vitals rather than give up the stolen things, like the one in ancient history; but when accused of the theft, with proof positive, his denials, were they paving-stones, would have built the Appian Way. Now, if you think he is honest, I do n't. I think he is a thief. Some men are naturally dishonest, and are honest from policy; some are naturally honest, and honest from principle. But the peon is honest neither from principle nor policy, but dishonest from both. The motives which induce his apparent favors are not unmixed with evil; down in his heart he sees, or thinks he sees, some way in which he can take advantage of you, and in the end injure you and help himself. Absolute necessity may force him to work, but it can never force him to do an honest day's work unwatched. He will either cheat in time, or faithfulness of execution.

There may be at times some excuse for stealing, certainly some palliation for it—to relieve, for instance, the pangs of hunger. But what can we say in extenuation of that other vice in the character of the peon, commonly denominated lying? Necessity does not prompt to this, as often it does to stealing, and hence it stands unrelieved in its moral deformity for this reason. He is a cold-blooded, heartless deceiver, who lies for a purpose, and that purpose to rob you of some object, or defeat you in some aim, by which from malignity or dishonesty he hopes to make gain. But wanting in moral principle, the peon does not hesitate to lie without scruple by wholesale and retail. His fathers did it before him, and he has never ceased to be a faithful follower of their bad example. Probably he now sees nothing wrong in it, so blunted have become his moral perceptions. To his responses to your questions there is always felt an uncertainty, and a hesitancy to act in the absence of confirmation. For some unaccountable reason there may be one in a hundred who may not deserve my criticism, but the remainder can not plead exemption from the righteousness of my animadversions. The little ones lie as well as the big ones, and often the little ones are the biggest of liars, exhibiting in this particular an amazing precocity. The more intelligent, the more inventive, and, I am sorry to say, the more reckless and unscrupulous. Education in and of itself will not prevent men from an indulgence in this disreputable practice, in the cultivation of this vice. I wish it were otherwise, but such is not the fact.

Superadded to the two foregoing evils the peon is also perfidious. You can never give him your full confidence. There is always a suspicion, rightfully entertained, too, that when the opportune moment comes to him he will betray you. For years they may give no evidence of unfaithfulness, and yet suddenly they will turn upon you, either to rob or kill. The more demonstrative in their attentions, pronounced in their expressions of attachment, the less reliance can be placed upon them. Protestations of unfailing friendship are likely, sooner or later, to be followed by unexpected treachery. And thus while abject menials, they are dangerous servants, for you know not the hour when their mean passions may plunge the knife to your heart. A sense of gratitude, if it exists at all, is reduced to the minimum towards those who have been their benefactors. They do not appreciate gentle treatment, but often take advantage to wrong you in some way. The more liberal you are towards them the less benefit it is to them and their families, for the extra compensation is immediately expended not upon their household, but in drunken excesses and riotous living. Your liberality stops them from work, for until their money is spent they care not to work, and will not do it, either for love or more money. Their own people understand them well, much better than others can hope to do with only a few years' residence in the country. To keep them regularly at work and earn some subsistence for their families, they give them barely living wages. When this is strictly followed your labor is prompt; when not, your mistaken policy results not only in an injury to you, but to them and those depending upon them. This may seem like a harsh rule to those who know not these people, but experience soon demonstrates the correctness of the treatment.

It may appear inhuman and unjust, but it savors of statesmanship, doing, nevertheless, the "greatest good to the greatest number." As they live principally upon corn, then corn becomes the barometer of their efficiency. As corn goes down, requiring less money to purchase the necessary supply, the excess of money is misspent in some species of debauchery, quitting work until the capital is exhausted. As corn goes up in price, it requires more work to buy it, and hence there is steadier employment to the benefit of themselves, their wives and children. No one fact is better understood than this, that so long as they have money they will not work. But the most efficient remedy to induce a return to employment is to put up the price of corn, and then it is the staff of life and becomes an instrument to chastise the idle and vicious for the good of themselves. Sentimental philanthropists may inveigh against the policy adopted, but that " man shall live by the sweat of his face," is as true to-day as when our first parents,

"Hand in hand, with wandering steps and slow, through
Eden took their solitary way."

And the apostle tells us, let him not eat that worketh not. So labor is the order of life, freely or compulsorily done, whatever to the contrary may be the theories of Utopian philosophers. But the peon has had hard task-masters for long periods of time, and this should plead something in extenuation of his present state of character. The hardships to which he has been subjected should perhaps induce a judgment leavened with charity. But I speak of him as he is, as I find him in business, and the relations of life, surely a fit subject, worthy of the efforts of the most ardent reformer. He is a great drunkard. But as for that, there is probably not one in fifty of the Mexicans in this section, peon or not, who does not get drunk. It is almost a universal custom. High and low, rich and poor, indulge alike in the Bacchanalian revels. And the poor peon, mistaking the fine examples to shun for fine examples to imitate, drifts with the sweeping current.

Then, in this condition, he is the very quintessence of meanness incarnated, the very embodiment of the evil passions uncaged. A drunken peon's ball is the revel of wild beasts. Probably the character of the liquor has much to do with the character of the performance. Here the most that is drunk is made from a native plant, and often made in such a manner that it "outvenoms all the worms of Nile." Not being copper distilled, it requires one to be "copper bottomed" to prevent his immediate consumption. One mouthful of it is said to make one's nerves tingle, as if they were jerked by a succession of fighting electric currents, while his brain goes wild in the delirium of the moment, causing the victim, like some blind giant, to strike right and left, smiting down friend and foe. Mescal and Tequilah* are the favorite drinks. The former sells for about three cents a drink, and its cheapness brings it within the capacity of the peon, and he gladly avails himself of the privilege, like many

---
* Pronounced Tekela.

in the higher walks of life, to make a nuisance and a brute of himself. With him the strength of this appetite can not be measured. It is his solace, chief delight, perennial joy. It matters not if his wife and children are shivering in tatters, and pinched with famine, something at least must go to purchase this accursed fire for his second nature. He is a fine subject for a temperance lecture. The picture of a drunken peon, with his repulsive surroundings, is enough to win for Prohibition universal approval. When unable to protect himself, the State should protect him from himself. It is a recognized principle that no one can use his property to the prejudice of others, nor should he use himself to the detriment of others, whether these be the State, or his immediate household, whose natural guardian he is.

We turn now to his religious life. Many of them, especially the worst of them, are most demonstrative in this respect. They observe with many scruples their numerous saints' days, but generally take occasion to wind up the day in some drunken orgies. But the saint is appeased, and on the morrow he is religiously prepared to meet the obligations of life, provided he is not still too unwell, and is out of prison. But did you ever think how often men are inconsistent in their worship? The anniversary of the birth of our Saviour, for instance, is celebrated throughout the Christian world, but in numerous parts in drunken carousals. It should be a season of fervent joy from the heart, but not for indulgence of the unbridled appetites. But to return, the peon has the utmost faith in the protecting power of his tutelar saint, and to it pays a blind obeisance. His or her image of very cheap material and rude construction he generally wears suspended about his neck, so that in any place and at any time he can make his invocations. How many saints there are which he worships I have not been able to learn, but I have sometimes thought nearly equal in number to the days in the year. If a child is taken sick before they can give it the remedy prescribed, the saint must be called upon to bless the medicine with healing power. And should it be restored all credit is given to the aforesaid saint; but should it die, the saint is none the less worthy of worship, but for some unknown reason was disinclined to interpose his power to cure, perhaps unappeased for some unintended affront. If a fire is burning the house over their heads, the women will run into the streets with crosses in their hands and calling upon the saint to extinguish the flames. But I have never yet known a raging fire to be stayed in its march, or put out by their prayers. But silly men and women will persist in using a spiritual weapon to control a natural element, and the consequence is, while they are without at prayers, their fireside altars within are sinking in the flames. I mention this to show the strength of their faith in their saintly existences, and how strongly superstition holds them in its grasp. Where this saint worship prevails to a large extent you may rest assured that its devotees are poor, ignorant and priest-ridden. The poorest and most miserable lazzaroni in the world, I presume, are to be found in a certain district in Italy, where it is said they observe about *sixty saints' days!* Think of these poor maccaroni-eating slaves, barely able with their daily wages to pin soul and body together, yet doing nothing for sixty days in the year but worshiping saints. No wonder they are poor and squalid, and miserable, and always will be until they revise and reduce the number of their saints.

CHAPTER XXIV.

MINERS.—PLAN OF EDUCATION.—INCEST.—INCI-
DENT.

The peon miners have some saint who is presumed to preside over the mine and to bless especially the miners who worship him and to keep them from harm while following their perilous vocation. A shrine, a cross, a lighted candle, bespeak the homage of their hearts, while a song of devotion from within echoes far and long among the rocky corridors of the mine. But this saint does not grant them salvation from danger, as will be shown from the many appalling mining catastrophes which sometimes take place. Upon this saint's days, some time in May, the miners will go in procession, under triumphal arches, decorated with evergreen, to the shaft of the mine, bearing the image of the saint, about the size of an ordinary doll, and having reached the mine will then engage in some devotional exercises. This saint is placed upon a small platform, over-canopied with some coarse material and borne upon the shoulders of some of the party, who frequently change among themselves in order to distribute the burden and the honor. A long retinue of straggling boys and women generally brings up the rear. The head of the procession is preceded by one of the number, attended by several boys, who shake the earth by exploding numerous charges of giant powder from time to time. Singular again, isn't it, to worship with giant powder! The observance of this day is rigidly enjoined, and under no condition could you induce one of these fellows to forego this religious festival. But like nearly all others, it ends in a promiscuous, universal drunk, and it is fortunate if you can get them to return to work for a week. It generally happens that several never return, as they have been numbered among the casualties of the festive occasion, and now sleep the unawaking sleep in the " Campo Santo," under the watchcare of their patron saint.

As to education, but the fewest number can read and write; in fact, there is scarcely one that can do so. They are veritable rough ashlers in the social structure; while at the very bottom, they make a very insecure foundation on which to rest the pillars of State, wanting in those two prerequisites, virtue and intelligence, declared by Washington in his farewell address to be indispensable to the perpetuity of a free government. But the peon has neither opportunity nor capacity for the acquirement of an education, and thus lives out his days in ignorance and moral bankruptcy. Nor so far as I can see, does he manifest any inclination to improve his condition, but prefers, from choice, the continued indulgence of his groveling tastes, vicious propensities, and general meanness. You can't make something out of nothing. That belongs to a higher power. You may polish the rough diamond, but it was a diamond before it received the touch of the lapidary. But you can't polish the peon unless you possess creative power, for he has been denied this susceptibility. Sometimes when I contemplate him, I almost conclude that he may at least be a kind of connecting link in the order of creation. 'Tis then, too, the couplet often occurs to me which was applied to the brilliant Sheridan:

> "That nature never made but one such man,
> And broke the die when casting Sheridan."

They are the prey of odious and unspeakable vices. Incest is frequently known among them, the father and the son cohabiting with the child and sister, thus, in the very wantonness of bestiality, outraging all the decencies of life and morals, all law, human and divine. But this practice is not confined to the peon class, others in higher stations are sometimes guilty of this monstrous iniquity. And yet, where it is practiced, it seems neither the law nor the moral sense of the community is sufficiently strong to abate it. Is there a deeper depth than this infamous degradation? Can sounding plummet line go beyond it? Open and notorious lewdness is seen on every hand. Were this confined to the lowest class it might be less censurable, but such is not the case. I am informed of one, an *honored citizen* (?), who has had a seraglio of his own, at one time, with half a dozen inmates, and suspecting the unfaithfulness of one of these, with a refined cruelty, he took a needle and picked out one of her eyes; the other one he spared, that she might henceforth recognize the mercy of her loving lord in not inflicting total blindness!

CHAPTER XXV.

A STYLE OF DRESS.—PEONAGE SYSTEM.

It may now be interesting to note the peon's style of dress, for you know it is said "the tailor makes the man." But whether to commence my description at his head, and go down, or at his feet and go up, I am somewhat puzzled. His sombrero is always broad-brimmed, and the finer the material the more suitable to his cultivated taste. If there is any one part of the dress upon which he centers his affection it is his hat. He wants it loaded down with yellow lace and big spangles, while conspicuous tassels fall in the rear. Had he money he would willingly give fifty dollars to get something in this line just to his taste. A twenty-five dollar hat and a twenty-five cents pair of guarachies for his feet, is the relative estimate he places upon his extremities. The sanitary maxim he ignores, to keep the head cool and the feet warm. He is looking after his head, and his feet, it may be like those of the peacock, are only seen to excite a feeling of shame, for he will instinctively contrast the poverty of his foot with the splendor of his head gear.

THE MOUNTAINS OF MEXICO. 175

But this is one of the peculiarities of the entire Mexican people, conspicuous hats, burdened with heavy and showy adornments. So in this particular the peon is but an imitator of the better portion of his countrymen, who often pay as much as fifty dollars for a Sombrero, when most elaborately adorned. It is "binding" enough in our country for the "old man" to plank down such a sum for a spring bonnet, or rather a nondescript termed a bonnet, and this is often done more in auger than sorrow; but if the male members, too, were to indulge in such extravagance the voice of wailing would soon be heard in the land. His zarepe, next to his hat, is that on which he sets the highest estimate. This is a woolen blanket, often very flashy and parti-colored. This is his invariable attendant in all seasons, and under all conditions, and is to him a jacket as well as it serves the double purpose of bed and bedding. So you see he presents this curious spectacle, if he goes to bed he takes his bed with him, and when he goes to work he does the same thing. If the weather is cold he wears his bed wrapped around him, and if it is hot he may loosen the fold, but wears it all the same. It is a partial protection in unseasonable weather, but an incumbrance when it is good. Were we to apostrophize it, we woud paraphrase Mrs. Hemans and say, " O zarepe, thou hast all seasons for thine own." But there is another garment, which is white cotton cloth, about two feet square. This is folded once, and to leave the lower points to cover the seat of his pants. It is a beautiful habit, and when thus folded and worn it is so suggestive of a baby clothes lines in the winter time stretched before the fire in the nursery room. A singular scene is presented when men and boys are seen, each thus arrayed, reminding one of big and little tadpoles ere they have shed their tails and grown into the proportions of frogs. But they utilize them by carrying within them their tobacco, handkerchief, and *stolen articles.*

The shirt of the peon is commonly of the flimsiest texture and worn *outside* of his pants. I think it was Sunset Cox, some years since, when making in Congress a speech upon the Chinese question, in reply to some inquiry why he didn't like the Chinese, said by way of a climax, that he didn't like any man *that wore his shirt on the outside of his pants!* And I fully indorse the *patriotic sentiment*. His pants are made of white cotton cloth, so very large in the legs as to cover his feet and remind one of a very small girl in very large pantelettes. His guarachies, consisting of a single piece of sole-leather tied to the bottom of his foot with leathern thongs coming up between his toes and finally fastened securely around his ankles, make up the *tout ensemble* of this gentleman's wardrobe. Thus accoutred, he presents an appearance of no ordinary attractiveness. With his winning ways, his engaging attentions, the heart must be callous indeed that would fail to respond in reciprocating terms to his soft palaver—his words of liquid sweetness. He may be uncomely, but "beauty is as beauty does," you know, and if I have failed to delineate him as he is, I have not set down "aught in malice," but have failed from want of sufficient descriptive powers.

However, it might not be amiss to say something of the system under which he has been reared, that of peonage, as it is called. The government, from time to time in the past, for distinguished military or other services ceded to individuals immense tracts of lands. And others in some way acquired great landed possesssions also. But these without tenants were of no value to their proprietors, and the poor own no lands, and to live must necessarily become the tenants of these great barons. They were compelled to pay such a price for the privilege of becoming tenants, that they became in arrears, and these, with their accumulations of exorbitant interest, made it thereafter impossible ever to extricate themselves from the yoke of thraldom. Henceforth, like a drowning chicken, the more they struggles the deeper they sank. Whatever supplies they needed, the actual necessaries of life, they must buy from their landlord, who was not scrupulous as to the price charged, but was careful that it should be so high as to keep his tenants in the toils. And thus it was they passed into the slavery of debt, and must remain upon the premises until the indebtedness was discharged. If a peon sought to escape from the condition of servitude he was pursued, arrested and remanded to the possession of his owner. That is what these proprietors were called, owners, masters, and they were spoken of as owning so many peons by virtue alone of having debts against them for certain sums. If the owner transferred his hacienda, his real estate, he sold with them the peons upon the place, for they were considered as a part and parcel of the possessions. You may readily imagine the treatment to which they were subjected under the system, compared with which that of former slavery in the South was an unmixed luxury. And to-day, in some parts of the Republic, the system practically obtains, for they are still imprisoned for debt, restrained of their liberty for its non-payment, should they wish to remove elsewhere, and this notwithstanding the present constitution of Mexico, modeled upon that of the United States, positively forbids, in civil matters imprisonment for debt. But these poor peons have not yet heard of such law, and will not likely hear of it, if they are to get the information from the lips of their masters. Some of the principal newspapers published in the capital are inveighing against the practice of these landed aristocrats continuing this peonage system, thereby acknowledging its existence; yet I apprehend it will take a long time to do away with the system, it has become so thoroughly ingrafted in exterior sections in the labor operations of the country. And then the peon has no interested friend at court to speak in his behalf, but the supposed interest of the more intelligent and wealthy who might befriend him, it is thought by them would be antagonized by his release from slavery. And as it is, he plods along, he and his children, unimproved in mind, morals, body, or estate, and probably in these incapable of improvement, to the undetermined destiny that awaits him.

CHAPTER XXVI.

CREDITOR CLASS.—EXTORTION.—CONSCIENCELESS.

I have adverted, rather incidentally to those Mexicans known as the creditor class, but now propose to submit some additional reflections as to these. I do so because they are worthy of at least a running commentary upon their idiosyncracies. I presume this last word is sufficiently large and significant to cover the traits of this Mexican type. In this treatment I must "hew to the line, let the chips fall where they may." His study by day and by night is how he may further entangle and oppress some poor unfortunate victim whom misfortune may have thrown in his power. He mercilessly devises all sorts of ingenious expedients the further to crush this helpless mortal. One of his chief instrumentalities is usury. He lends, renews, compounds, and then, just for "accommodation," he relends, re-renews, and re-compounds. It takes but a very short time before the chains are forged and the manacles are riveted. And then the *accommodating* gentleman becomes the haughty tyrant, his demeanor and spirit having changed with increase of power. Thenceforth, unless relieved in some unexpected way, the poor debtor is as helpless to escape as the wounded, fluttering bird to break the bars of its wiry cage. As there are no laws against usury, the lender takes what he can get, and he gets to the fullest extent of the debtor's capacity to pay, which is seldom ever as great as his promise to pay. The non-payment in part does not at all embarrass the creditor, for he had rightfully calculated that there would be something wanting, and upon this default he grounds other exactions. In this way he winds around and around his victim his ingenious net-work, and makes secure the fastenings for his life. He is now a serf and his wife and children slaves. So far as an emotion of pity is concerned for the helpless ones, you might as soon expect the hawk to release the frightened dove, or the wolf, the trembling lamb. He has them, and holds them, and leaves them to his equally cruel-hearted descendants.

Should you owe one of these Mexican creditors, the bee is a poor symbol of industry compared with him in his timely and untimely efforts to collect it. He consults the proprieties of no time, place or occasion to urge his importunate demands. To collect his money, his bond, he would not have hesitated, like Shylock, about the pound of flesh, but "would have taken the risk in the home office," his excessive cupidity with him outweighing the probable death of the debtor. This creditor acts as if he had received the same injunction the father in Horace gave his son when he said: "My son, make money honestly if you can, but if not honestly, then I say to you, my son, make money." We may here pause long enough to remark that this is nowadays too much the case, outside as well as inside of Mexico.

But returning to my theme, should one be so unfortunate as to have several creditors then, he can truly enter into and catch the spirit of the orator when he exclaimed: "Hard, hard, indeed, was the contest for freedom and the struggle for independence." No relation of circumstances, however reasonably calculated to induce forbearance will abate their efforts, and these soon become annoyances, and these in turn often repeated are aggravated into persecution. The Mexican creditor never "lets up;" he is ever in the pursuit, however hopeless may be the effort to secure possession. If the poor debtor falls a martyr to his ruthless attentions and falls into the grave as a refuge at last, the creditor condemns him for this *dernier* resort, and in his disappointed wrath now turns upon the unfortunate widow and hounds her remorselessly to the verge of despair. He is unfeeling as an Apache butcher. Payment or death are the only alternatives of relief. His soul-absorbing thought is money, how to get it, and how to keep it, whether by fair means or foul. Certainly the love of money is the root of all evil. Its inordinate love is soul-killing, drying up all the noble parts, and leaving all the evil ones to flourish in their rank, wicked luxuriance. The truthfulness of this is fully exemplified in the case of these Mexican creditors of whom we are now writing. Seeing their persecutions, their crystallized meanness, I have often thought, and I speak without irreverence, had these Mexicans existed at the time of the exodus of Israel, the Almighty would have withheld them, and sent in their stead the flies, lice, frogs and serpents upon Egypt in tender mercy to a rebellious race! Now, I think I may truthfully affirm that history fails to record the life of a more heartless, conscienceless gang than the subjects of this sketch. Were I called upon to write their epitaphs historic truth should speak in marble.

CHAPTER XXVII.

LARGE LANDED ESTATES.—POLICY AS TO THESE.—
TRANSFER OF PROPERTY.—TAX GATHERERS.

We now pass on to other themes. The large landed estates deserve particular mention. It is sometimes the case that one man may own land extending in a body for more than fifty miles. Especially is this the case in the mountains. He can afford to do so, as he pays no taxes upon these vast possessions. These are practically exempt from the burdens of government, which must fall upon personalty, merchandise and other things. In thus being relieved of the weight of taxation, he can afford to keep his large estates from the market and collect from his numerous tenants the means of livelihood. This policy of the government is certainly a mistaken one, for it fosters a class of men who, for the most part, are unworthy of such a special privilege, and this to the detriment of the well-being of a large body of citizens. It prevents the settlement, the growth of the progress of the State socially, in wealth and political advancement. The axiom is, that "population is power," but population will not increase under such discouragements, such forbidding circumstances. The consequence is that immense tracts of territory, as is often the case, are but sparsely inhabited, leaving untouched some of the fairest fields for the industry and enterprise of man. Were the lands subject to taxation the consequence would be that they would soon be thrown upon the market and bought in by numerous parties, who would cultivate those which were tillable and become a source of considerable revenue to the government. Beside the parties purchasing feeling then a greater interest in the welfare of the country would become better citizens. The policy would also lighten the grievous taxation upon those articles which are now so heavily oppressed as almost to amount to confiscation. While these changes have been agitated to some extent, yet, up to this time, the agitation has only served to awaken some thought upon the subject, but no legislation has been had looking to a correction of the evil. It would break up, too, in the course of time that system of peonage of which we have already spoken. The poor illused tenants, or some of them, would probably become small landed proprietors and set up small establishments of their own. If anything like a moderate tax were imposed upon these lands by the government, the present sources of revenue to the owner are so limited that they could not hold them, and they must revert to the government unless privately disposed of. It is a vicious system as it now exists, but time, better financiering, better statesmanship, in the near future will supersede it by reform legislation, more in accord with the public requirements and the spirit of the age. This land question is becoming more, from year to year, not only in our own country but in other sections, a vital one. Mexico, too, is not now oblivious to it importance, but has begun to study the matter of late years preparatory to legislative changes in the future. Some of the large tracts are already changing proprietors, bought up generally by American, English, French, German and Scotch syndicates. This is more particularly the case in the northern part of Chihuahua, the States of Sinaloa and Coahuila. Many millions of acres within the last two years have changed titles, and the sales instead of diminishing are steadily on the increase. The sections mentioned offer the finest inducements to the capitalist, where investments are almost certain to meet with ready returns. These sections, for the most part, are abundantly supplied with water and the finest pasturage, and the seasons are so mild that there is no risk to the stock grower, where animals unsheltered may run the entire winter without injury. What political changes may be wrought by these inflowing colonists is a problem for state-craft to anticipate. But these subdivisions of territory result in an increase of population, and this increase is encouraged by the present administration, at least by colonization, and invitation to capital with guaranties of protection. It may be that these large estate holders may be induced by the tempting offers of capital to break in sections their domains, ere the government by legislation has compelled them to do so. It is certainly a singular policy of the Mexican Government to exempt from taxation these lands, so far as I now remember, without a precedent in other countries. At this time it may be well to remark that as to taxable properties, these can not be transferred until all taxes upon the same have been paid. Until the condition is complied with the proper officials will not give their necessary services, nor will the conveyances be received into the custody of the public registry. This is a most effective mode for the collection of the public revenue, and if it were adopted in other States, they might then say to that supplemental officer, known as "Back Tax Collector," henceforth "Be no longer officer of mine," for like Othello, his occupation would be gone.

But enough has been said in reference to these large land owners, and the non-taxation of their estates, and the viciousness of such a governmental policy, and also some suggestions made, that if a change were adopted it would increase the public exchequer, and promote the general welfare, and by an easy transition we now approach the real subjects of taxation and the character of their imports.

It may almost be truthfully affirmed that nothing escapes the vigilance of the tax gatherer—and these individuals carry with them the same popularity here that the publicans did during the reign of the Cæsars in the land of Judea, or the rent collector among the Irish tenantry of to-day. These taxes, under one designation or other, are classified as government, State or municipal. Each make their levies, and when each shall have been satisfied it leaves the owner in a very unsatisfied frame of mind, for he feels as if he were paying the price of robbery for protection. Taxation is always unpopular, and not less so here than elsewhere. Men dislike to yield what is in sight for a theoretical protection which is too often all they get. They prefer retaining what they have and taking their chances with the multitude as to losses, or, as is often the case, they selfishly prefer that if taxes must be paid then let the "other fellows pay them." They can stand the imposition upon others much better than when placed upon themselves. It is rarely in a group of wealthy old citizens the subject of taxation is not freely discussed, now and then, by some of their number, the conversation being interlarded with denunciatory expletives, condemning in the strongest terms the taxation policy of government, State and municipality. They cry out that the burdens are more than they can bear, and that business and property, though flourishing as never before, are taking to themselves the wings of the morning. That Mexico has her croakers, too, is only natural to suppose, and goes to prove that this sentiment of aversion to the revenue collector is deeply implanted in the human heart.

CHAPTER XXVIII.

DUTIES.— SMUGGLERS. — INCIDENT. — IMPORTS.— STAMP DUTIES. — STATE TAXES. — MUNICIPAL TAXATION.

The chief revenues of the government are derived from importation duties. These, in many instances, are so enormously high as to fall little short of prohibition. The article of ready-made clothing, to illustrate, pays one hundred and thirty-two per cent! So excessive are these duties upon fabrics, as a class, that the art of smuggling along the border is greatly practiced, and nothing but the greatest watchfulness upon the part of the government keeps it within moderate bounds. These smugglers are well armed and organized, know well along the line the places of rendezvous, and are well prepared, in case of pursuit, either for flight or fight. If too closely pressed and outnumbered, they can well afford to abandon one train, if they can escape with two, for then their great profits will more than compensate them for the loss of the one. Were the taxes less, the temptation to smuggling would be also correspondingly decreased. But high taxation stimulates the illegal traffic. There is such a thing as killing the goose that lays the golden eggs, and there is also such a thing as making taxation so grievous as to defeat the ends sought to be attained. Upon this subject Mexico has much to learn, as well as it would seem, her northern sister republic. The chases after these smuggling bands are at times very exciting, ending frequently in conflicts and in the loss of many lives. When captured everything is confiscated, and the offenders subjected to the severest penalties. There are but few merchants who do not sympathize with the smugglers in their contraband trade, and are willing to take great risks if they can only come into possession of these goods, out of which they realize enormous profits. The banks of the Rio Grande have been the theater of many daring exploits, many fights, captures, and escapes. But of late, so vigilant have been the officers of the government, that the traffic has greatly diminished. This, however, may in part be due to a reduction of duties upon articles imported, thus lessening the profits upon the contraband articles. I can not here undertake an enumeration of the articles imported and the duties imposed upon the different classes of articles; it would be unnecessarily tedious and tiresome to the general reader. These taxes are often imposed not only as a source of revenue, but also as a matter of protection to their own "infant industries," which they are seeking to foster and build up. The mining industry receives the especial favor of the government, and to stimulate this as much as possible many of the articles needed are relieved from importation duties. Mining machinery, steel and quicksilver, fall within this category. Medicines, as a class, are heavily taxed. Articles of luxury share the same fate, which is nothing but proper rather than the necessaries of life. Cooking stoves pay import duties equal or exceeding in amount the prime cost of these artices. Flour is heavily burdened, I presume, to protect and encourage the native production.

Speaking of stoves, I can not forbear the recital of a little incident which occurred only a short distance from this point in the household of one of the best families in the mountains. The lady of the house had at last come into possession of an American stove, costing, too, a good round sum, but abandoned it after a few days' trial, alleging that she did not want it any longer, as it *brought and bred roaches in the house!* And no amount of persuasion could induce her to reconsider her resolution, and the innocent stove was expelled from the house as a guilty culprit. But this only shows some of the vagaries of the mountain Senora. To prevent the avoidance of these duties the goods are sometimes examined by a series of custom-house officials at different points in the interior along the line of their transit. And even irregularities are taxed with heavy fines, these being paid to the vigilant official in part as a reward for his efficiency. Being paid out of the fine, induces them to search for the most trivial irregularities, and to inflict upon the well-intentioned importer vexatious annoyances and unjust fines. It former times these custom-house incumbents have been guilty of the most flagrant corruption. A vessel freighted with a cargo of assorted merchandise, for instance, would stand out to sea, and would not put into port until an interview had been held with the *proper parties* on shore, and unless a satisfactory bargain could be made the captain would set sail for some other port with more accommodating custom-house officials. Of course the government with such representatives could not hope to collect legitimate charges, but these appointees gave to the principal only so much as they felt inclined. For the one who will deliberately cheat only lacks the necessary opportunity to deliberately steal. But this old time practice has been superseded by the introduction of a more efficient service from which the government derives its proper revenues in a reasonably honest and satisfactory manner. Examiners make inspection tours, to look into and report as to the conduct of their custom officials and to keep them in remembrance of the fact, that they are under the constant supervision of the department at the capital.

Upon the whole, I may here remark that the tendency of federal legislation is to lower the import duties, and this policy receives the sanction of some of the ablest men in the nation. Mexico is in no condition for free trade and she must raise her revenues in a great measure from the sources indicated. Yet the burden might be more equitably distributed by heavier imposts upon articles now lightly charged, or new imposts upon articles now wholly free. But time, experience and the observation of the practical workings of the present system may ultimately suggest its own corrective, which its leaders, it is hoped, will have the courage to apply.

There is scarcely anything exempt from stamp duties. I have seen these stamps affixed to each separate piece of shelf goods offered in the stores for sale. All kinds of bales, packages and bundles must receive them before they can be exposed for sale and for a non-compliance with which the severest penalties follow. All kinds of transfers, conveyances, invoices, acknowledgments, receipts are invalid unless properly stamped.

These stamp duties are in many instances excessively high, graduated according to the value of the subject matter, a promissory note for five thousand dollars requiring stamps to the value of one hundred dollars! I have thought that this class of taxation indicated the distress of the government, and was resorted to only in times of great financial stringency. But upon more mature reflection I am not so sure but that it is a means of raising money less felt than when directly imposed.

The States, too, are grievously exacting in the extent of their tax demands. Doubtless, much of this is to be attributed to ill-advised taxation, malversation in office, misapplication of the public funds. While commerce between the States is, under the Federal constitution, exempt from State taxation, yet it is notoriously true that the States, or many of them, act in open violation of its plain provisions, and so far, it seems, the central government has either been too weak or too indifferent to correct the abuse.

The municipalities come in lastly for their share, and by this time the taxpayer is glad that his life is spared and that he is permitted to go hence with the blessings of the revenue collector upon his head. The poor man can not bring a little corn to town without he and his cargoes are escorted to the office of the collector and taxes paid upon the same before he can sell it to buy some needed supplies. One can not kill a beef without paying tribute to the municipality. There is nothing brought to the village for sale but must give up a part for the privilege of selling the remainder. Producers labor under the greatest discouragements, for they feel as if they labor in vain, so heavily oppressed are they with these iniquitous taxes. The reason assigned for these exactions is that the city officials must be paid and the prisoners in jail supported. Misgovernment is the real ground for such unjust proceedings. And as an instance of how they manage these municipal affairs, murderers, prisoners, may sometimes be seen guarding in the streets some unfortunate drunken wretch. The murderer, then a prisoner himself, the rapist, keeping watch over the helpless sot! And this is the kind of a municipal government which levies exorbitant taxes upon those who would furnish bread and meat to the half-famished population!

These remarks give but a feeble description of the actual hardships undergone by the poor taxpayer, for he is a veritable hewer of wood and drawer of water for those in position who squander in maladministration his hard-earned dollars. While this is the case to some extent in other parts, yet it probably prevails here to a more alarming extent than elsewhere. The average Mexican official does not regard a public office as a public trust, but as private property for the time of his incumbency, and to be used for his own aggrandizement. He seldom goes out as poor as when he went in, however meagre may be the salary, for somehow or other what this lacks in quantity, he manages so to multiply the perquisites, legitimate or illegitimate, as to be numbered among the grandees of the land. One can hardly imagine a more corrupt set of officials than the ordinary municipal ones existing in this country. The Tweed regime was more brilliant, for it had more brains, and more money was at stake; but for inward rottenness and unblushing debauchery, it could not exceed some of these Mexican municipal dynasties. If articles are in transit from one State to another, and they should pass through one of these villages, the petty officials pounce upon them for their contributions, as they are called, like the eagle upon its prey. If they were organized to cripple trade and impede commercial relations generally, they could not have devised more efficient measures to that end.

CHAPTER XXIX.

RESOURCES.—POPULATION.—AGRICULTURAL PRODUCTS.—MINES.—MEXICANS AS BUSINESS MEN.—SECURITY OF LIFE AND PROPERTY.—FOREIGNERS MISTREATED.

While our observations have more particular reference to these mountain districts, and while some casual references have already been made to the resources of Mexico, yet I now deem it a matter of entertainment, if not of instruction to the uninformed, to speak a little more at length as to general resources of Mexico. Manufactories are now being established in the greater number of the States of cotton, silk, woolen, paper, glass, earthenware and shoes, which will give an increased impetus to the well-being of the country. The present population of the republic does not exceed ten or twelve millions at the most. It is said, were all its territory populated as thickly as Guanajato the census returns would show nearly sixty millions of people. But immense tracts of territory, in consequence of a scarcity of fuel and water, are but sparsely inhabited. The value of the real estate

THE MOUNTAINS OF MEXICO. 199

will approximate $400,000,000. Corn is grown in every section, wheat in the table-lands, rice along the river and coasts in the hot sections; in these also are raised coffee, tobacco, vanilla, sugar and cotton, all of which, superadded to the tropical fruits and other products, will aggregate, I should think, much more in value than $100,000,000. If the available soil of the country could be utilized by an active, thrifty and intelligent population the benefits which would flow to the country would be incalculable. In this estimate I have not even adverted to her immense mineral deposits of almost endless variety, which have excited the wonder of the mineralogist, and the history of which to-day reads like the creation of vivid fiction. Almost unworked are her mines of copper, iron, zinc, lead, magistral, antimony, arsenic, cobalt, copperas, salt and sulphur. There also exists alabaster, some coal, marble, white and colored, carbonate of soda, many precious stones, such as opal, topaz, agate, amethyst and garnet. The quicksilver mines are also now coming into prominence and adding to the national wealth. It is impossible to tell accurately the product of her mines, for this reason, that the laws originally required that all bullion should be sent to the city of Mexico to be coined, and the transportation being so high from the greatness of the distance the result was the product of the mines in the border States never went through the mint at the capital, but was smuggled out of the county, leaving no record of its value. But sufficient reliable data exists to show that more than *three billions* of dollars, gold and silver, have been produced.

The possibilities of such a country, with such a climate, such a soil, such unexhausted mineral resources, *with a population revitalized*, can not be overestimated, can not be prophecied. This, of course, presupposes the existence of a popular government, with all the civil blessings which flow from such a benign institution. Mexico, too, is the bridge between the continents. The far East and the far West must cross her territory as a highway, to be brought into neighborly intercourse. The Interoceanic Canal, inspired by the genius of the great Frenchman, is within her borders, and to her, from its smitten rocks, "abundant streams of revenue will gush forth" when completed.

I have given but an inkling of her resources, and cannot pass further into details, to weary you with statistical information and tabulated statements. These may be learned from the official reports on file in the different departments, but the details here would only tend to encumber this volume contrary to its design.

Leaving now this interesting theme, the resources of Mexico, we pass to the consideration of some popular ideas entertained abroad as to this country, and some of which I can not more truthfully describe than by characterizing them as popular delusions. I speak now in reference to Mexicans generally, and do not limit my remarks as heretofore to those isolated sections outside of the centers of trade and travel. One idea seems to obtain that the Mexicans are a low kind of people, easily imposed upon, deficient in knowledge and business abilities. This is an old civilization, well-informed in the centers of population and the marts of trade, and eminently conservative in its modes of business. They proceed cautiously, take but few risks, calculate closely, and consequently are seldom overtaken by "the flings of outrageous fortune." The firms of other nationalities go to pieces in this country, but exceedingly rarely do the financial storms overwhelm the natives, those "to the manner born." The speculation craze in stocks, gambling on margins, comparatively speaking, secure but little favor, while legitimate business is pursued in such a conservative manner that it seldom fails to reap its legitimate fruits. I presume that there are no safer houses in the world than some of these old Mexican firms. Some of them have been in existence more than a century and have remained unshaken in their solvency during all the revolutionary times through which they have passed.

This is strange, but speaks volumes to their credit, to the preëminent ability with which they have been managed. Integrity, intelligence, activity, vigilance must have been the foundation on which such a permanent structure was reared. Of course the original members of the firm had long since died, but the business went on the same, often in the name of the original firm; and often in the name of successors. And thus, through successive generations, the house has stood, even growing in influence and strength as it grew in years. I would accordingly dissipate that fallacy that they are limited in their business capacities, if an unbroken success is to be the criterion of such things. I am now speaking of the best class of business men, those who are an honor and ornament to the vocation which they follow, and not of these sharks which shoal in shallow waters and prey on all that comes within their reach. These exist unfortunately everywhere, but by such standards we should not judge the others.

Another idea obtains abroad that nowhere do the laws give adequate protection to property and life. It must be confessed that in certain localities the laws, while good enough in themselves, in their spirit and scope, can not enforce themselves, and the officials charged with that duty are neglectful, indifferent, timid; in a word, absolutely worthless, and for this reason property and life have not the safeguards of the law. This is especially so in the mountains, and in some other sections, but it is not generally the case; but with the exceptions named the reverse is true, and property and life are generally secure. I think it can be said as much so in the main as in other countries. Of course there are some individual hardships, but these happen everywhere, and are departures from the law, and not in accordance with it. I believe the general sentiment of the better class is the enforcement of law and the dispensation of justice through the regular constituted tribunals. Mexico, like the United States, has her wild, thinly settled sections, where, at times, the lawless element are in the ascendant, and where terrorism reigns to the insecurity of property and life. The authorities are weak, and the law-breakers set them at defiance, and pretty much have their own way. But in view of her past history, her numerous revolutions instigated by ambitious leaders, the disturbing elements which have been present in her society, I can but think that a greater respect is being cultivated for law and order, and that these, at no very distant day, will rightfully assert their proper places in the government of the republic.

There is another idea which prevails: that traveling in Mexico is unusually dangerous, and that it is necessary to insure safety to have a strong escort. This, too, I believe is a delusion, for I apprehend that upon the public thoroughfares traveling in stages or upon the railroads is attended with as little danger as anywhere. In fact, as already stated, the punishment of the offender for making an assault when so traveling, or otherwise traveling upon a public road, is death, the penalty to be inflicted within a few days at that by the official living nearest the place of the assault. He may be some petty officer, not more important than a justice of the peace in the United States, yet to suppress such villainies is invested with such extraordinary power.

But in speaking of the enforcement of the law in this country, I omitted to say that formerly the administration was much more lax than at this time. Foreigners coming to this country, too, were sometimes thrown into prison, and lingered there for an indefinite time for some alleged violation of law, upon some suspicion, or upon the accusation of some irresponsible nobody. Often these foreigners deserved punishment, for if a nationality is be judged by the character of some of its tramps passing through the country, then such a nation deserves commiseration. In the abstract and concrete there does not exist a more trifling gang of vagabonds. But now and then it so happened that good men as well as bad men were cast into prison, and remained there for a long period of time without a hearing. This was wrong, for the accused, be he ever so vile, is entitled to a speedy trial, that he may be punished if guilty, and discharged if innocent. In civilized countries the meanest criminals are entitled at least to this right and privilege. A Mexican prison, with its filth and vermin, is a miniature reproduction of the blackhole of Calcutta. Americans, probably more than all others, were incarcerated in these prisons. For many months, and I am told sometimes for years, they languished in imprisonment without a sentence, without even a trial. Appeal after appeal, remonstrance after remonstrance, went up to the representative of the American government, and after so long a time they came back through red tape channels, asking this or that, but bringing no relief to the imprisoned sufferer. Of course the customary diplomatic correspondence would take place sometimes, voluminous, but this generally ended in nothing, for the Mexican minister is generally an official of superior address, great courtesy, with the gift of procrastinating anything, thus wearing out the patience and life of the complainant; and, moreover, he can be easily furnished from his own country with the *exparte* statement of others, that it is an act of mercy to the complainant, though innocent in fact, that he is permitted to live even in a Mexican prison.

The explanation is satisfactory, the American

representative now assuming to be as courteous as the Mexican, half apologetically retires and leaves his countryman severely alone in his dungeon, the curtain descends, and his government's last official act in the drama is ended, and death or deliverance from some other source must force his prison bars. Unfortunately for the reputation of our country this is no mere ideal sketch, but can be vouched for by many American residents. They hardly now expect any kind of redress from the American government, whatever may have been the wrongs they have suffered. At least without referring to the present administration, such supineness on the part of former ones has been displayed as only to make one feel that "hope deferred maketh the heart sick." In this respect the policy of our government, among the American residents, has been a by-word and reproach. Relief asked, and to which he is entitled, if our representatives were not hoodwinked, seldom gets beyond the high-sounding correspondence, however meritorious the application. Somehow or other the Mexican blarney, with his "mañana"* manœuvers, outwits the American man, gains his point, in fact, "takes all the tricks." In the meantime the American official felicitates himself upon the fact that by his brilliant diplomacy

---

* Pronounced Manyanna.

he has cut the knot of a threatened complication, preserved the national honor and the friendliest international relations. But the wronged American sojourns in prison still.

CHAPTER XXX.

DIFFERENCE BETWEEN OUR GOVERNMENT AND ENGLAND AND GERMANY AS TO THEIR SUBJECTS ABROAD. — INCIDENTS. — TRAVELING IN THE MOUNTAINS.

The English and German governments, to their credit be it spoken, immediately upon information being furnished them that some subject of their country is under arrest or in prison in Mexico at once investigate the matter and take steps that he shall either have a trial or be discharged. They do n't permit their subjects to lie in prison for months, but demand for them a hearing at the shortest notice. The contrast between their action and that of the United States is, not only striking but humiliating, to say the least of it, exhibiting an indifferentism misbecoming a great power.

Some years since, I learn, an Englishman was arrested and held in imprisonment for some time in Guymas on the Gulf of California. He had no trial. The captain of an English man-of-war heard of it, and he moved his vessel up in front of the town, communicated with the authorities and laid down his ultimatum, that if that man was not tried or discharged within so many hours he would bombard the place. The Englishman was discharged, it is needless to say. A similar case also occurred in the city of Mazatlan, some years since, when the captain of a man-of-war came to the relief of his countryman, as it was his duty to have done. The same result followed his demand. Germany, I believe, proceeds in the same way. "Short settlements make long friends." When rightly viewed, it is no little matter, wrongfully, to imprison the subjects of a foreign power. The honor, the whole force of their governments, are pledged to their protection, and in doing this, vindicating the national escutcheon, the majesty of the nation. Injure a British subject abroad, and the British Empire, feeling the wrong, is moved to action, and it unredressed 't is then " her morning drum-beats may be heard around the world." In the rights of the subject are wrapped up the rights and honor and good faith of the nation.

Now each nation has a right to live, to protect itself against the machinations of crazy madcaps, filibustering expeditions which, for the time, go to unsettle the peace of the country and threaten, by an alliance with malcontents, the integrity of the existing government. When such men are caught they should receive a punishment, and this promptly, commensurate with the gravity of the offense. The incursionists deserve no better fortune than an abandonment to the fate which their misconduct has induced. So it is not with reference to this class of malefactors that the foregoing remarks are pertinent, criticising the action of our government towards its citizens when imprisoned abroad. But as to this matter it is sincerely to be hoped that an era of reform has been inaugurated, and that now no steps will be taken backward. Let us, at all events, place ourselves abreast with the nations referred to, Germany and England, and see that our citizens in the maintenance of their rights are not neglected.

It sometimes happens that American citizens are wronged in some locality remote from an American representative and they are held in durance vile without the knowledge of the Minister or Consul. Then, again, there are others of these officials who scarcely know what steps to take in the matter. They exhaust themselves in profitless correspondence. The truth is, I do not think that our foreign representatives compare very favorably with those of other first-class powers. They are not, as is the case with some other nations, brought up in a diplomatic school, but untrained politicians thrown to the surface by a change in the administration. And so frequent are the changes that the incumbent holds his office by such a slight tenure that he scarcely has time and inclination to prepare himself for the place before, it may be, he confronts his successor, properly accredited to relieve him of his charge. To insure efficiency, the service by all means should be more permanent, not so shifting, and a compensation adequate to the dignity and requirements of the position should be awarded to him by a nation with an overflowing treasury, thus, too, inducing the most capable men to fill these responsible places.

I have said this much in reference to the changes in our Ministers and Consuls in foreign countries, following the changes in the administration, for it seemed naturally to rise up out of the plan of the subject I was discussing.

Now, retracing somewhat our steps, we will make some further remarks as to traveling in this country, as to which many feel a lively interest. My former remarks as to the comparative safety of traveling here and in other countries, were not intended to include the mountains. There is always more or less danger in passing over these. The lurking-places are so numerous, the places of retreat also, that one must be ever vigilant, always on the alert. A set of barbarians live in these rocky fastnesses, and, living by plunder, although having some ostensible means of honest livelihood, are always on the watch to surprise and rob the unwary travelers when suspected of having valuables, and not well attended. I have had some experience with these mountain robbers and a narration of the incident might serve to diversify these pages; and if this is done I am sure I will earn the thanks of my readers. Of this, in my next chapter, I will speak.

CHAPTER XXXI.

AMBUSCADED BY ROBBERS. — CAPTURED. — TIED DOWN. — ROBBED. — ESCAPED. — OBSERVATIONS.

On the morning of the 6th of December, 1885, I left the village of Guadalupe y Calvo, for the city of Parral, some one hundred and eighty miles distant. After an absence of more than two years I had started home to see my wife and children in the State of Tennessee. I expected to make Parral in five days, there take the stage some sixty miles to Jimenez on the Mexican Central Railroad, thence for El Paso, and thence to Memphis, Tenn., and be with my family during the Christmas holidays.

After such a long absence my heart was bounding with joy in anticipation of seeing so soon my loved ones once more. It was a bright, cold morning, but all was warm within, nature—everything seemed to give auspicious omen for the journey. The carols of the few songsters heard made musical the mountain path, and my trusted mule went on his way up and down the rugged mountains as if he knew the mission, and shared the joy of his rider. I had two mozos (servants) with me, selected by reason of their supposed fitness for such a journey, with a thorough knowledge of camp life and familiarity with the trail. We had two pack mules and two riding animals, and each of us was well armed. One of the pack-mules was loaded with two bars of bullion, weighing about one hundred and fifty-five pounds and valued at near five thousand five hundred dollars. These, for special reasons, I desired to take with me to Parral, and there leave them. I did not apprehend any particular danger, except I thought it probable I might be intercepted by some straggling members of a mountain raiding party, which but a short time before had been broken and scattered in fragments. In fact, a few of these had been seen only a few days before near the village from whence I started. As to these I had resolved to take my chances and go through, if possible. For several days we journeyed on very well, meeting only one or two persons, Mexicans, but feeling better and better as I drew each day nearer my destination. The nights were quite cold, sleeping on the bare ground, the stars shone to me as if in ineffable beauty, and the glad waters went by and soothed me with their musical numbers into tranquil sleep, the sweet sleep of the weary and hopeful. In times like these dreamland is peopled with the purest and best. On the night of the fourth day we camped near a small stream, about forty-five miles from Parral, determined to reach that point the next day. So far we had proceeded uninterruptedly, and our trip up to that time had been a pronounced success. The next morning we had a big frost, but started about six o'clock. Our trail ran over some high narrow mountains, with many sudden ascents and declivities. So winding, too, was the road that your companion, only fifty feet in your rear, in some places, could not see you. It was a lonely, desolate, uninhabited region, of all others the most suitable for the lair of the robber and the sally of the murderer. We had been on the road probably an hour, and I was in advance of my servants, who were with the pack animals some fifty or seventy-five steps in the rear. Just at this time I was out of sight of my servants by reason of a quick turn and sudden descent in the road, but passing along unconscious of any danger near me. Nor did my riding mule give any signal of danger, contrary to the custom of that animal, when such is at hand. But so it was riding along slowly that my companion might catch up, and unwarned, with head cast down in a meditative mood, I was suddenly confronted by two robbers at a sharp angle in the road, immediately in my front, within a few feet of me, the one a little to the right and the other to the left, and each with his rifle leveled on me. The sound of their voices, I think, had broken my reverie, and I beheld them for the first time in the position described. Speaking in Mexican, they advanced the few feet on me with rifles aimed, compelling me to dismount, and while one kept his gun against me the other took away my pistol. It was fortunate when they told me to surrender my arms I did not make an effort to deliver my weapons, for my action then might have been misconstrued as an attempt to defend myself, which would have cost me my life. I permitted them to find and take the pistol. Under the circumstances, to see such an apparition with disguised faces, as if painted devils had suddenly risen out of the earth, makes one of those thrilling episodes in life seldom seen, but never forgotten. They had blackened their faces for the occasion, and this intensified the chill of horror, for the recollection for many nights afterwards of the vision, when first presented, started the half-sleeping, half-wakeful shudders. I saw at a glance that resistance was vain and that I had better take the risk for the time, and watch for a better opportunity, and the sequel fully justified the wisdom of this course. They immediately marched me back, with rifles in dangerous proximity to my head, to a point just below the crest of the hill down which I had just gone, and there made me lie down, as they did also, to await the arrival of my servants, coming up on the opposite side. In a few minutes the heads of the animals could be seen coming where we were hidden, and in a few feet more my captors had their guns against the breasts of my surprised servants, reinforced by two other robbers, who rose up immediately in their rear, and whom I had passed unperceived, as they were hidden in the grass on the side of the path. Thus surprised and surrounded by four of the robbers they, too, offered no resistance, but were captured without even the firing of a gun. The field chosen, the plan of the attack and its admirable execution displayed no little generalship. Others circumstanced as I was, and as we were, might have acted differently, but the probabilities are, had they done so, they might not now, as I am doing, be writing recollections of this stirring incident. They at once tied our arms behind us and drove us before them away from the road a considerable distance down into a deep gorge along with the captured animals. When we had reached a certain flat spot on the side of the deep canyon the animals were stopped, and then they took us a little farther down towards the bottom of the canyon when they commanded us to lie down. When my mozos had done so, then they tied a strong rope around one of their legs, just above the ankle, and drew the leg up under them closely to the body and tied it to the rope with which the arms were tied. They then ordered me to lie down, and I was subjected to the same humiliating treatment. While this was being done, one was officiating while the others were present with arms ready to enforce obedience. When we were flat upon our backs, then one of them was stationed as a sentinel some thirty feet above us, near the spot where the animals were stopped, but in such a place as he could command us with his rifle. And so attentive was he that from time to time he would leave his place and come down and examine our fastenings to see that we were still secure. And then he was so solicitous about us, too, he would now and then ask if we were still tied, and make other inquiries which I then thought were ill-timed.

While he was filling the time with these "side-bar" remarks, I could distinctly hear him chewing away on some of my provisions they had captured, and this was not well calculated to favorably impress me with the newcomer. While he was keeping watch, I could hear him talking with the others, or some of them, but these I could not see from the position I occupied. Every now and then he would retire for a few minutes beyond sight, hold a conference with some confederate and then return and take his accustomed place. Once or twice he came near where I was lying and asked one of my Mexican servants what old "gringo" I was. He held his gun about half raised toward me, as if in the act of firing. My servant commenced begging for me in the most plaintive tones, and telling him I was on my way then to see my family, whom I had not seen for more than two years, going, as he expressed it, to my own land, and that I was "*un muy buen hombre,*" one very good man. From some unknown reason his countenance, with its mean scowl, relaxed as well as the hand upon his rifle, and he turned around and went back to his place as sentinel. Just at that time, when my servant was pleading for me with the wretch, and he looking as if in the act of firing upon me, my feelings can neither be imagined nor described. There tied down in the mountains, as helpless as an infant by a band of robbers, gave but little promise of a family reunion again. The happy anticipations of the few days past were lost in the sudden change of the situation. To all appearance our fate was still unsettled in the hands of the villains. I asked in an undertone, as we were all three tied near each other, one of my servants, who had been saying his prayers and invoking his saints, what these fellows were going to do with us, but he, in a despairing tone and look, replied he did n't know. Now it is said that a man in the act of drowning has passed in review a panorama of his past life. I do n't know how that is, but I am willing to indorse the couplet of the poetess when she says:

"There are moments, I think, when the spirit receives
Whole volumes of thought on its unwritten leaves."

When that rascal held that gun on me, as if about to fire, not only *whole volumes*, but a whole Alexandrian Library went through my mind! I have faced death on many occasions, amid the clash of arms on the battlefield, in the pestilence, when the very air seemed laden with the missiles of the Great Archer, and against which there was no protection, on the flying, disabled train, on ocean waters angered by the winds, but never before did death seem so near as on that December morning in the Sierra Madre. At best it is bad to die away from home, unsoothed by affection's voice, untended by affection's hand. But the thought was almost intolerable to be tied down and shot like a dog in the desert of the mountains, in one of the loneliest and most dismal spots, by a gang of desperate, murderous ruffians. In that event there is hardly a probability that any tidings from that sequestered canyon would have gone over the mountains to tell of the cruel fate of the harmless travelers. I presume we had been thus confined for nearly seven hours on our backs, our limbs swollen from the tightness of the cords, causing great pain, when one of my mozos said to me in a whisper, he thought he could untie himself. This was said during the temporary absence of the sentinel. I replied to him, "Then do so immediately."

He attempted it and succeeded, how, I am not able to tell, and then he untied the other mozo, and then the two jumped at me and untied me. While it occupied but a little time, yet I thought it took much more time than it did. We three then "sorter fell" down the side of that mountain towards its bottom, keeping between us and the position of the sentinel as many big rocks and other obstructions as we could, for we expected the crack of his rifle every moment. Whether he returned to look after his charge, I know not, but if he did we were beyond the reach of his aim, and with fleet feet hastening down and up the rough mountains. Stunted undergrowth grew in our course, and thus furnished a friendly covert for the fugitives. In this way we made our escape, pronounced by Americans and Mexicans familiar with the habits of these robbers, to be the most marvelous one of which they have any knowledge. Their habit is to kill, for "dead men tell no tales." But whether such was their ultimate purpose in our case, no one can ever tell. The truth is, I have now no curiosity on the subject, and felicitate myself more upon my escape than I care to indulge in idle surmising as to what might have been my fate. Luckily they did not take from my person any of my clothing on that cold morning; but we lost our animals, our bullion, our clothing, blankets, watch, some silver dollars—everything, in a word, and nothing has ever been recovered. It was a wholesale and retail robbery. I had in my possession a passport from the State Department at Washington, but these chevaliers did not then permit it to pass me. I had quite a nice collection of mementoes which were all lost.

After our escape, in a few hours night came upon us, but we traveled on through brush and timber, and over the great boulders, going up and down the steep mountain sides in the direction of our destination. We walked and walked until a late hour away from the accustomed trail, for fear of being again intercepted by our captors. At last we came to a light near the path, having tramped that day, it is now learned, about twenty-five miles. To that light we turned our steps, and it proved to be some timbermen in camp for the night. With them we remained until morning, they giving us something to eat, for since early morning we had eaten nothing. Two days afterwards we reached Parral lame and weary to exhaustion—such was the pain and roughness of my tramp that two of the nails of my toes came out.

The night after the day of our robbery one of my mozos went on to Parral with information to the authorities there of the robbery, and with a request than an expedition would immediately be sent out after the robbers. The prefect replied he had none to send. After my arrival, however, he did send out some policemen, I paying their salary in the meantime; but these found neither thieves nor property, which is *sometimes the case with policemen,* as you may know. It is but proper to say that the Prefect of Parral sent my exhausted mozo on as a messenger to the chief authority of the canton, some fifty miles or more, from where the offense was committed, with instructions to him to fit out an expedition and dispatch it after the robbers, and that such was the celerity in which this was done the parties went out to the place where the assault was made and arrived there just eight days after the commission of the offense! They immediately, on arrival there, returned by the same road to their starting point in the morning, and then were disbanded, but whether complimented or not in orders, I am not advised. From Parral they could have reached the place in less than twenty-four hours, instead of eight days, which it took them in the end. But the violent exertion of a more vigorous pursuit would have been a rank departure from a time honored usage. The matter is now pending between the respective governments, and some interesting correspondence has taken place, calling into play diplomatic niceties and manifesting the warmest international relations. Of this I am glad, for I should dislike to be even the innocent cause of any disruption, the occasion of any grave State complication, much less a " *casus belli.*"

Such, imperfectly sketched, was my experience with the mountain bandits. I hope not for its repetition. I only wish that the hand that traces these lines could more faithfully portray the scene and more vividly describe at that hour my surprise, my feelings and all the attendant circumstances. But such a picture would require the genius of some literary Raphael, some Washington Irving, to write it as it was. On the minds of others the pen paints it in imperfect colors. In my own memory it will remain undimmed by the dust, and uneffaced by the flight of years. Of it I have ceased to dream, but never to think. On several occasions since I have passed over the very spot with emotions that caused the unbidden tears to start; and with a thankfulness swelling up from my heart over my happy deliverance. Association was then busy with the past, evoking the images, locating the different characters here and there until scene followed scene in swift succession, and there was a reproduction of the startling drama.

CHAPTER XXXII.

MURDER OF AN AMERICAN IN THE MOUNTAINS.—CROSSES.—MURDER OF SENATOR COOPER.—NATIONAL SYMPATHIES.—IMMIGRATION DESIRED.

Not more than two hours distant from the place of my robbery, and nearer to Parral, is a lonely mountain grave. There was the scene of a brutal tragedy in the spring of 1886. Two Americans were going out to Parral and to the United States by this route, named respectively Preston and Houser, when they stopped at this place, near which runs a small stream, in order to eat and rest their animals. After having dismounted for a short time, and while preparing their little repast, with their arms and effects scattered upon the ground, two Mexican boys approached them and made inquiries respecting some lost cattle. This conversation, as it afterwards turned out, was a mere ruse to engage their attention and divert them from their premeditated purpose. Old man Houser was from the State of Iowa, Council Bluffs, and knew nothing of the language, and Preston but little. One of the Mexicans picked up the pistol from the ground, asked questions which Houser did not understand; but just then Preston's attention was called to what was transpiring, when he gave some signal of warning to his companion. Just as he did this the Mexican fired upon Houser, killing him instantly, and turned upon Preston, firing also at him and shooting him through the wrist. Preston, although disabled to some extent, closed upon the assailant and threw him down, wrenched the pistol from his hand, but in the scuffle, being crippled so much, he could not then fire the pistol. The Mexican in the end escaped, but not before Preston had fired at him several times. Some months afterwards the two Mexicans were captured, the reward for their capture being offered and paid by Americans. They have been in jail ever since, having confessed the crime, but for some unexplained reason they yet live, enjoying the hospitalities of the prison in the city of Parral. It appears the motive which prompted the cold-blooded murderer was simply a desire to possess himself of a pistol. The younger of the Mexicans fled when the firing commenced. The fiend was perfectly willing to take a human life, one whom he had never seen before, if he could only rob him of a pistol. Such is their estimate of the value of a life, and the long-delayed punishment also indicates the standard of official efficiency in this country. The old man was going back home, but his purpose was thus untimely cut off, and near the spot where he was so foully murdered they dug a hole in the ground and laid him away to his final rest. Some Americans passing by the spot some time after this, and seeing how exposed and neglected the grave was, took up the body and re-interred it in a more decent manner near some overhanging oaks, and there he now sleeps a stranger's last sleep amid the mountain solitudes. The ax has hewn a face upon one of the oaks which stand as sentinels near his sleeping form, and upon that smooth face is a rough inscription traced in pencil lines, telling of his name, residence, birth and death. In a brief time the action of the elements will efface the pencil record, and nothing save the rude cross and the little hillock will tell to the passing traveler the burial here of a human being. Anxious friends were awaiting him at home when, in the mysterious providences of life, his course was changed and he took his journey to a more distant land. The sight of the lonely grave awakened sad reflections. He must be buried where he fell, for his removal from the country was a physical impossibility, as well as contrary to the law, until after a lapse of a certain period. Had he thus died young the pang of sorrow might have been less acute, but that an old man, thousands of miles away from home, should thus have perished calls for the saddest memories. The little stream at his feet will continue to make with its symphonies a sorrowful refrain, and the stars overhead in the long ages to come will see ungraced by affection's flowers this lonely tabernacle of the dead. He was a stranger to me, but such a fate awakens a stronger sympathy for the living and sorrow for the dead. He had been lured away from his quiet home in the North by some oily-tongue adventurer upon extravagant misrepresentations as to mineral wealth at some point in the Sierra Madre, and it was when the pictured scene had dissolved and he was on his return journey that death met him at the hands of the assassin.

I have thought if such things ever happen, that near this spot will the belated traveler, as he passes, hear the voice of a troubled spirit, mingled with the moaning, midnight winds, as o'er this lonely mountain grave they dirge the requiem of the dead.

Here and there, scattered over the mountains, in the most out-of-the-way places may be seen over a little upraised earth some little crosses, fashioned in rudest manner from some limb of tree, the upright planted in the grave, split above and the transverse wedged within, and in which the moss of long years has gathered, as if to soften thus that symbol our faith. The cross! the cross! what a hold it has upon the human heart! It takes us back more than eighteen hundred years to the Man of sorrows, to the Son of God. From whence came the cross save from the brow of Calvary? Its teachings have compassed the sea, and gone out to the ends of the earth. So that to-day its mission is being proclaimed in almost every land and clime, amongst every kindred, tongue and people. Its lesson is felt in the midst of waters, the deepest valleys, the highest mountains. I have seen them on top the highest mountain, there with outstretched arms, proclaiming in the wilderness the story of the crucifixion, the sweet evangel of divine love.

The story of the cross is now as omnipresent as the atmosphere which surrounds us, giving life to all breathing things. Then no wonder here its heralds have told its rise, history and mission, and that the children of faith should plant it over the tombs of the dead, and link it with the thought of immortality. I have seen them carved upon the trees. This at times to indicate directions or the supposed vicinity of buried treasure, and again I have seen them upon the loftiest rocks overlooking the adjacent country for miles and miles away. But the thought was there; it came down upon the tide of the centuries, and its reputed origin is now well-nigh universally received. Here the Indian tribes associate it in some way with the Great Spirit and revere it as a holy emblem. The rudest nations do the same and overhang it with garlands of flowers as votive offerings from the heart. So interwoven is it now in our being that to push the thought from our hearts is to leave them without chart or compass, sail or anchorage in the storms of life.

But it is needful that I hasten to other things. There is another grave which has around it sorrowful associations. I refer to that of the Hon. Henry Cooper, buried in the cemetery in the city of Culiacan. He was formerly a senator from the State of Tennessee, in the Congress of the United States. He was in the prime of life, universally beloved, and died universally regretted. He was president of the El Cuervo Mining Company, not far from this place, and accompanied by another gentleman and a faithful mozo, he had started in the interest of his company to transact some business in the city of Culiacan, expecting to return within a short time after his departure. When he had reached a point in the immediate vicinity of that city, and being a little in advance of his attendants, two Mexicans were seen to be approaching him with pistols in their hands and as if they were half-drunken. His companion from behind him cried out to him they were robbers, and just as he did so the Judge received a fatal shot through the body, falling from his horse and expiring immediately. By this time his friend had opened fire upon the attacking party, and had wounded and disabled one of those, who continued his fire, notwithstanding his wound, until the mozo who, at the commencement a little distance in the rear, ran up and killed him with his pistol. The other Mexican had managed for the time to escape, but in a few days was captured, found to be badly wounded, was put in prison, tried, and, I believe, condemned to be shot upon his recovery; but taking advantage of his situation, died in prison, and thus escaped the sentence of the court. On several occasions I have seen the ground whereon that good man's life went out; it is in the outskirts of the city, and, strange to say, rather a populous district. Judge Cooper's death produced a profound sensation, not only where killed, but in certain parts of the United States where he was so well known and highly esteemed. It was, I suppose, just one of those unfortunate occurrences which are liable to take place in almost any country where pistols are worn and liquor is sold.

It must be said in behalf of the authorities of the State of Sinaloa, that they then acted in the matter with the most commendable dispatch, evincing an honest determination to find and punish in the most summary way his murderers. In that State crime is much more certainly and severely punished than in this. But a few days before the Judge's departure for Culeacan, I had received with much pleasure the promise of an extended visit, and was, as were we all, much shocked at the reception of the news of his death a few days afterwards. With heart-felt grief, kind friends and sympathizing strangers performed for the honored dead the funeral rites, and thus he was numbered with those who people the silent city of the dead. But I never think of his untimely " taking off," unmixed with pain, of his grief-stricken family, without anguish of heart. Once I walked out from the plaza a considerable distance to see his grave, but on the hour of my arrival the gates of the cemetery were closed and my purpose was defeated. From the same State, several thousand miles away in a foreign land, I desired, at least in some humble manner, to leave some token of memory, and to testify my appreciation of his exalted worth. And here, may I not ask, have you never noticed how this State fraternity of feeling outcrops when seen away from home, and especially how sympathetic it is when felt on foreign shores.

And now having paid my feeble tribute to the departed, let us pursue this line of thought just suggested a little farther. Probably distance from the same country nowhere binds men in closer union, if possessed of anything like similar habits and tastes, than when formed together in this republic. The national bond is strong, and compatriots naturally gravitate toward each other in sympathetic union, unless repelled by the most unlovely traits, or a base abandonment of all the noble virtues. And this is none the less true in this remote section, as I have often seen it exemplified in the conduct toward each other of the members of the the same nationality. And while I do not wish to indulge in hypercriticism of Americans, yet it is the truth to say the strolling ones seen in these parts are generally of the hardest class, the toughest genus, the most worthless species. Botanically considered, they are for the most part that kind of timber, out of which nothing good can be constructed. And yet this kind of floating riffraff seldom fails to touch a responsive chord in the American heart, and he gives him food and money and sends him on his prospecting rounds. Two Germans, meeting here for the first time, will meet as brethren and of the Fatherland, will talk and talk until night has come and night has far advanced. Two Irishmen, like melted wax, will run together, especially if warmed with "a bit of the craythur," until the words run into notes, and the notes into a song about the " Gem of the Sea," and the " Land of Erin go Bragh." In loving embrace they are happy once more, and tell over and over the scenes of the long ago, when as " spalpeens of boys" in the old country they frolicked for life and fought for fun. The grasp of the Frenchman is something more than a mere theatrical performance, and needs but the inspiration from the vintage of his own France to make him once more a member of the old Empire and an inheritor of the honors and glories of the great Napoleon. The Scotchman and the Englishman are also clannish, and each thinks in his own favored land, as nowhere else, the sun, moon and stars rise and set. Members from the same State of our Union feel for each other a close relation, a tender feeling. The Virginians here believe in their mother State with a fonder devotion and intenser filial affection. "Old Virginia never tire," never tires with them, and no change of circumstances or place can ever change their affection. I doubt if any other than members of the "first families" ever left the "Old Dominion" to roam or dwell in other lands. And however low in condition he may become from the changes of fickle forture, he never loses his first love, and a fellow-Virginian, wherever he meets, is his "long lost brother," whether he 'has or has not "a strawberry upon his left arm." And so it goes. We take with us to foreign parts these inter-state partialities, and a long time must transpire ere these different constituents become fused into a homogeneous whole. Even for our acquaintances, the familiar brutes, seen by us when we are far from home, we have more affection. Our neighbor's dog, when seen away, we like much more, and then wonder why we once so much disliked his nightly howls. Our neighbor's cat, which for hours on neighboring roofs and walls concertized to sleepless eyes, when seen in exile is *poor Grimalkin then*, and with soft words and gentle strokes we fain would make amends for spoken words and unspoken thoughts!

While Mexico is desirous of immigration, she prefers colonies from different countries, so that the influence of no one may be controlling, but that of the one may to some extent counterbalance that of the other. Many of her people are watching with no little distrust the large influx of foreigners. They fear that they may come in such numbers that in the course of time they may be able to control legislation and introduce radical changes in the State policy. And particularly are these fears entertained by some in reference to the border States, into which so many Americans are now pouring, and who have already bought up such immense areas of land. Some have expressed a preference that these border lines might be peopled with German rather than American immigrants, as the former are regarded as more conservative than the latter, less likely to excite disturbances along the frontier. But in the absence of positive prohibition I apprehend that the Americans will continue to cross over the border and fringe the frontiers with long lines of settlements, introducing American habits of industry and life, and gradually with their approach, leavening with their thoughts and ways the contiguous communities. Energy and brains will triumph over inactivity and numbers. Such is the history of the past and will be the record of the future. New blood will give new life and new life will put in quicker motion the wheels of State and national progress.

CHAPTER XXXIII.

RECIPROCITY TREATY.—ITS AIMS.—MEXICO AS A MANUFACTURING COUNTRY.

Having now spoken in outline of the different classes of taxation, government, State and municipal, we pass to make some few observations in reference to the proposed Reciprocity Treaty between the United States and this country. This was conceived with the view of making more intimate our trade relations. And in doing this it would at the same time tend to bring into more intimate social relations the people of these countries. An interchange of trade would be accompanied by an iterchange of thought, and an interfraternity of feeling. The railroads penetrating this country had aroused its leading men to the importance of closer commercial relations. Railroads are the harbingers of trade, and in fact create business in the desert places. And so it was thought by the Mexican statesmen that such a treaty would be highly beneficial to the development of the wealth of their country, and it with but feeble opposition received the legislative sanction. I am sorry to say it met with a dissimilar fate in the Congress of the United States, for, after having been approved by the Senate, it was defeated in its passage by the action of the lower house, which hampered it with some provision requiring an enabling act to make it effective, and this has never been passed.

And thus it is that the Reciprocity Treaty sleeps to this day, and there are no very favorable indications that it will ever pass such a body as the last Congress of the United States. But in some essential particulars, it is to be hoped, such a body will never again convene to direct the foreign policy of the government. I belief the chief reasons urged against the treaty is that it would militate against the sugar and tobacco interests of some of the States. So far as sugar is concerned, for the fiscal year ending January, 1886, the statistics show that Mexico actually imported more from the United States than she exported to it. During that year the refined sugar exported was of the value of $640,730. Central America, during that year, sent sugar to the United States in value of $441,876. I am sorry I have not the tobacco statistics before me for same period, except those as to leaf tobacco, and this was valued at $173,654, exported from Mexico. I find leaf tobacco, during April, 1887, imported by Mexico from the United States, to have been $18,861. This is taken from the report of the Treasury Department at Washington. Returning to the article of sugar, in 1875 Cuba sent to the United States seventy-five per cent. of this product, while in 1885-6 she sent there ninety-four per cent. of the same. The product of the United States, compared with that grown in other countries, and on which duties of importation are levied, is the merest fraction, and yet a tax of several cents in the pound must be paid by the people of the United States upon the enormous amount imported in order to keep alive within one or two States this languid industry. Sugar, as an article of daily consumption, has become a necessity, and the many should not pay to the few such an extravagant premium, millions in the aggregate, for their protection. The treaty proposed was experimental under its term of limited duration, and assuredly within the time specified the articles on the list of Mexico asked to go in free could not have greatly injured the United States. Mexico proposed to admit free from the United States seventy-three articles if the United States would admit free twenty-eight of her articles. This treaty was signed by the American and Mexican commissions on the 20th of January, 1883, met with the approval of the President and Senate of the United States, and was defeated by the lower House, and now has been again postponed for final action until some time in the early part of 1888. Of the seventy-three article referred to above Mexico has already placed forty-one of them upon her free list, which tariff went into effect on the 1st of July, 1887, thus manifesting a liberality which should evoke a corresponding spirit. Seeing the apathy of the United States to meet her overtures for closer commercial relations, as demonstrated in her treatment of the proposed Reciprocity Treaty, Mexico, despairing of its ultimate passage, has already entered into commercial treaties with Germany and France upon the most advantageous terms for these countries. Within the last ten years the exports from Mexico to the United States have been doubled, and it is estimated at Washington that the imports by the former from the latter are about $20,000,000, gold, or $26,000,000 in silver values. The policy of the present administration of Mexico is to extend in every practicable mode her trade relations to foreign lands as well as to stimulate, by proper inducements, her domestic industries.

Certainly Mexico presents a most inviting field as an outlet for the overflow productions of neighboring nations, and none could or should so readily avail themselves of the auspicious opportunity presented as the United States. Her geographical position furnishes superior advantages, shorter time is necessary to make her commodities marketable, and cheaper freight obtainable by reason of proximity. The manufactured products of the United States, in excess of the actual needs of the country, must find a market somewhere, or stagnation supervenes, and no fairer field is offered for these than her sister republic. It would appear to be the part of wise statesmanship to have entered on the "goodly land" while the gates were thrown open. But American statesmanship thought otherwise for the time, perhaps too much absorbed in some matters merely of local nature to lift themselves to the "height of the great argument," and take a broader view than is circumscribed by the imaginary lines of congressional districts. It is a sad commentary upon the average Congressman of to-day that he lowers himself into the mere politician, and into all that this term implies in its modern acceptation, and subordinates the whole to the part, his country's interests to those of his section.

So upon the whole I can but think that the action of the American Congress was a mistake in reference to the Reciprocity Treaty, that the reasons assigned for such action were not tenable in view of the actual facts, and that the manner of its rejection, so far, has not been well calculated to increase and cement the fraternal relations between the two countries. But it is still to be hoped that other and broader statesmanlike views may yet be taken of this most important matter, that better counsels will prevail, and that better results will follow their adoption. And here it may not be ill-timed to suggest that if the United States would take the import duty off from many of the raw materials which go into that country, and are manufactured there, it would greatly benefit their manufacturing interests, thus enabling the manufacturer to compete successfully with those of other countries which admit free of duty the articles mentioned. In fact then the United States would have the vantage ground, her lines of communication being much shorter, her markets nearer home. Wool is a notable example, of which great quantities from Mexico might be exported to the United States with great profit to our manufacturers, if it were only relieved from the import tax with which it is now burdened, and from which it is disburdened in England, enabling her people to distance ours for this reason in their competition for the commerce of our neighboring nations. But some local interests must be subserved to the detriment of the general good. But when the futility of such a policy has been demonstrated by experience, it would seem the wiser course in the future to inaugurate legislation having a broader basis and of more general application. These are simple suggestions, but, we think, if adopted, far-reaching in their beneficent results. Outside of the mountain districts, the resources of this country are yet undeveloped, its agricultural wealth, particularly, untold, but time, experience, civilization and improved methods of labor must, from its wonderful fertility, call forth surprising results. There, such of these as were desirable, by enlightened legislation, by easy transit, would pass into the domain of the United States, exchanged for some of its surplus productions. Thus beneficial results would flow to both countries, the surplus of the one finding its disposition and equivalent in that of the other.

I hardly think this as a manufacturing country can attain first rank, as water and coal are wanting —indispensable conditions to manufacturing centers, and hence in the end must rely upon her soil and its products for greatness as a nation. At all events, her water-courses are limited in number and ability, and her coal fields, if existing in sufficient quantity and quality, are yet unexplored. The disposition of the better class of the Mexican people is for better relations with the United States, social and political. Of course there are some who disfavor such a course, but these are generally found among the more ignorant class, in whose hearts rankle envy and hate. Some, too, uninfluenced by such motives, yet have an undefined fear that the cultivation of more friendly, social and business relations with the United States will prove in the end the introduction of the Trojan Horse, and that absorption must follow at no remote period. These views, I think, are not shared by many, although some of the periodicals give out such intimations; but these papers, as in our own country, often are more the expression of the sentiments of the individual than a reflex of the public feeling. The advocacy of such a course in this country would cost one his life, and its advocacy in the United States meet with no general favor, and hence the absorption theory is the merest *ignis fatuus*, the chimera of a distempered brain. But the two peoples can live side by side where nature placed them, in the friendliest intercourse, with no dreams of conquest and absorption, each in its sphere pursuing its own appointed ways, and fulfilling its "manifest destiny."

CHAPTER XXXIV.

AMUSEMENTS.— BULLTAIL PULLING, ETC.—EGG-SHELL PERFORMANCE.

The amusements of a people often proclaim their tastes and character. The Olympic games proclaimed a physical culture, and the wrestlers sought iron manhood. Effeminate games bespeak effeminacy, and bloody and cruel ones a bloody and cruel race. Innocent sports, unlike cruel ones, are never reflexes of bad hearts, but speak of good and gentle natures. I think the chief amusements of the country, as now practiced, came from old Spain, the mother country. There is a day set apart in the year, almost generally observed, in which male and female repair to the country to witness a certain game, which, in the absence of a better name, I will call "The Bull-tail Pulling." This is regarded by highest and lowest, male and female, as one of the most exhilerating sports in the country. They come from far and near, and sometimes remain for days, in order to witness, if not to participate, in what is reckoned the splendid sport. A minute description will be helpful to a proper appreciation of the game. Out some miles from the village, on some chosen spot in the mountains, an enclosure is made on level ground, running about the width of an ordinary lane several hundred yards. The upper part of this lane connects by drawbars with an adjoining lot, in which are turned for the occasion a number of bulls. The fiercer the animals the greater the sport. When the drawbars are pulled down a watchman permits any one or two to pass into the lane at a time. The animals, as they come out of the lot into the lane, are punched by a spear in the hands of the watchman, and frightened and maddened by the unexpected assault, they make a break at full speed down the lane for liberty, the further end of which is closed. Inside of the lane, and at the drawbars are stationed horsemen, who dash after the bull as he dashes down to the further end of the lane. Now I will venture no one is wise enough to anticipate where the fun comes in unless he has seen or heard of it before. Why, the object of the rider is this, that he is to outrun the bull, and as he nears his tail, both going at full speed, the horseman stretches out his hand and seizes the bull by the tail, drives his horse suddenly forward by, just then driving into him his cruel spurs and throwing his right leg dexterously over the tail of the bull, held by the right hand, he turns the bull a terrible somersault on the ground, the rider in the act relaxing his hold and rushing forward a considerable distance before able to check the speed of his steed. Sometimes bulls and riders go down together in a promiscuous heap, attended with great danger to man and beast. The fence and fence corners on the outside are lined with curious spectators its entire length, while great numbers of men and women on horses, in convenient proximity, view the exciting chase. When the poor animal has been crippled or exhausted from his repeated falls he is then driven back into the pen and a fresh bull is sent forth for fresh sport. The young men dress themselves and their horses fantastically for the occasion and hope by their clever agility in throwing the bull to elicit the coveted applause from friends and lovers. This thing sometimes for days goes on. My sympathies were always with the bull in the race, and the bull in the fight. I thought the brute was less brutal than the brutal sportsmen. How ladies can look on such scenes and enjoy them for hours is to me a matter of profound surprise. I never attended but one of these games, but this will be sufficient until I see another, and this I shall never do if I can avoid it. During the performance the neighboring villages are nearly deserted; great and enthusiastic crowds are present with cheers and shoutings. Of course these performance teach no lesson, and do no good. They may serve to exhibit a creditable horsemanship, but at the same time a discreditable cruelty. To call that sport which does violence to other creatures is a bad misnomer. But the heartiness with which these people seem to enjoy these things tells of a coarseness, roughness and cruelty better befitting some dark age. I saw the priest present on the occasion of my visit, and he was there not to discourage or rebuke his parishioners, but himself gave countenance to the game. "Like priest, like people." There is need that the schoolmaster should be abroad in the land, call him what you may, whether teacher or preacher, is immaterial, so he lights up the dark places, and plants in the heart the lessons of a sweeter humanity.

The games in this section of the country are limited in number. The classes of amusements are few, and inferior in quality. Why, would you believe it, no circus with its clowns and sawdust and spangles, has ever made its "grand entry" into these mountains and pitched its big tent on the neighboring lot to the wonder and inexpressible joy of the half-grown urchins. In the absence of the circus they must amuse themselves as best they can, but for the circus there is no counterpart in the life of the young. With them it is ever ready to fill "a long-felt want," and a long-felt want is ever ready to be filled. Occasionally some strolling acrobats make their appearance and for a few days take the town by their gymnastic feats.

THE MOUNTAINS OF MEXICO.

The matter to Mexicans is simply inexplicable how men can do such things and be nothing more than men. Exhibitions of strength, feats of agility, and slight of hand performances excite the profoundest admiration. These wandering mountebanks gather in all the loose change from male and female, and often to the stint of the back and stomach. Hunger and cold must wait, but the appetite for the marvelous must be gratified. And in this the Mexican shows a great deal of human nature.

Here there are no theaters and operas. The love of them may indicate high culture, but these mountains are too high for such æsthetic entertainments. No traveling agent has yet, with flaming hand-bills, advertised the approach of such companies in these parts, and the young man may yet call the dollars his own, which, were it otherwise, might go to the evening's entetainment of his fair senorita. I do not mean to say that there is a want of musical taste and culture, but the opportunities are wanting to the indulgence of them to any great extent. Here all classes are fond of music. I might truthfully say, inordinately fond of it. There is scarcely a village but that has one or two bands, and there is scarcely a week but on one or two occasions they do not parade the streets and make the welkin ring with their music and noisy demonstrations. Like the brass band everywhere it draws to itself in its march all the straggling loafers in town, not excepting the inevitable small boy, who either heads or skirts the procession in its aimless marches and countermarches. Their open air soirees, with their attendant crowds, present in dress and appearance a grotesque sight. Some Mexican, with a few dollars in his pocket, gets drunk and he immediately wants a band of music to go up and down the streets and stop in front of the houses and stores and play for glory, the glory of his being drunk! It is then or never he relaxes his purse strings, and his soul floats out on the wings of song, or it finds its heaven in a band of music. Night and day he will keep up the performance, and keep the village awake until his funds are exhausted, or music no longer sooths his tired nature. The authorities of the place seem to catch the spirit of the occasion, and however annoying and detrimental it may be to others, they never think of abating the sweet nuisance.

Liquor of some kind generally starts the *trouble*, keeps it alive until it dies from sheer exhaustion after the lapse of some days. In the meantime it must be borne by all as the free musical treat of some eccentric drunken villager. Sometimes I have almost wished for the power to abolish brass bands, even at the risk of incurring the charge that I was "fit for treasons, stratagems and spoils." Even too much sweetness, ill-administered, palls upon the taste and sickens the hearer. The cultured young ladies discourse sweet music with guitar and harp. The men take to the violin and brass band, the noise from the latter of which we seldom fail to hear in the busy hours of the day or the tranquil hours of the night. I think somebody says that "Orpheus' lute was strung with poets' sinews;" that is not exactly the case here, but for equipment of their instruments they find a never-failing substitute in the twisted entrails of poor Puss. Music I love, but not affectedly so; like many young men who, upon the rendering of some difficult opera, not one note of which they properly understand, will split with their clapping all to pieces a pair of bran new kids. I don't think I undervalue music and its harmonizing influences. In speaking of music, I remember and recognize the words of Eliza Cook when she says:

"It is the silver key to the fountain of tears
Where the spirit drinks till the brain runs wild,
The softest graves of a thousand fears,
Where their mother care like a drowsy child
Is laid asleep in flowers."

But a Mexican can make too much of a good thing out of the best thing, by heroically overdosing at inopportune intervals his surfeited listeners. And of this I complain without underestimating the art or its value to the human race.

There is another amusement which may be designated as the egg-shell performance, from which they derive much enjoyment. For many months they will save up the egg-shells preparatory to the festival and paint them in variegated colors. In fact such is the demand that egg-shells become quite an article of merchandise before the appointed day approaches. They take different colored paper and cut it up into fine powder and introduce this within the shell until nearly or quite full. When the company assembles its members, good-humoredly, commence breaking their shells over the heads and faces of those present and covering them with the fine powder from within the shells, so that within a short time you would scarcely recognize your nearest neighbor and best friend, such changes in appearance have they undergone in such a short time. The egg-shells and their contents are ground into the hair of the participants in such a manner that repeated applicacations of water, brush and comb must be made to relieve one of the offending particles. Egg-shells are the weapons with which they engage in these spirited contests, and he is lucky who comes out of these friendly encounters with, unbruised face and unpained eyes. To brighten the interest of the occasion, during the peltings of the egg-shells, bottles of Florida water are dashed into the faces of the contestants, and while they smart under the sting, it is seldom the least ill-humor is ever shown, but each takes the part he receives with a smiling complacence. Old men and old ladies, young men and young ladies all mingle in the sport, and enjoy with much satisfaction the hours of fun, their triumphs and discomfitures. Of course the little ones are transported with the entertainment and enter into it with a zest. And thus they pass a quarter part of the night in this frolicsome sport. But there is generally a dance on the occasion, and as is usual this contributes to the enjoyableness of the festival. It is a season corresponding to what is known as Mardi Gras in some of the States, and each one is on his good behavior, so that the festivities are seldom marred by unpleasant occurrences. Once or twice I have been in attendance, and remembering that I was in Rome, I became for the time a Roman, and added as I best could to the gayeties of the hours by crushing egg-shells on others and by others crushing egg-shells on me. To crush them on the head of an American is rather an unusual privilege and considered the height of felicity. Sometimes this festival continues for days, during which it is no exaggeration to say that bushels of painted egg-shells are used. In these friendly altercations the girls are regular "Tomboys," and from *favored ones* submit to the crashing and crushing without a ripple of dissatisfaction. But naturally you know how they will do, and why should my pen persist in a description of the parts they play in the frolicsome scene. So I will right now submit to a chastening, rather than scatter, any more unappreciated pearls before you.

CHAPTER XXXV.

DANCE.—DRESS, ETC.

If there is one thing which the Mexican enjoys more than another it is the dance. In his youth he was brought up to it, and in his old age has not forgotten it. Nor will he forget it while the blood courses, or the muscles play. He looks upon life as one great big frolic, to be filled up with Mescal, music and dancing, and the end of life as some elysian ball-room where he may sip heavenly Mescal and dance the eternities away. His head and heart may remain undergraduates, but his heels must take the first diploma under the practical professors of Terpsichore. The education of the feet, so as to move in grace in the labyrinthine mazes of the dance, is of the supremest importance, and for this he expends his time and bends the energies of his nature. And so, from a professional standpoint, they are accomplished dancers, having made other things subservient to the attainment of this accomplishment. Sometimes they will begin a dance here in the evening, continue it all night, the next day and the next night, rest a few hours, and continue it until everybody is broken down, and nature refuses to take another step. They generally commence these dances on Sundays. Dancing and drinking go together, and when dancing fails, drinking never fails to floor them. On these occasions the ladies seldom are guilty of improprieties, but the men often make beasts of themselves. Men in liquor will do that everywhere. The music continues unbroken during the long hours, and until the campaign is ended the little fiddles and big fiddles, the little horns and big horns are tortured for their harmonies. They spend their money freely for the music, for this wafts them toward the ecstatic land. While the gentleman and lady dance together, yet, when the sets are ended, he escorts her to a seat and then retires until they commence again, when he solicits again the same hand, or that of some other partner. The ladies generally sit on one side of the room and the gentlemen on the other. The lady goes to these gatherings, notwithstanding she may have an escort, attended by some other friend or member of the family. He is not privileged to go with her alone from her residence to the place of entertainment, but some other lynx-eyed person must obtrude himself or herself upon the young people, much to their embarrassment and dislike. Often it is the mother that thus shadows the girl, to her annoyance and that of her suitor. No man with any taste and spirit wants a mother-in-law before he has a wife, "for sufficient unto the day is the evil thereof." At the dance, the only time the gentleman gets to talk to his partner is when actually engaged on the floor, for so soon as the dancing ceases the conversation ends. Herein may lie the fondness of both sexes for the prolonged exercise, as it affords ample opportunities for divulging long pent-up heart secrets. The gentlemen do not shrink from the intoxicating waltz, and the ladies are equally as courageous, and, not to be outdone in the boldness of performance, yield themselves to voluptuous embraces of their partners, and are whirled and whirled to strains of music, as "they chase the glowing hours with flying feet." At times his whole expression indicates he is weary of his burdensome charge, but she "fashioned so slenderly, young and so fair," as the ivy with twining tendrils around the oak, clasps him the closer for continued support. And the poor thing seems to need assistance too, as she floats in the dance—some manly heart whereon to lay her weary head, while the whites of her upturned eyes have a far-away look, reminding one of the frightened, motherless calf. In the contest of endeavor he can claim no advantage, for what she lacks in toughness of fiber and suppleness of action she is more than compensated for by the delicious privilege of swooning away in the arms of her protector, who unmurmuringly must at the close bring the precious freight into port in gallant style. The body grows weary, but the spirit never tires. The dresses worn are not ill-suited to the occasion. While I am not aware that Mr. Worth has ever built outfits for these high altitude lasses, yet, in some ingenious manner, they manage the thing so as to array themselves in vestments of rare texture and beauty. It will be late in the season when women are left on the question of dress. This matter of dress addresses itself not only to her taste, but to that of her adorers, and she makes it ever a study to adorn herself in comely and graceful attire. Knowing the condition of many the wonder is, and this grows as I wonder, from whence came these costly fabrics, fashioned in such bewildering style. One would suppose that from the poverty of their resources they could not pay the duties of importation. But woman's ingenuity tackles the question, and the thing is settled. Of course the old man now and then groans a big groan and grunts a big grunt, but the girl, reinforced by the old lady, attacks the stronghold with their invincible weapons, and the man once more capitulates, dropping from his nerveless grasp the shining coin. Against their eloquent importunities there is but feeble resistance and no defense, and their demand for an unconditional surrender is tersely expressed in these words, "down with the dust." Fashion magazines, with latest plates from Madrid and the Capitol, are found even here upon the drawing-room tables of the fashionable senoritas. From these they take their lessons and make their rehearsals. I am not sure that the Mexican girl is very different from her sisters elsewhere, except, if possible, she may be more fond of style. But now ‚I tread upon the boundaries of a debatable land, and dismiss the subject to other more curious investigators than myself. The foregoing are some of the more noticeable features of the Mexican dance and dancers.

CHAPTER XXXVI.

BULL FIGHT.

The most exciting sport in Mexico is the bull fight. This had its origin in Spain, but has been practiced here for centuries. It may be rightly termed a national game, recognized as such in all sections and by all persons. While in the city of Mazatlan some years since, I once attended an exhibition of this character. On that day I was the guest of the German Consul, an elegant gentleman, and after we had dined he insisted that, as I had never been, I should go with him to the bull fight that evening. Fearing I might give offense to my host by a persistent refusal I consented, and went with him and witnessed the performance. There is a large amphitheater which will seat thousands, with rows of seats rising one above the other, in the enclosure of which are driven the bulls through a gate from an adjacent lot, one at a time. The larger, fiercer, and more vicious the animals the more exciting the sport and the more valiant his slayer. In this ring passes the *matador*, as he is called, the bull fighter, attended by several others, whose part seems secondary to that of the matador. All these are dressed in tight stripes and glaring colors, and with little flags or a banner or blanket in their hands. As soon as the bull enters the amphitheater he is stricken with a sharp-pointed iron several times, causing the blood to flow freely, and he plunges forward, maddened by the blows towards the parties. But he is received by the El-picador, a mounted spearman, for whom he then makes a headlong plunge, and if the horseman can not avert his course his life is in imminent peril; or if he escapes, the poor horse may be horribly gored in the side, and often from the ghastly wound his bowels fall on the ground, and lengthen from his now shrunken sides as he drags and kicks them in his short circuit ere he drops dead in his tracks. To elude the furious onset of the bull, by an agile movement the flag-bearers shelter themselves behind little stations provided for that purpose within, but at the outer circle of the enclosure. And were these stations not made so secure the violence of the assault made by the bull upon them would result in their demolition and the death of the refugee. Having expended some of his force in the vain endeavor to overtake the first fugitive he now turns to the others, who are irritating him by shaking flags in his face or making menacing gestures. These too are soon compelled to find a refuge from his fury. Becoming wearied from repeated efforts to punish his tormentors his passion for the time somewhat abates, and then to arouse him to a crazy fury some of the attendants are each provided with small flags, the staffs of which are iron or steel, the heads or lower portion of which are sharpened and barbed. These flags, one in each hand, the attendant will take, and while the attention of the bull is directed by some other participant in the fight, will approach the bull by a surprisingly active movement and plant the barbed flags in the shoulder or neck of the animal and leave them securely fastened there in the quivering flesh. He shakes and shakes to rid himself of the painful things, but the vibrating flags only lacerate and pain the more, the more he moves. With distended nostrils and glaring eyes he now and then stops to paw the earth looking like madness in agony. The flag-bearers must now look to their safety in their activity and sure-footedness. For should they stumble or fall they might not rise again from the pursuit of the furious beast. But as opportunity presents itself some one of the attendants will drive more barbed flags, wreathed with festoons, into his body, augmenting his torture. The matador, in the meantime, has not been a silent spectator, but with a large flag in one hand and a sword in the other, as the bull would rush toward him, he would throw the flag over his face, and jumping aside, thus avoid the blow. This flag, at times, the bull would dash to the ground and trample it under his feet with an air of wild triumph. These scenes are witnessed with the noisiest demonstrations, the excitement of the spectators increasing with the flow of blood and the shifting dangers of the situation. In the course of time the body of the animal is thickly studded with the metal arrows, some bearing flags and some wreathed with artificial flowers which have opened up fountains of blood, with which his sides are reeking as it goes dripping in pools below. Now the sight is sufficiently sickening and shocking to the strongest nerves. All this to furnish amusement to gratify the coarsest taste. From exertion and loss of blood, exhaustion at length comes on and the matador, armed with a long, sharp dirk-shaped knife, by a few alert strides unharmed, reaches the bull, and with a well-directed blow drives the knife at some fatal spot deep into his neck, and upon its withdrawal the blood jumps from the gaping wound. The poor animal, stunned and sickened, reels and sinks to the earth another trophy of the wicked sport. 'T is then the spectators indulge in the loudest huzzahs, and the matador receives their loudest plaudits. 'T is thus he retires from the ring bowing his acknowledgments to his enthusiastic admirers with an *Io triumphe* air about him. One bull after another is thus slain until as many as six or eight may be killed during one evening's performance. But when you have seen one you have witnessed the whole thing, with possibly some minor variation of incidents. As soon as one is killed he is dragged out of the ring by horsemen, who are near for that purpose, and the flesh on the morrow to the assembled spectators of the day is regularly retailed at market rates. So the game may have a double aspect, meat and sport. Such sights must leave a bad impression upon the young hundreds who are in attendance as witnesses of the cruel spectacle. Young ladies, too, elegantly dressed, belonging to the higher classes, are present and give countenance and approval to the proceedings. Not only with unshocked hearts, but with manifestations of pleasure, they look at the bloody drama. Gentlemen take their wives and children and make it an enjoyable pastime, varying the every-day occurrences of life. But I am glad to learn that of later years the sport in many parts of the republic has gone somewhat into disuse, indicating, I hope, the approach of a better time for the bull and for his persecutors. On the evening of my visit one of the participants in the ring was a lady. I beg pardon of the sex, a woman, an unsexed one at that, who, by the fullness of her limbs and the fewness of her skirts, which were also short and showy, made herself shockingly conspicuous. She narrowly escaped with her life, as she stumbled and fell to the earth, but by rare fortune regained her footing, and found safety in the protecting station. She was nothing more than a female brute, with the lowest and meanest habits, passions and tastes, a libel on her sex, and a disgrace to her race, and as between her and the gentlemanly bull, he had my warmest sympathy as much as if he were "the under dog in the fight." And this is the national amusement of which the Spaniards and Mexicans so much boast! People, male and female, abandoning their business occupations for the time, will spend hundreds of dollars and travel hundreds of miles by private conveyance, in order to see these revolting exhibitions. What a standard of taste and morals it foreshadows! But let us indulge in the hope that this relic of barbarism will soon pass away with the civilizing outgrowth of the land, and that it will find its appropriate burial-place beside the inquisition and other cruelties of the dark ages. The nineteenth century, with its wonderful tendencies, is unfavorable to its growth, but favorable to its death. As the reign of cruelty gives way may that of love increase, until the coming years shall see a lovelier earth, peopled with a sweeter and lovelier race. And to this sentiment will not all my readers respond a hearty affirmative?

CHAPTER XXXVII.

DRINKING GENERAL.—EVIL EFFECTS.

Let us now turn and speak of some of the habits and customs of this people. The first habit which arrests our attention, by reason of its universality, is that of drinking. The fewest number are exempt from this vice. It is strange to see men, otherwise good citizens, to this thing yielding submission. For this reason those who, by virtue of their social position, should be good exemplars in society are bad exemplars in morals. Men are generally imitators. Few men have sufficient strength of character to be independent in thought, and speech, and action. Hence, if the best in the country are drunkards, the worst can scarcely be less. They will follow the example before them, and jump unchallenged with their leaders into perdition. As here the leaders all drink and become drunken, so their followers do the same. And the same evil consequences flow from drink here as flow from it the world over. By this curse the poor are made poorer, and the better conditioned worse. The poor peon, with scarcely any raiment to his back, and no shoes to his feet, goes staggering in the street, having put his wages in drink instead of family supplies. He falls upon the street, or reels to his hovel and sleeps the stupor off, while his wife and children are starving by piecemeal. He robs others and those the nearest to him by blood and affinity that he may selfishly gratify the meanest appetite. In liquor his meanness is fully developed. What was before suppressed or hidden now is revealed with all of its deformities. Liquor is the magician's wand which brings treachery into light, and murder in the heart into murder in the act. It serves as a magnifying lens to the character of these drunken wretches, breaking reserve, piercing disguises, and painting in true colors what manner of men they are. In the wide universe I venture to affirm there is no tougher character than the drunken peon. Life, property, wife, children, nothing is sacred to him; his hand is that of a regular Ishmaelite, against every one, and boldly sets at defiance the peace of society and the laws of the land. In him the worst elements are so mixed as to make the very worst citizen. The meanness latent becomes the meanness open, defiant. Nor does it seem to be regarded as a disqualifying vice for the better positions in society, but looked upon as something to be expected in the life of all, and in no manner to be reprobated. And so general is the custom it may almost be said that the Mexican who does not drink and get drunk is the *dead Mexican*. One unaccustomed to such a condition of things can only, with much difficulty, accommodate himself to his changed relations. A good deal of wine and brandies are imported into the country, and much of this of a very inferior quality. It sells high, but is bought with eagerness and drunk with avidity. Of course it is only the better class which can afford such expensive indulgence. The poor class, for the gratification of this appetite, rely upon the products of the soil, and I might add are the best of patrons. From a certain plant, which in certain sections grows well, a liquor they call *Mescal* is manufactured. The plant is most extensively cultivated for this purpose, and from its manufacture immense fortunes are made. It is indigenous to the coast and warm lands, and when cultivated grows luxuriantly. It sells, after heavy freight has been paid upon it, for three cents a drink, and is thus brought within the reach of the poor. When tasted for the first time it is simply villainous, and the wonder is how men can ever so educate themselves as to crave it. But such is the fact, and the desire becomes so strong after a little while that it claims a preference. The practice of drinking is so common that it demoralizes labor and makes it inefficient and unreliable. It is immaterial how urgent may be the necessity for prompt and vigorous labor, liquor may thwart all of your purposes and upset all of your calculations. The injury received at the time can not be repaired, and you must bear in silence your injuries as the inevitable. Elsewhere you might have some recourse for damages, but here such a proceeding would be the silliest measure, for from it no praclical good could result. "Sue a beggar and get a louse." As poor and wretched as these people are they are made more so by liquor, which is to-day not only here, but in other portions of the world, the greatest *crime* of the age. It destroys more homes and lives, brings more misery, ruin and wretchedness and deaths, than all things else in the world. If ever prohibition was needed it is right here and now. If people will not save themselves, the law, then in mercy, with its protecting arms, should be long enough and strong enough to reach and reclaim them. The State has an inherent power to protect itself and to prevent its members from committing suicide, and it is derelict in its duty if, when the occasion demands it, it should fail to discharge this obligation. Liquor, poverty, ignorance and crime are the most intimate associates, and wives, women and children the greatest sufferers from the unholy association. But it is not my purpose to descant at length upon this vice, but rather to notice its existence, its extent and evil consequences. I fear many years must pass before a reformation can be here effected, so wedded are the people to the prevailing vice. Nothing short of a great moral revolution can ever break its strength and force its devotees from this body and soul-killing tyrant. At best reforms move slowly. Much time is consumed in planting seed-truths, in their germination, cultivation and growth before they flower and bear fruit for the healing of the people. Much time is needed in preparing the soil of good and honest hearts for the reception of those truths which, when received, will in the end diffuse themselves through the different strata of society, and confer untold blessings on a living and an unborn race. So upon the whole, in this particular, I see no immediate prospect for many years to come of a change for the better. I wish I could indulge more hopeful views, but the signs of the political zodiac forbid at present this entertainment. Nothing short of the power of the nation can stop such supplies from gratifying such appetites.

CHAPTER XXXVIII.

PROFANITY.—BURIAL CUSTOMS.

The habit of swearing, as indulged in in the United States, does not here obtain. It is probable the American can use more oaths in a shorter time and with a greater variety of tone, gesture and meaning than any other person. In this line he is unquestionably an *artist*. If you disagree with me, I refer you to Jack the sailor, the mule driver, and the young man on a July morning breaking up a new ground with a yoke of young steers. While the Mexican has not yet learned in this way to give vent to his feelings, yet he has a vocabulary of billingsgate, which, for vulgarity and course ribaldry in the nomenclature of no other nation finds its equal. The presence of ladies somewhat deters the American from giving expression to his voluble oaths, but their presence is no embarrassment to the Mexican, when in words he would relieve his mind of its weight of filth. Nothing shocks him, and, in this particular, there is a poetic equality between him and the burro; the sense of decency he does not recognize in the burro, nor does the burro recognize it in him. I do not mean to say that every Mexican acts thus, any more than every American swears; but this, that the expletives of the Mexican, are unapproached, and unapproachable in outrageous obscenity. The flexible language is twisted into terrible anathemas, and becomes the vehicle of concentrated wormwood and gall. So, as between him and his neighbor across the border, in shocking invective and profanity, there is not much difference, doing the same thing through the employment of different vernaculars. I think this habit is confined principally to the men, but now and then a female interlards her Castilian with some unrhetorical excerpts, such as have been described. But in this line she is a feeble imitator, as her masculine prototype disdains all competition. One of the most distasteful of all repulsive objects is a cursing woman. In defiance of the ordinary decencies and properties of life she cuts herself adrift from human sympathies.

The burial customs are peculiar. These people have their Potter's field, wherein they inter the poorer classes, those unable to pay the expenses of interment. Those who die in the hospitals and prisons have but little ceremony and lamentations made over them. A detail of prisoners (with guards), takes the body to the grave, borne upon their shoulders; these constitute the funeral cortege. A public coffin is kept in readiness for the purpose, and, as they die, this is called into requisition to carry the body to the graveyard. When it reaches the grave the body is taken from it and uncoffined, the body goes into its resting-place, while the coffin is returned for the next unfortunate. This public coffin I have seen on several occasions, as it rested on the shoulders of the pall-bearers, going and returning to the cemetery. It is rather fancifully painted in stripes and colors. Armed soldiers attend the prisoners who bear it to and from the grave. And thus, from the prison of life to the prison of death, sadly recurring thoughts will come as we reflect upon the theme suggested. A shallow grave is dug, the rock forbidding further depth; no song, no prayer, a profane word, a hollow jest, and then unwept, the dust goes to its fellow dust, and the spirit to God who gave it. How truthfully spoken in the play is the sentiment of Joe Jefferson, " How soon we are forgotten when we are dead and gone."

But there are more pretentious cemeteries in which it costs something to be buried. The ground must be paid for, and other incidental expenses which are felt and remembered by the family of the deceased. The cemeteries which I have seen are unornamented, and are left in a comparatively neglected condition. It is necessary, in many places, to deposite the bodies in tombs above ground, constructed of rude masonry, because of the solid rock underneath. Often these works are left in a badly dilapidated condition, through the broken arches and apertures of which may be seen the skeletons of the buried. I think I observed in one of these no less than three skulls, and this inspection having satisfied my curiosity, I cared not to prosecute further my examination in that direction. But when the ground will permit they are buried in the earth. When the coffin is lowered, some dirt is cast upon it, a foot or more, and then some one jumps down into the grave, and, with a large rock, he rams time and again the earth upon the coffin. Now and then the rock, weighing probably twenty or twenty-five pounds, he will raise as high as he can and then let it fall upon the dirt to be certain that the earth is sufficiently compacted. He then comes out. More dirt is cast down, and then he again descends with his rock and goes through the same actions; and this he continues to repeat until the grave is filled. While this is being done those standing around are talking and laughing as if nothing more than the commonest occurence of life was transpiring. No funeral obsequies, no air of solemnity is seen, nothing to indicate a sense of loss, a feeling of grief, unless, perhaps, by the bearers of lighted candles, tied with bits of black ribbon, and mechanically held in their hands during the burial. Those who attend must, of necessity, walk, or at best, attend upon horse back, as there are no vehicles and no roads for the same. There are reliefs of pall-bearers if the distance is considerable, for upon their shoulders they carry the wooden, decorated coffin. These coffins are buried with the dead. The members of the family do not go to the grave at the burial. These take their last look and say their last farewell at the home of the deceased. I am not sure but this custom is a good one. It saves the further pangs inflicted in the presence of the grave, the lowering body, the rumbling earth, the closed sepulcher. The briefer the services, to be decently appropriate, is often a mercy to the sorrowing survivors. I was once invited to attend the funeral of the little child of a Mexican acquaintance; when I went I was surprised to find no member of the family present. I then learned, for the first time, such was not the custom. The little coffin, with quite a profusion of flowers, was borne on a litter by strong persons, over-canopied with rich hangings, and a long retinue of little children made up the funeral procession. A few older persons were present, friends of the family, to direct the funeral, but the little children were the chief mourners present on the occasion. There is also this tendency here, where the ability is present, to have expensive funerals. I knew one instance where the family of the deceased were almost impoverished by the extravagant outlay at the funeral, costing many hundred dollars, when, at the same time, they were compelled to borrow money to meet the actual necessaries of life. The folly of such a thing must be apparent to the least observant. We should not rob the living to enrich the dead with an idle pomp and gorgeous pageant at the grave. There is an empty vanity in this, which the dead, were they living, would rebuke, and the living should do the same. It is a species of pride, vain glory, that should perish with the growth of better ideas. It does no good to the dead, and much inconvenience and often harm to the living. The graves have over them many curious inscriptions, quaintly, at times, commemorative of the deceased. Cemeteries everywhere, I suppose, perpetuate many lies cut in stone and marble. We under-estimate the vices and magnify the virtues of the dead, and, through the softened light of charity, read the lives of the departed.

CHAPTER XXXIX.

MARRIAGES.—HOW CELEBRATED.—COURTING.

I should not fail to say something in reference to the marriages in this country. Their celebration by the civl magistrate is all that the law now requires. However, the rites are generally solemized also by the priest. The females, for the most part, insist upon this latter solemnization, while the men are more indifferent to it. The law requires that some civil functionary should perform the marriage service, to preserve the rights which flow from such a relation, for instance, the rights of property and the legitimacy of children. Something like the bans are published for a given time before the event takes place in the parish church. It costs something to get married in this country, and especially is this the case if the priest has a hand in the affair. Often, I am told, for his services he will charge several hundred dollars, and the cash must come down ere the two hearts can beat as one with his permission. The truth is, the fees are so high in some parts that it exceeds the ability of the contracting parties to consummate the marriage. I believe the poorest peon must pay about *eleven dollars* in order to make some female peon as miserable as himself. It really, in some places, is a virtual inhibition upon the institution. The girl *will* have the priest if she marries, and the fellow, not being able to pay for such a costly luxury, the consequence is, they either quit, or, which is more frequently the case, they live together for years, rearing a family of children, and then, on some fine day, when a change of good fortune has overtaken them, they are regularly married according to law and the canons of the church. Thus it is often the case that the father and mother are married in the presence of their numerous children. A singular state of affairs, you may say, and I agree with you, but it is one of the customs of the country. In the United States the cost of marrying is insignificant; it is the cost afterwards that makes the perspiration flow. If many of the young men there were compelled to pay as here, a few hundred dollars for the privilege, it might check hasty marriages and shorten the perquisites of the clergymen. The fee of the priest is graduated by the position and ability of the bridegroom. He sets his figures, and he sets them high, too, and the poor fellow must come up like a "little man" and plank down the cash, or else the good Father will not ferry him over the river. If possible he pays the priest, and then whips himself, if not his wife afterwards, for his enforced liberality. But now he is at least married, and for the future he can afford to live hard and die poor. The marriage occasion is generally attended with festivities—some dance or other public entertainment. There are but few people who adopt the custom of the ancient Thracians, who wept at the cradle and danced at the grave. These dances at marriages are generally protracted ones, and liquors flow freely until the guests often find their level *on the floor*. Presents too are given; some souvenirs for the future.

There is also this custom, which is an unusual one, that the young lady's outfit should be purchased by the bridegroom. This is considered the desirable thing, and the young gentleman has, for once, an opportunity of exhibiting his taste, and if he would please his affianced he should make no mistake at this point. And then, too, it pleases the old people to see their daughter starting out in life well provided for—*by another*. Should they at once commence housekeeping, a few household goods are given them, or the young man is advised where he can *buy* them from some other *member of the family*, and then they go out into the world with the benediction, " God bless you, my children," resting upon their heads. If, in our country, it were intimated to the young man the necessity of purchasing the girl's trosseau, I apprehend he would hie away to the " hills of Hepsidam." But here it is all right, everybody is pleased with the beautiful custom, and the bridegroom knows the character and cost of the rich apparel and "fixings" before the eyes of the bride have seen the sweet vision. I do n't believe our girls would submit to such treatment, and would rather remain unmarried (*for a time*) than to yield such a first sight to their intended. There is a delicious mystery about such things, the first sight of which should be unseen, save through the veil of maidenly modesty.

But the courting comes before the marriage, and this is always an interesting chapter in life, however uneventful in other respects. Doubtless my young lady readers may have more than a passing curiosity to know how the thing is done in this country. In some respects it is different, in many, similar to those since wooing was heard with the songs of the birds in the bowers of Eden. It is one of those blessed things which must remain forever unpatented, and in which there are no exclusive rights or privileges, and on which no improvement has ever been made since, for aught I know, the morning stars sang together. The senoritas (young ladies), are never permitted to go out unattended. Girls ten and twelve years old must have some one to go with them across the street, to the school-house, to the nearest neighbors; and to go to any public gathering, church concert, or ball, without some member of the family or other chaperon, is never thought of, and, were it done, would set the tongues of all the gossips to wagging, and these are always graduates in the "school of scandal." What an occupation that must be to have one's ears converted into courtship funnels, into which must be poured all the trashy verbiage and unreportable silliness of kittenish lovers! And, up to this time, no soporific has been discovered which brings inattention to the wakeful eyes and ears of such chaperons and sentinels. So, really, the opportunities for *sure enough, down right, good, honest courting* are rather limited, as what is done must be done quickly and to the point, and in the unguarded moments of the watcher. No excursion parties, nor walks in the garden among the flowers and bees and humming birds, no moonlight strolls, no naming of stars, are permitted unwatched by some family policeman. The young man must study his astronomy in his own studio or in his lonely walks, unembarrassed by his sweetheart's presence. That it is so may be good for science, but bad for the lover. Again, the houses are so constructed that gratings of iron are placed in the windows perpendicularly in position so that while the windows reach to the floor they do not permit ingress or egress. In the evenings those windows are favorite places where the young people meet, but on either side of the intervening bars. Situated thus, with the protection of the iron railing, she is not subject to the customary espionage. And, if the lover is liked, the old people permit the young people to hold " sweet converse" for an indefinite time. Before the matter has progressed so far, he will simply wander along in front of the window where she is stationed, and, with a bow and smile in Chesterfieldian style, make his salutation. From the manner in which she returns his advances, he can but know whether his attentions have been favorably received or otherwise. Her smile may bring hope or her frown despair. But receiving encouragement of some kind he is emboldened to approach nearer, and linger longer. If possessed of any address and he then can gain her ear, the chances are that, with melifluous words, he will gain her heart. To her his charm of manner, the persuasive witchery of words, and earnest purpose make him invincible. They talk about a thousand sweet nothings, and a thousand other things of which we know nothing, and yet their store of talk remains unexhausted. " I would just like to know what those children can find to talk about so much," says the old lady, and the old man replies, " I wonder too, but I 'll be blest if ever I will tell you." So soon have they forgotten they were children once, and then, as children now, did such childish things. And so it is, and was, and ever will be, till the end of the world. If the young people should live at some distance from each other the mails are burdened with these perfumed missives, just like it is everywhere else. Here the embarrassments are more numerous and annoying. Yet he recognizes the aphorism that "a faint heart never won a fair lady," and his redoubled courage and persistency win in the end. No studied phrases nor set forms of speech can reach the heart like earnest love's impromptu talk. Where this is mutual, and "the time is up," *the thing just courts itself.* No art is needed when heart seeks heart; the welding process has begun, and union is the end. Of course she has called him this and that, "a bad thing," "the meanest man in town;" told him "to go away from here," and "not to call again." Yet eyes and smiles are better tell-tales than such words—woman's words—and he goes again, to find a warmer welcome than ever before. They have their little quarrels, too, from some little somethings, which explanations cure. Sweet reconciliation comes, estrangements go, and life is a dream until the marriage day. *And this is the way they court in Mexico.* There are some artificial obstructions-some man made barriers, but when these are out of the way, then nature proceeds upon the same line, to the same object, irrespective of geographical divisions. The haughtiest grandee, in the presence of proud beauty, becomes the veriest knight of gentility. She puts her hand upon the warrior, statesman, poet, earth's mightiest magnates, and as a lit-

tle child " leadeth them whithersoever she listeth."
It is so here, there, everywhere, her God-given
power to guide us though we govern, " to lead us,
though she follows."

CHAPTER XL.

HANDSHAKING. — CUTTING TREES OUT OF THE PATH.—CIGARETTE SMOKING.

Let us now speak of another custom which is generally observed and prevails to such an extent that it is almost annoying. I refer to that of handshaking. This would seem to be an innocent habit, but when practiced as they do, it often becomes a nuisance. If they meet each other twenty times a day they must shake hands on meeting and shake hands on parting. It matters not how you may be circumstanced, or how inconvenient it may be to do so, yet he considers it a slight if you do not shake hands with him as often as he offers to do so during the day. The commonest peon with dirtiest hands must meet with the same kind of recognition, or else he is insulted and then insults you. I have seen ladies and gentleman seated at a dining table, when some messenger would come in to make some announcement or bring some note, and he must go all around the table and shake hands with the guests who had risen to receive him; and when he had finished his salutation after this he would immediately go all around and shake hands with them again, saying to each one, "*Adios,*" and then departs. It matters not how much the company may be disturbed by his uninteresting visit, he must " get his hand in " before he returns satisfied. Such is the custom of this part of the country. Should one come into a store to buy a few cents' worth of things he must shake hands with the proprietors and the clerks as he enters, and repeat it as he leaves.

Unless you have been subjected to this thing you can not imagine what a nuisance it becomes. A bow of recognition on frequently meeting is generally thought sufficient with most people to fill the requirements of politeness, but these fellows think it discourteous unless you make a pump-handle of their hands.

If you meet them twenty times a day you know the programme and you must play it out, otherwise you forfeit their good feelings. This handshaking business is often attended with a kind of half embrace, male and female indulging in the habit. It is not exactly a hug, but a kind of "half hamond" approach to it—just enough in that direction to be disappointing to those who were expecting it, or who loved such a demonstrative salutation. This they also do when they leave as well as when they arrive. While quite a number of them were going through a dress parade of this kind, an Englishman who had lived in the country a long time, and knew the Mexicans by heart, remarked to me, "You see all this foolishness; it does n't mean anything." It is the shallowest pretense, the merest mockery of affection, the one for the other, and deserves to be remembered among the other hollow hypocricies of the day. I have no respect for such vile shams, deceits under the guise of pretended friendship and affection. The fellow who is unusually demonstrative in his embrace, who will pat you two or three time on the back, watch out for him, and feel when he lets go if your watch and other valuables are still in your possession. If so, and you are traveling, he has missed his opportunity; but if he journeys with you after that you will be lucky if nothing is stolen from you. Under the garb of personal devotion, he is an arrant hypocrite, if not a thief or murderer. As I fear the "Greeks bringing gifts," so I fear these superlative manifestations of esteem. But enough on this topic.

As you are traveling, you will often find that trees have fallen across the trail, and that great notches have been cut into them at the crossing, but seldom have they been "cut in two," and thrown aside. The reason of the thing is this, the Mexican does not wish to do more work than is absolutely necessary, *has n't time you see*, and therefore he cuts down far enough in the log to enable his burro train to pass over it, and thus accomplishes his object. In this way he saves muscle and time, and the sooner goes his way rejoicing. The foolish American would do otherwise than the economic Mexican, but the latter is religiously opposed to doing any more work than the present generation requires, and the future generations must take care of their own roads as well as themselves.

The practice of cigarette smoking exists nowhere, perhaps, as it does here. The old and young of both sexes follow the practice. Boys and girls of tender years do the same. The first thing on meeting is to take a smoke, the last thing is to take a smoke, and between times is to take many smokes. And thus the days and the nights, the months and the years, are filled up with much smoking. While the cigarettes come in packages, yet the Mexican seldom smokes them as received, but he prefers to unwrap them, and then in his artistic way reroll them before use. He will consume great numbers in one day, and while comparatively cheap, yet the quantity makes up a considerable aggregate. Of course the injurious effects can not be calculated, but must be very great when the habit is so general. It matters not what he may be doing, if he wishes to smoke he drops everything and *smokes*. The time employed in preparing his cigarette is just that much time out of which he cheats his employer, and this many times repeated in the day is no inconsiderable amount. If the importance of the matter demands much haste, this does not in the least hasten the Mexican, except it may be to smoke the more frequently. You can't hurry him except with the prospect of an early smoke, and this often repeated. I imagine that in his fall down a shaft one of the sources of his regret would be that he can't stop on the way and take a smoke. I know he would if he could. The urgency of business, uncertainty of life, imminency of death, never interferes with the enjoyment of his smoke. It is very aggravating at times when so much may be depending upon prompt action, but the Mexican doesn't see it in that light, and he moves along as much undisturbed at one time as another, as if he held in his hand a fee-simple to the centuries. I repeat, you just can't expedite him out of his smoke, whatever may come to you or upon the land. He is ready for it, and will smoke away with supreme satisfaction, while you are filled towards him with supreme disgust. Why I verily believe that there are some of them who, if the life-blood of some member of the family were ebbing out from a cut artery, would not tie up the artery until they had first unrolled and rewrapped their cigarrettes. Things may come and things may go, but cigarettes they will smoke forever. Cigars are not ignored, but as these are more costly they can not be bought in much quantity by the poorest classes, who must content themselves with the less expensive cigarettes. The tobacco used is produced and manufactured in the country, and for the production of it there are some of the finest lands in the world, probably not even excelled by those of Cuba. With proper encouragement and tillage, it is only a question of time when these shall be made to yield to their owners and the government a large revenue.

CHAPTER XLI.

RAWHIDES. — USES. — WOODEN PINS. — ADOBE HOUSES.—SANITATION.—DISEASES.

But there is another thing which I must not omit to mention, and which is peculiar to the Mexican. I refer to his many uses of *rawhides*. This would, at first view, appear a small matter, yet in the business life of the Mexican, cuts no unimportant figure. What he can't do with this useful article is not worth doing. With it he yokes his oxen for the plough. With it he binds on his pack-mules their cargoes. Many articles he sews with it, and it is seldom he ever loses these stitches. His fence rails he will tie together with it, and for years and years it will weather the elements. The very rafters on his house he binds and holds in place with it for half a century. It dries and hardens, but does not seem to weaken. To a great extent it supersedes pins and nails, is always on hand and purchased cheaply. A Mexican without rawhide is deprived of one of his chief resources, but with it his stock is nearly full. A good stock of rawhide is a good patrimony. While the rafters, as stated, and the cross slats are tied with rawhide, yet the roof proper is put on with small wooden pins. These are used in the place of nails, and last a surprisingly long time, more than a quarter of a century. These pins are about five inches in length and made of pine. Nails are too high to be used for such purposes, costing here as much as thirty-seven and a half cents a pound! Thus, you see, a few pounds of nails would break the ordinary Mexican, and consequently, instead of driving nails "he sets his pegs." But he is not fastidious about his roof; like the story of the man seen by the Arkansas Traveler, when it rains he can't fix it, and when it don't, he does n't need it.

And here in this connection I might remark that the architecture of the mountain is inferior to the designs furnished by Sir Christopher Wren. The houses are made of adobes, large sundried bricks, one story, and on the top, from wall to wall, laid transversely are rows of poles, and these all covered with dirt one or two feet thick, and over this comes the roof proper of thin pine boards. The houses are warm in winter and cool in summer, and well adapted to the warm countries. In many places there is great scarcity of timber, and these houses are made from necessity, but they are often made where timber is obtainable.

The construction of dwellings has no little bearing upon their sanitation, but as to this matter the common Mexican has no ideas whatever. He knows nothing of the laws of health, and your efforts to teach him these, were you so inclined, would be misspent time. The thought would be too big to find a lodgment in his cranium. His dress does not vary with the seasons. I have seen them often with the thinnest white cotton pants and without shoes, when the snow was several inches on the ground. The zarape, a single blanket, is the only bed-clothing with which they are provided, let the weather be as it may. Often he will wrap himself up in this and fall upon the cold ground, without fire, "and sleep the gentle hours away." In the coldest weather you will find them sitting around in the sunshine with their blankets wrapped around them, concealing the whole body except the head. The little barefooted children pass through the same hardships, endure the same privations. But these things do not prove their exemption from disease, but only their ignorant, reckless mode of living. The fact is but few have perfect health. I think it no exaggeration to say that the majority have inherited vitiated blood; and then long exposure has developed the seeds of many ailments. They are forever wanting some prescription, some medicine to take, and the first inquiries upon the arrival of a new American is if he is a doctor. They will take anything you will give them, if you call it some kind of "doctor's stuff," and express much confidence in the efficacy of the potion, and *say nothing as to payment for the same.* If but little is the matter with them, their groans are noisy in the extreme; but when seriously injured, I have seen them submit to surgical treatment causing great pain, without scarcely wincing. I have assisted in some of these operations, and under the torture of a blunt needle they scarcely flinched. They know nothing as to diet in sickness or health, except to take what is given them, and never changing the quantity. Personal cleanliness is one of the lost virtues, and this contributes no little to the increased bills of mortality. Uncleanliness, superadded to bad living and great exposure, makes a heavy death rate in the healthiest localities.

Were not the water supply in quantity and quality so good, and the air so pure, their habits of life would kill them in greater numbers. Filth and stench fill their hovels, and the wonder is how they survive so long the unwholesome conditions. When attacked by fevers they do not show that tenacity of life which so many possess, but succumb to their influence in a brief period. They do not possess the constitutional power of long resistance to the inroads of disease. The precautions against unhealthfulness are scarcely known, or if known then unrecognized. Even in the most populous cities the sewerage system is most imperfect and little understood. And to-day, for instance, the city of Mexico, which should be one of the healthiest places of the world, is far otherwise. It is only very recently that anything like sanitary reform has made any headway, but even as yet to such a little extent that the death rate percentage continues alarming. However, some project is now on foot, I learn, to drain that city on a scale and in a manner commensurate with the importance and magnitude of the undertaking. Some scientific engineers and sanitary experts are engaged in the great enterprise, and it seems the necessary means have been already furnished, or satisfactory arrangements have been made to secure them. But so stupeudous is the undertaking that years must pass before its accomplishment. Chills and fever are rarely known on the mountains. Now and then one is developed after the person had sojourned for some time in a warmer latitude and then comes here; but they seldom originate so high above the sea level. Colds and the ailments in consequence of cutaneous affections and blood poisons prevail to a great extent. In some sections sore eyes, in others *goitres* predominate. These goitres are not unknown in the United States, almost every practicing physician has seen them, but here the singular phenomenon is presented that in some neighborhoods nearly every other person is so affected. It is an enlargement of the neck; seems to be an engorgement of the blood vessels, as if contained in some kind of a sac, and has the appearance of an excrescence, and if not painful, at least quite inconvenient. The young and old of both sexes are similarly affected. Why it should prevail in certain localities so much more than in other places, is said to be on account of the character of the water. This, at least, is the reason ascribed, but whether well founded or not, I am not able to say. The water, it is said, in these places possesses such constituents as are favorable to the outgrowth of these things. It is at least an interesting study, worthy of the investigation of the medical expert and scientist. Upon examination it may be ascertained that there are certain other local causes which induce their origin.

CHAPTER XLII.

YELLOW FEVER.—SMALL-POX.—MOUNTAIN DOCTOR.

Some of the coast cities of Mexico are, at times, visited by that dreadful scourge, the yellow fever. Guymas Mazatlan and Vera Cruz have, from time to time, felt its severest visitations. Culiacan, a city interior from the Pacific coast some forty miles, has also suffered much from its being carried thither from the sea ports. The seed brought and planted in a bed of filth, under a hot sun, germinate rapidly, spread alarmingly, and kill frightfully. If the conditions are favorable, the sun and the germ soon start the pestilence on its mission of death—when the conditions are predisposing the germ introduced is the explosive spark. The smallpox sometimes visits these denizens of the mountains, and in numbers sweeps them into the grave. Their imprudence is such that they perish numerously and rapidly. Again there is a want of proper medical attention in such cases, and ignorance and neglect run up the figures of mortality. Having now alluded to the sanitation of the country, and to some of its prevailing diseases, it may not be amiss to refer to that professional character known as the "mountain doctor." I have spoken heretofore in reference to the "mountain lawyer," and it would hardly be just now to leave the "mountain doctor" and his characteristics unchronicled. And here I would preface my introduction to him by saying that my remarks apply more particularly to the native "medicine man." Now and then an intelligent foreign physician may be found, but rarely a native. In all my acquaintances I can now only recall one Mexican doctor in these parts that has anything like respectable attainments. He was a student at some medical school, and a man of much more than average intelligence. Some of the American doctors here are models in their way, and subsist by a kind of professional bushwhacking. With his potions, and lotions, and lozenges, he coins his subsistence, coppers, and keeps the wolf, not from his door, but from eating him up. And in this he is lucky, for poor patrons, poor doctor. But of all places in the world for humbugging this must be the paradise. The doctor is a kind of neighborhood boss in most parts, and his counsels sought, which are given, too, in such weighty words and with such weighty emphasis, that they impress his hearers as but little short of the oracular. Here he is "El Capitan" of the whole gang. He carries no solemn-looking saddle-bags, nor pocket-cases, the relics of former times, but what he has is generally "done up in a rag." And when this comes out, the business proceeds. This native of the woods shrinks not from the responsibility of human life, but he meets that responsibility like a man of courage, and his patients, unlike those of Doctor Sangrado, in Gil Blas, die, but not according to "established principles." "Saul hath slain his thousands," but how many these fellows have killed will remain unrevealed till the last day. These mountaineer practitioners "get in their work," notwithstanding the laws of the republic forbid any one from practicing medicine or pharmacy without a diploma from the government. Is not a useful hint here suggested by this legislation to our people by which the standard of the medical profession may be raised? There is one good thing here for the people, and in this fact is the salvation of many, the fewness of these medical shysters. Were they more numerous the population would soon be decimated, and as it is, it takes the wonderful fecundity of the people to preserve the equilibrium between the living and the dead, the births and the deaths. He has a few native herbs and roots, and unpatented nostrums with which he medicates his faithful people. If they die, it is the act of Providence, if they live it is the mighty doctor! Here and there among the little ones he shoves in his "teas and things," and with grave face and sage words retires to learn on to-morrow that the little sufferer "has joined the angel band." The old women regard him not only with admiration but affection, and in the contemplation of his stores of knowledge, wonder how one small head contains it all.

Among them "he weeds a broad row," and while with them, from them he is loth to tear himself, but lives upon the "fat of the land." And why shouldn't he? They believe in him, and he, to return their confidence, receives their numerous favors, but not "without fee or reward." He knows nothing as he ought to know it, and is simply the prince of humbugs. But isn't it strange that people will be deluded with such arrant frauds, such outspoken, self-advertised knaves? And yet they will be, will slip in and get remedies from such characteristic quacks, and somehow or other feel as if it were a good thing upon their regular physician. They have saved a visit and taken a short cut to the restoration of their health! But these fellows neither know the a b c's of their profession, nor some even the alphabet of their own language, and yet with a temerity only equalled by their stupidity, essay the healing art. They are not so bad in surgical cases, for malpractice here "leaves its wreck behind." Their favorite cases are those which sweetly sink to rest, and "give no sign," and leave no trace of the professional cunning. But there are humbugs in every profession, but I reckon the acreage is larger in the medical than in any other. There is more privacy, more opportunity for concealment, and fewer opportunities for exposure. He does his work, and *the work is done*, and that is the last of it. No public board to which he must go and answer, but to the family residence, and not beyond. Nothing but praises follow his good practice, but his mistakes are buried with his patients, who "softly lie and sweetly sleep low, low in the ground." The practice of the lawyer is more exposed to public scrutiny. And the public, knowing gold and baser metals when they see them, seldom fail to give due fineness and weight. Their mistakes live to proclaim their demerits, and lessen their influence. The charges of these doctors, or rather, I should say, empirics, is not according to any known schedule, but they are a tariff as well as a law unto themslves, and what they do n't get is not for the reason that they have not charged it. Perhaps they remember the words of Shakespeare, " that we lose much by not asking for it." They will die with no regrets on this score, by reason, in a word, of having in a pang of conscience placed an undue estimate upon their pre-eminent service! For the real good he may do in a case of sickness, I would as soon place myself in the hands of the Voodoo doctor, with his rabbit foot, snake rattles, cat hair and owls' ears, with which to exorcise the spirit of the disease, or drive it away as a necromancer with his medical incantations. But he lives according to the law of supply and demand. Unless there was a demand for his wares, he would not supply them, but he will supply them as long as there is a demand for them. And there will be a demand until ignorance goes, and intelligence comes to stay. And this shall come to pass when the mountain tops shall greet the sunlight of the millennial morn.

Here I should not fail to note one peculiarity about the Mexican. It matters not how he may be injured or disordered, he must tie up his head! If his arm, leg or foot is cut he must bandage his head, whether the injured member is bandaged or not. If his stomach, kidneys, liver or "melt" is disordered, he must put up some unbruised green leaves, or other tomfoolery, in a rag and then tie this to his senseless noddle. In this he regards the head as the seat of the ailment, whether constitutional or local, and with him, I reckon, it is true, for the poor fellow's head is terribly befogged, and we may, without any diagnosis, reasonably conclude he suffers much from that "aching void." So whether he has the toothache or toeache it is all the same—"*binding on his head.*"

Now, in the large cities, I learn that there are some eminent physicians, excellent surgeons, men who have qualified themselves at the best schools in

Europe and America, and are real ornaments to their profession and benefactors to the race. But of this class I am not writing, and leave them to their well-earned reputation. But my pen is after these mountain medical bandits, who cause you not to stand and deliver, but place you on your back, and then take both life and purse. These are the shameless wretches who deserve the most stinging excoriations. But as of these I have now given you a charcoal sketch, I leave them with you, that you may think more charitably of them than the writer can hope to do.

CHAPTER XLIII.

SERVANTS. — GALA DAYS. — POPULATION. — FECUNDITY.

These sketches would be incomplete were I not to say something as to the servants of the country. This is a matter of considerable moment, as well here as in other parts of the world. The peace and prosperity of the household depend in no little measure upon this branch of the domestic economy. Here what is wanting in efficiency in the individual servant is sought to be supplemented by the numbers employed. And the numbers engaged, as a matter of course, vary according to the pleasure or caprice of the employers. The poorest families think it necessary to have from one to three to do a minimum service, and give a little style to the decayed family. Those in little better circumstances must have a few more servants to share with the family their meagre rations, and help hold up the family escutcheon. Those who are well to do in the world have a regular retinue of servants; as many sometimes as from twelve to fifteen, and the more they have the less valuable they are, as they are in each other's way. But then this is thought to be the proper thing for a gentleman of means, and less than this fails to catch the appreciation of his acquaintances. When one of these grandees moves through the country his approach appears like the vanguard of a caravan. He has one servant to attend to his stock, another to cook the meat, another to grind the corn, another to make tortillas, and so on, assigning a separate servant to the discharge of a separate duty. The one must not interfere with the other in the performance of his task, but every man attends to his own business. The female servants are similarly looked after, and, in view of the multitude, it is a tolerably "happy family." The servants here are not altogether so exacting as in some parts of the United States. They do not demand, as a condition precedent to continued service, that the mistress of the house shall furnish them with a piano and the parlor during certain evenings of the week, for the exclusive entertainment of their visitors. They do not bargain in advance that the humble proprietress shall not give them any of her "slack jaw" if ill pleased with their household management, which, during their reign, must be entirely entrusted to them.

She does not undertake to give the head of the house "her place," and around it draw the cordon of her authority, and, beyond which, if the lady thoughtlessly ventures, she is considered a trespasser, and, unless apologies are made and received, she gathers her things, and, with the air of a queen, marches forth, shaking the dust from her feet "as a testimony against that house." The thing is better managed here than that; and fewer "scenes" transpire to disturb the harmony of the household. A lady with three or four children will often have a nurse for each child, and then one or two house servants, in addition to the cook and assistant, and one or two errand boys. And it is thought that they can not get along with a less number and support the dignity of the old family name. And even this is so when they are, from sheer necessity, compelled to live upon about the poorest the land affords. People often compel their stomachs to pay tribute to their backs, but here a change takes place, and the stomach is sacrificed to the love of display. I reckon this is carrying the thing about as far as it can well be done without earning a straight jacket and a home in an asylum for lunatics. These servants do not improve each other by association, for the blind can not lead the blind, and it is only stupidity mixed, confusion confounded. In many instances the difficulty is, not to retain them, for they are not possessed of such sensitive natures as American servants, but to get rid of them. It is true they sometimes leave without note or warning, but this is the exception to the rule, for they must live somewhere, in order to get something to eat, and, when once well settled, they are disinclined to change their abode. The wages received, too, are not so high as to permit many luxuries in the way of living, dress, or travel. The number of the faithful are few, but that of the unfaithful many.

I must not omit some account of Mexican patriotism, as it is displayed on gala days. The 16th of September is the anniversary of Mexican independence, when they whipped the French army and overthrew the Empire of Maximilian. They commenced this year its celebration on the 15th, continued it through the 16th and concluded it on the 17th of the month. In the mean time, you may say, that all business was suspended, except liquor selling, and the streets, for a portion of the time given up to drunken revelers, imperiling the safety of those who dared to venture upon them. It would seem, to come up to the patriotic standard, one must become patriotically drunk, and the more frequent, and the longer he remains in this condition, the more intensely does he manifest his love of country. Country often requires sacrifices, and these choose to make them in this way. It is a singular exhibition of loyalty, but one now incorporated in the custom of this portion of the country. It conforms to the tastes and conceptions of the people, and, while we may not admire the mode of these commemorations, yet, in heart, we applaud the sentiment which induces their observance. On this national anniversary, many speeches are made by the fiery young orators from improvised stands, decorated with the national colors; songs are sung, and salvos thunder forth. Music is heard on every side, and the national air is encored time and again. The Mexican air is charged with an electric patriotism, breathed and felt by all classes. Nor is the "small boy" wanting to fill up his part in the exercises of the day, and give eclat to the anniversary display. The 16th of September here, is the Fourth of July in the United States, as formerly celebrated, characterized by many of the same excesses in speech and song and conduct. As time passes, these things will be succeeded by fewer extravagances, and give way to more temperate exercises and better reflections.

Here a few observations as to the population of the country may not be out of place. The population has increased but little in many years. Until within the last decade the immigration has been very small, but, of more recent years, this has considerably increased under the encouragement given by the government. Again, the loss of population from the continued revolutions which agitated the country, was very great. For many years it was exceptional when there was not some conflict raging in some part of the land. The victims of these perpetual strifes were very numerous; so much so as to weaken the physical forces of the country, and retard its growth in population and power. Had not the birth rate been very high, the losses from the causes stated must have been seriously felt. In these mountains, often in the same household, fifteen and twenty children may be seen, having the same parents. Even by the same parents, twenty odd children, in some places, are not considered an extra allowance of the domestic bounties. In fact, I knew one man, a shriveled, attenuated specimen, who claimed the paternity of *thirty* children, living and dying with a serene satisfaction that he had "multiplied and replenished the earth." While, as stated in some former chapter, the mortality among them is great for many reasons; yet, if reasonable chances were given them, the wars having ceased, the land would soon be filled with the increase from the native population. This presupposes to some extent, however, more personal care, cleanliness, and a better recognition of the laws of health than are now observed. Better education in the future will bring better sanitation, and this will lessen the list of mortality and lengthen the period of longevity. As human life depends so much upon the mode of living, I may be permitted to make a few remarks additional to those made in some former chapter. Exercise, eating, sleeping, dress ing and drinking, are those things on which, more than all others, health depends. As to some of these we have already sufficiently remarked. The ordinary Mexican, with plenty to eat, is not disposed to indulge in violent exercise. Under such conditions he prefers the sunny side of some house, where, in the ascending fumes of his cigarette, he can build his castles in the air. With an empty stomach, he will follow a band of vagrant musicians, with the hope that, by quenching his thirst, his appetite may be satisfied. The land lies untilled before him, which would yield an abundant supply at his invitation, but he lies and gently slumbers on the top of a rock, wooed by its warmth to fairy land, where hunger never troubles and cares never come. Let him eat and let him sleep, and things as now may go on forever. He will neither start nor change a current, but, with folded arms, will flow on with the stream, he knows and cares not whither. To think is to exercise, and hence he prefers not to think, for he cares not to labor, and thus break his rest. He rightly calculates that his life is short at best, and, in the measure of his days, would compress as much *solid rest* as possible. This is an inkling of his ideas of exercise, and how it should be indulged so as to bring to him the most substantial good, and *compact comfort*. Others may hurry to and fro, here and there, up and down the earth, something to make, and turn, and change, but he serenely sees them pass, and from his labors rests, ere his labors have begun.

CHAPTER XLIV.

TOURNAMENT IN SOUTH.—SOME OF OUR OWN FOLLIES COMPARED WITH THOSE OF THE MEXICAN.

While upon the follies of the Mexican I have written in a vein of harmless irony, yet we must remember our own people have not been at all times wholly free from criticism. But we are prone to see in others what we fail to see in ourselves, the mote is bigger than the beam. But to be consistent we "shoot folly as it flies," whether in our own land or out of it. We can but smile a good-natured smile when we recall some of the scenes witnessed in the South soon after the late war. The habits of the people had so long been fixed that it was with extreme difficulty they could accommodate themselves to the changed conditions of life. In numbers from the neighboring farms they would repair to the country depots on Saturday mornings, and there pass the entire day in profitless games and follies, to the neglect of their growing crops. An old man in faded black, with the bloodless prefix of "*Col.*" to his name, and three grown boys in "store clothes," might have been seen superintending one little stumpy negro digging a post-hole for the new gate made by the colored mechanic. Had you asked the old gentleman how he was getting on, he would have replied, "O, not at all, sir, not at all; the labor is wholly demoralized, not worth a continental." The last word of the sentence is here suppressed by reason of its inelegant strength. And the boys would heartily have seconded the statement of their father while their hands were in their breeches pockets, and they squirted tobacco juice towards the hole being dug by the aforesaid little negro. Ask them about the crop in the spring of the year and they would have said, "O, you can't get the negroes to work; labor no 'count, sir; it is all in the grass, and I fear old Uncle Peter will have to 'turn out' some of his crop, the old man just can't keep up with it." At this very time, at the little depot near by, had lain the tombstones of his father and mother for many months, not able to pay the freight and take them to the cemetery. The depot agent, on several occasions, had spoken to the boys about the marble slabs and asked them to take them away, but they had replied that he would have to wait until the crop was gathered and sold first. That referred to old Uncle Peter's patch. Again, when addressed upon the subject, one of them replied, "Just let them stay there for the present; they are not hurting, and the old folks don't need the slabs as bad as we need the money right now, and it will all be right after awhile anyway."

This, too, was the season of the tournament, and this in preparation took up a good deal of time, or rather I should say, it did look like work interfered with almost every kind of enjoyment, if they would have permitted it, which they didn't. "O, that riding tournament" was a big thing in that time. The young men from far and near, fancifully dressed, dubbed themselves knights with chivalric names, resurrecting some of the heroes of medieval ages. They carried long poles in their hands, yclept in the nomenclature of chivalry lances, and with these poles astride their mettled chargers they sought, under full speed, to poke the rings from the posts planted on the outer edge of the amphitheater. The best poker punched off the most rings, and thus the hero of the hour received the huzzas of the crowd. Some simple girl was crowned by him as queen of "Love and Beauty." The Rozinantes ridden upon the occasion had been browsing on native grass, but for this exhibition had been rounded up a little on *bought corn*. The boys went into the sport with an able-bodied fervor —with the spirit of the Knight of La Mancha— while admiring Rebeccas gazed on the rivals for their hands with bright eyes and soft hearts. Such a pity there is no Walter Scott to write their exploits, their windmill expeditions, and thus embalm in history these modern heroes of chivalry! Many of the boys amusingly pronounced the word tournament, as if it were written t-e-r-n-a-*ment* with the emphasis on the last syllable, in absolute contempt and utter defiance of orthoepy. Old women sometimes called it "tornment." But I must now forbear. Enough has been written to soften the heart of my Mexican friend to prove that he is not alone in his weaknesses and follies. Glass houses are poor fortresses to stone throwers. However, while my own countrymen are not free from faults, it is due to truth and justice to say that those of the Mexican—of the *proletaire* class —are so numerous and so general that not to notice them in a good-humored way would be violence to the true character of this people. I would not knowingly caricature them, but paint them as I see them with their vices and their virtues. I write not in malice, nor much with "Attic salt," but a little satire now and then will poison no one's joy, and may correct a wrong.

CHAPTER XLV.

SCENERY.—ROCKS.—MOUNTAINS.—FLOWERS.—ATMOSPHERE.— MOUNTAIN TORRENT. — RAINBOW SCENES.

In the past I have said but little as to the scenery of Mexico, as viewed in the mountains. Of course, different localities present an endless variety of scenery. The great plains outstretching to the farthest verge of vision until the mountains come down and wall them in, are scenes at the loveliness and grandeur of which the pen falters, and the pencil falls. On these broad acres thousands of cattle may be seen, lazily feeding upon the luxuriant grass. In the far distance some winding stream may be traced for miles and miles by its fringe of trees. Now and then, to diversify the landscape, herds of antelope may be seen far off quietly grazing. But to me these mountains have a greater charm, a wilder beauty. Ridges on ridges piled higher and higher, as you penetrate the interior, tell of nature's mighty throes in those upheavals of an early age. Here and there may be seen columns of rocks shooting upward hundreds of feet, standing like grim-visaged sentinels at nature's gates. These I have sometimes seen crowned with a single loose stone, weighing thousands of pounds, resting like a crown on a monarch's brow. On it had fallen the rains and snows of centuries, around it had played the storms of long past ages.

Far up the sides of these monumental rocks the verdure grew, plants and flowers found a rooting place, and thus here in the wild solitude, strength and beauty dwelt together. The mountains lift their heads for thousands of feet in the air, while they bathe their feet in rivers at their base. These rivers, through a long succession of epochs, have hewn their channels through the solid rock for hundreds and hundreds of feet in depth, and left the mountain side as an abrupt wall of rock, nature's solid masonry. From the rushing waters over immense boulders and cascades, the thunders leap, and the echo from the neighboring hills and canyons comes back to swell the grand minstrelsy in this temple of God. It is hardly a wonder that the ancients peopled the glens and grottoes with genii, the reigning spirits of such abodes. But here enter these grand amphitheatres of nature, and we feel that we are in the presence of some living spirit that awes us into silence and awakens a feeling akin to reverence, if not to worship. Communion with nature leads us heavenward. We withdraw from the petty strifes around us, and for the time observe with wonder and delight the beauty, and harmony, and glory of those unchanging laws which govern alike the tiniest atom, the travel of a star, the mighty universe. Here is beauty without a blemish, truth unmixed with error, strength without weakness, and all things in sweet accord moving to the "music of the spheres." Alone, we like to contemplate the wonders fashioned by the grand Architect, and strive to read within their revelations the purposes of their Author. From earth the creature looks through them to heaven, to their Creator. No place have I ever seen like these mountains to arouse such thoughts, induce such meditations, and to see my own insignificance and the majesty of Superior Power. It is well for those who have never been, to go to the mountains, forget the things below, commune with higher spirits, and, for once, see transfigured before them celestial shapes. They will then descend as if emerged from a new baptism, the better fitted to meet the fortunes and misfortunes of the future. Here not a sound is heard from a breathing thing, no voice save from the maddened waters and the hastening winds. You stand awe-inspired, a solitary listener to the strains of their wild melody. No silver-throated choristers warble their notes with this orchestra, but these fly away to quieter retreats and there raise their voices in exultant joy and praise. The waters are very

THE MOUNTAINS OF MEXICO.

bright and flash like polished mirrors in the sunlight, while in their depths disport schools of the finny tribe. Often as you ascend the mountains, you will find the oak, small, gnarled, like stunted undergrowth, so that when mounted, and by its side, your head will be higher than its tallest bough. But ascending further you leave the oaks behind, and come within the zone of the pines which flourish in the higher altitudes. The solitary traveler, listening near nightfall to the winds sighing through them, is reminded of some sad dirge in the memory of by-gone years. Then the distant light, the gathered flock, the barking dog, are welcome sights and sounds to him, for soon and near a shelter is found, and the day's journey is ended. The curtain of night does not shut out the music from those harps of pine, but once shut within, there is somehow a securer feeling, and when stretched for rest the sad refrain heard through the openings seem the sooner to waft the spirit into dreamland.

The number and variety of the wild-flowers are few, and these, though beautiful to view, seldom exhale an odor—have no incense offering. We seldom see the climbing vines as in the lowlands, tieing themselves higher and higher as they grow, but the modest creeper in this place dwarfed by the frigid earth. Standing on some lofty Pisgah and straining the vision beyond, the intervening mountains look like great billows suddenly fixed on a great sea. Nothing greets the eye but the sky above, the eternal mountains ahead, no change save a variety of form. The omnipresent mountains,

" Many as the billows, but one as the sea."

The atmosphere at times is most remarkably transparent; great distances, in fact, appear compressed into short spaces. So clear is this that the stars at times have a familiar nearness, and these jewels of night flash with unwonted radiance. More beautiful than words can tell when earth is filled with the golden sheen, it is here, to see the moon leading her " virgin host far up the eastern sky," and then adown its western slope, till light is lost in darkness. In the valley below I have watched with rapture the ascending moon, first appearing as a silver crescent upon the mountain's brow, with its pencilings of light; a little later, full orbed, it burst in view and filled the world around me with its effulgent glory. At times in midwinter, when cold and clear, the heavens seemed almost afire with the pyrotechnics of the stars, luminous from their scintillations. The silence that prevails adds to the impressiveness of the scene, no voice, save, perchance, the sound of a distant waterfall. But how noiseless are the greatest forces in nature. Gravitation holds in harmony the revolving suns and sytems. The pent-up internal fires are unseen, unfelt, save where an earthquake starts, or the sea is lifted into mountains, or the mountains sunk into the sea. Electricity, that subtle agent which pervades all things, is hardly known, save in the manifestations of its power. And so it is I have looked upon such scenes as faintly described, until I stood speechless in the presence of their sublimity. When I gazed about and around me I saw evidence of a Supreme Power, and when I gazed upward to the stars, with Newton I could say :

"The undevout astronomer is mad."

These are some of the mountain scenes one may witness and carry their impression with him through life. Some less poetical than others see these things with scarcely more than ordinary emotions, while others, with a little coloring of the imagination, invest them with the gorgeousness of a dream. To me the reality is sufficiently distinct and impressive to excite my homage and wonder, and an earnest wish that others might share with me the enthusiasm, inspired by such visions of grandeur and loveliness.

There is another thing here which, to be appreciated, must be seen. I now refer to the mountain torrent, and which only comes in what is termed the rainy season. This commences about the 20th of June and ends about the first week in October.

During the interval there is scarcely a day in which it does not rain, sometimes but little, and then again as if the fountains of the upper deep were broken up. The heavy fall may be far up the canyon, and the first intimation of its approach will be a sudden, fearful roaring, and then a high black column, rolling and surging in its maddened fury, sweeping everything before it in its headlong march. The grinding rocks in the seething waters, as they go tumbling along, may be heard a great distance above the din of the dashing torrent. The watershed of the mountain is so precipitous that the waters are collected and poured down as through a funnel, carrying death to every living thing in its pathway. At times only a few minutes are sufficient to cause the avalanches of water, for they come down in volumes, as if being emptied from inverted buckets. Generally the fury is of short duration, the clouds retire, the sun comes forth, and nature smiles again. One of the loveliest scenes I ever beheld was a rainbow on the mountains. The sun dying in the west, was struggling with the falling raindrops, when there appeared in the east a magnificent rainbow, with deepest colors, and with its extremities resting on separate mountains. These, with their broad shoulders, seemed to uphold this celestial arc bent from mountain to mountain. I thought its form and colors never so beautiful before; the storm had passed, and there it stood in the heavens, an emblem and a promise. From the chambers of memory came the lines of Campbell:

> " 'T is the bow of Omnipotence bent in His hand,
> His grasp at creation the universe spanned,
> 'T is the presence of God in symbol sublime,
> His vow from the flood to the exit of time."

Soon the sun sank to rest, the jewelled raindrops ceased to fall, and the beautiful apparition vanished away, and I was left to muse on its "faded loveliness." Thus seen spanning the intervening chasm, bent in glorious beauty from mountain to mountain, made it for earth's pilgrims the arch of a gorgeous gateway to brighter realms beyond. But it was a picture that I shall long remember, and never elsewhere hope to see again, having its extremes resting on the pillared mountains. Doubtless the immediate surroundings framed the scene in greater splendor, and photographed ineffaceably the picture. But that one must be unpoetic, unsentimental, indeed, who could not enjoy a scene like that. Almost as cold and utilitarian as the one, who, when asked how he enjoyed a view of Niagara, seen for the first time, replied he saw nothing in that, *except a great waste of water power!* If any of my readers are so intensely practical as that one, then I shall lament a recital of the rainbow scene described.

CHAPTER XLVI.

COOKING.—"CHILE CON CARNE."—"CALABASA" EDIBLES.—HOGS.

Often the stomach is the door to the heart. Once in possession of the former there is a broad avenue to the latter. This is so well understood by adroit housewives, who would raid the plethoric exchequer of their liege lords, that, as a preparatory movement, they first give substantial satisfaction to the appetite and then they pass on to ulterior conquests. They first seize the lines of approach and then they carry the fortress by assault. A hungry man seldom grants favors, or, if done, seldom gracefully granted; but break this hunger down, and his rebellious nature melts, and favors flow, for he then feels as if "he was at peace with all the world and the balance of mankind." A hungry man is rarely a happy one, but to make him happy, first satisfy his appetite, and frowns are followed by smiles and joys chase cares away. This is the observation, if not the experience, of nearly all. But the culinary art is the very handmaid of happiness. Bad cooking means bad digestion, bad temper, household disturbance, and too often domestic infelicity. No one can calculate the consequences of an ill-cooked steak. It may unseal the fountain of domestic discord, to be followed by estrangement, separation and disgrace. The trite maxim has no more apposite application than when applied to cooking, "What is worth doing, is worth doing well."

While by no means epicurean in my tastes, but far otherwise, yet I must say that the Mexican cooks I have seen will not favorably compare with those of any other nation seen by me. It takes many to do the work of one, and when done we feel, " would it were done otherwise." As for cleanliness, I prefer not to speak in the main, but as I have heard that it has been decreed that each one should, in his life, eat a peck of dirt, I will only add if that be true, then this must be a short-lived people, as this quantity is early obtained. But in this respect I must say I feel I have been specially blessed, living for much of the time in the neatest and best of families, and consequently fear no early demise from the cause stated. The cooked mixtures sometimes served are puzzles to the uninitiated. Onions and pepper are their favorite vegetables. The former are cooked with almost everything brought to the table. It is in the soup, in the rice, and, occasionally, cooked with eggs. I have seen them cooked in deserts, puddings! Onions in puddings—what a compound! But a dish more generally eaten than any other is meat cooked with red pepper, called "chile con carne." It is perfectly red, and, at times, even strong enough to sear the throat in its downward passage. Should tears come in the effort to eat it, just let them flow, but go on with the mastication. In this, as in all other things (perseverantia omnia vincit), 'perseverance overcomes all things. It is truly wonderful how the human system will accommodate itself to such edibles, but it does, and survives the burning ordeal. I have seen the red pepper pods cooked themselves, and these are eaten with a great relish. They are fried or baked, and have the appearance of cooked tomatoes. These, I have thought, are not so strong, so fiery as the red pepper we find in the States, and hence, the eater survives his meal. This red pepper is served with dried jerked beef, and I must say makes it more palatable, "When the dose is given in moderate quantities." There is a plant called the "calabasa," the flowers of which are eaten as a species of salad. These are highly esteemed by the natives, but contain little nutriment, and are almost tasteless. They belong to the pumpkin family, but not so succulent as these. Sometimes the melon is cooked with sugar, baked, and then it is endurable, but always with the idea (when eating) that it is a vegetable fraud. The meats for sale are cut in strings, running with, and not "across the grain."

The hog is never put up in bacon; they do not understand the art of curing this, but he is cut up in strips, and out of these lard is made, and such parts as have no fatty substance are converted into sausage meat, thoroughly charged with red pepper and other " taking ingredients." This, when somewhat advanced in age, in smell, has the strength of the sepulcher. But some folks like it, and so they do putrid meat, and hence, at last, it is a mere difference of taste, for which, it is said, there is " no accounting." Some few of the rancheros make cheese, some of it is moderately good, and some of it, to be known, should bring a letter of introduction, as unaided without identification, it must remain an indefinable compound. Such a treatment has it received, I am sure the honest cow, could she recognize the metamorphosis through which her milk has gone, would bellow a disclaimer of the fradulent substance.

Eggs and potatoes are cooked as elsewhere, and have this advantage, that when served with their natural coverings, the interior remain unaffected by unclean vessels and dirty handling. But eggs are so eagerly sought by the peon owners of hens that, as a fact, I have sometimes seen them chased and caught, that manipulation might verify the anticipated outlay. Here hens must do their duty, and not trifle too long with the patience of their proprietors. The Mexican thinks they go to bed early, and at the dawn of day must alight and bestir themselves the task of a daily contribution to the family supplies. While disposed to be idle himself he submits to no idleness in the farm yard; there is too much at stake, a little 'dereliction here is too vitally important to his peace and health. He keeps none other than business hens, for, when they cease to perform, but, as widow hens, become envious of the attentions of rival chanticleers, he kills and eats them without a pang or scruple. There are a few berries in the mountains—raspberries and strawberries—the former mature in August and September. Were these cultivated they would be very fine, but like tomatoes, they are found wild in woods. Peaches are seldom permitted to ripen on the trees, but are pulled and eaten green by the natives. And the quantities they can " store away " would amaze an eastern fruit-gatherer. The tomatos found in the woods are very small and inferior in quality, but from good seed I have seen a superior species flourish here.

Milk is but sparingly used, and, from long training, " Biddy " puts herself in position to have her hind legs tied to undergo the milking operation. Her master and mistress have no faith in her heels, and adopt this precautionary measure to avoid injuries and losses. The cattle, while of no improved breed, are yet better than one would be led to expect, and equally as good as the stump tail steer chased through the pine thickets, referred to by Governor Henry A. Wise, in an agricultural address delivered some years since before his fellow Virginians. But few sheep are raised, and these by the Indians, who are more pastoral in their tastes and pursuits than the Mexicans. From the wool these Indians make a coarse blanket, woven in a loom of crude and queer device. They market but few, but follow and watch them on the mountains, giving them much care and attention. The native hog is a queer looking specimen, his members seem out of proper proportion, those in front much larger than his hinder parts. He appears to have been left incomplete behind, while in front he is so driven together as to give his head and neck a swollen appearance, reversing the order of the kangaroo, which is stronger behind than before. He is an unique looking porker, and may have been fashioned in this way the better to enable him " to root hog or die." He has the shoulders, as a turfman would say, of a " quarter horse," and the hams of a greyhound. A Chicago packing establishment would hardly place him in the price current list, but remand him to his native hills to grow up and develop with the outgrowth of the country. He is of the old *red blood* species, claims no fancy name, like Berkshire, or Irish Grazier, but claims a parentage lineally descended from the pair which Father Noah housed in the Ark, and of such a variety that it was considered then the "survival of the fittest," Vegetables exist in considerable variety, but are only cultivated by the few, the others being so occupied " in *resting*" that they have n't time to devote to such pursuits. They have but few iron vessels for cooking purposes, but use earthen oyers,* as they are termed. In this way, and upon such things, do these Mexicans live. His quantity is scant, and its quality, as served, is to the fastidious, at least, rather an uninviting repast. But, such as it is, he takes it with a relish, though it neither feasts nor fattens. As heretofore stated, his staple table commodities are beans and tortillas, and, without these, the human machinery is thought incapable of moving. Much may be learned of men from the mode in which they live. This, and their surroundings, have much to do in the formation of character. These things impress themselves naturally as the bent twig becomes the bowed tree. But as to these things, I have sufficiently spoken, at least enough has been said to roughly outline the Mexican character, as influenced and shaped by his habitudes and modes of life, and we now leave him for the study, if not the admiration, of my readers.

---

* Pronounced O-yers.

CHAPTER LXVII.

STORMS. — CONSTITUTION OF MEXICO. — IMPORTANT PROVISIONS.

The heavy rainfalls suggest the storms which, at times, prevail in the mountains. If storms elsewhere arouse painful apprehensions, here their approach and continuance come and leave the soul terror-shaken. They seem like some irresistible power unchained, with a mission of destruction. Traveling once in the month of June, I was overtaken by one of them, but not of the severest character, and when it had passed and left me alive, I felt as if my escape was almost a marvel. Their suddenness and the hopelessness of escape from their rude peltings when caught, beget a fear which makes the stoutest heart quake. A black cloud is suddenly seen moving toward you with the swiftness of the wind, some large raindrops as outriders heralding its coming, and almost before they have ceased to fall, the storm in fury has broken upon you. The wind becomes a furious gale, the water falls in blinding sheets, and the vivid flashes of lightning, amid the crashes of thunder, reveal the madness of the tempest. The great centuried pines, with rock-tied roots, bend and break before the blast like reeds, and are hurled down the mountain sides, together with the loosened rocks, weighing tons, which go thunder-ring below. The pitiless hail comes down with the rain torrents, to add to the grandeur and terror of the scene. The flashes of lightning are so frequent and so blinding as to remind one of that realm of light seen by Milton's Angel,

> " Who saw, but blasted with excess of light,
> Closed his eyes in endless night."

The earth trembles as if quaking with fear in the elemental war. The frightened beasts and birds have, instinctively warned, sought their hiding-places or found their doom. The fallen forests, the dislodged rocks, the rushing flood, bespeak the circuit of the storm. Its genius rides in a chariot of desolation, drawn by the steeds of the wind. In the presence of such an overriding power man feels his utter nothingness, his boasted greatness the chaff of vanity, and his life the merest fleeting vapor. He stands abashed at the exhibition of such majestic power, and feels, when retreating within himself, that none but God can rule the storm. It is well to see such things; it takes us from ourselves and makes us feel there is a Power that in his own good time can destroy the earth, melt the heavens and imparadise the blest. Such, briefly sketched, will give some conception of the force and terror of these mountain storms; but a far better conception might be gained by witnessing the phenomenon itself, as words are feeble instruments with which to paint such scenes in nature's colors. And now, with these pen tracings as mere outlines, I leave my readers, from colors of their own, to fill up and complete the scenes.

And at this time and place I may as well refer to the Constitution of Mexico, the fundamental law of the land. Elsewhere I have stated it had its model in that of the United States, but it is well here to note its most important provisions with the guarantees they embody. The constitution of the country indicates to no little extent the genius of its people. This constitution, like that of other nations, deals in general outlines and leaves legislation within the purview of its limits, to deal in details. Certain great principles are recognized and their observance enjoined, which are for the well-being of the State. These must find a place in every government instituted for the welfare of society.

The first declaration of the Mexican Constitution recognizes that the rights of man are at the foundation, and are the object of social institutions. And, as a consequence of this truism, it declares that all laws and all the authorities of the country ought to respect and sustain the guarantees that the constitution concedes. This is certainly a good pillar upon which to rear the fabric of constitutional government, the rights of men, a principle imbedded in the very nature of things, a most fit starting point in constitution building. This principle can not be ignored, but must be recognized at the very threshold, and to attempt to do otherwise is the supremest folly.

It recognizes that all men are born free, and, as such, are entitled to the protection of the laws. The principle of liberty, if untrammeled, will assert itself in every land, and sooner or later, by every people. But liberty in theory and liberty in fact are two different things, and while each one has a constitutional right to its enjoyment, yet in fact each one does not so enjoy it, and that this is the truth no one will deny. The principle is right, yet in too many cases the practice is wanting. Perfect equality, in fact, although aspired to, yet can never be attained under human institutions. Inequalities flow from human imperfections which enter into human workmanship, more or less, of every kind. But liberty to the citizen is one of the guarantees of the constitution and finds a front place in the organic law.

Education is free, each one is privileged to seek it as he sees fit, and no one shall hinder him in the exercise of this right. The intelligence of the people is one of the foundations on which is raised the superstructure of government. It is left, however, to the legislators to determine what professions require a license for their exercise, and the requisites of the same.

It is announced that every man is free to labor in his profession or at his calling, it being a useful and honest one, as he may think proper, and avail himself of the products of his labor. And in doing this he can not be molested unless he invades the rights of others, when by the action of the government or judicial sentence pursuing the law, he may be restrained.

No one can be compelled to give his personal services without his consent and without, at the same time, just compensation. The law will not authorize any contract that has for its object the loss or sacrifice of the liberty of the citizen. Nor will it sanction any agreements in which the party may agree to his own proscription or banishment.

The publication of one's thoughts can not be an object of judicial or administrative inquisition, except when he attacks the morals, the rights of a third party, provokes a crime, or disturbs the public order. I am disposed to think that this wholesome provision is not as broad in practice as it is in theory, judging from the manner in which some of the publishers of papers are treated, when it is supposed their criticisms of the government have transcended certain limits. But Article 7 says, the liberty of writing and publishing writings upon any subject is inviolable. The offense of printing will be passed upon by a jury, which will determine the fact, and by another which will designate and apply the punishment.

The right of petition by writing is also inviolable when done in a pacific and respectful manner, but in a political matter, only the citizen of the republic has this right. The right for the people to come together for a lawful object in a peaceful manner is duly granted. But no one but the citizen of the country can do this, in order to take part in political matters. Nor is it lawful for any assembly of people, armed, to come together to deliberate.

Every one has the right to possess and carry arms for his own security and legitimate defense. The legislatures will determine which are the prohibited cases and the punishment incurred. Every man has a right to come into and go out of the republic, to journey through its territory, to change his residence without any necessity of a letter of security or passport or safe conduct of any kind. But the judicial or administrative authorities can pursue him in cases of criminal responsibility.

There are no titles of nobility, nor prerogatives, nor hereditary honors recognized in the republic. It is said that the people alone can, legally represented, decree in honor of those who may give their eminent services to the country or to humanity. No one can be judged by special tribunals. Nor can any person or corporation enjoy privileges or emoluments that are not a compensation for public service and are fixed by the law. There are no retroactive laws. Nor can any one be judged or sentenced except by laws in force before the fact, and applicable strictly to it, and by the tribunal established by the law.

There shall be no treaties made for the extradition of political offenders. No one can be molested in his person, family, domicile, papers, possession, except in virtue of a written warrant, from competent authority that sets forth the legal ground of the proceeding. And in case of a flagrant offense, every person can apprehend the offender and his accomplices, "putting them without delay at the department of the nearest authorities."

Article 17 reads: No one can be made a prisoner for debts of a character purely civil. No one can exercise violence in order to regain his rights. The tribunal will always be open for the administration of justice.

Nor can one be detained in prison for a longer period than three days without a judgment condemning him to such imprisonment.

In criminal cases, the accused has certain constitutional guarantees: 1. He has a right to know the ground of accusation and the name of the accuser. 2. He has a right to make his preparatory declaration within forty-eight hours from the time he is in court. 3. That he may face the witnesses against him. 4. That he may be aided in obtaining the facts and the process necessary to prepare his defense. 5. He has a right to be heard in his own defense or by his counsel.

The punishment of mutilation, of infamy, marks, stripes, torment of every kind, excessive fine, confiscation of goods, and any other unusual and excessive punishment are prohibited.

Correspondence through the mails is strictly guarded and protected. In times of peace, without the consent of the proprietors, the military can not for purposes of lodgment, take possession of private residences.

Without consent, property can not be occupied except for a public purpose, and it first having been paid for. The death penalty is abolished except in a few cases. No one can be judged twice for the same offense. Monopolies are disfavored. The President, with the consent of his minister, can suspend the guaranties conceded by the constitution in certain public exigencies.

CHAPTER XLVIII.

CONSTITUTION CONTINUED.—INTERNATIONAL BOARD OF ARBITRATION.

It is declared, in the Mexican Constitution, that all sovereignty resides in the people, and all government is instituted for their benefit, and they have the inalienable right to alter or modify the form of this government.

The supreme power of the Federation divides itself for its exercise into three branches—legislative, executive and judicial ; nor can two or more be united in one person or corporation, nor the legislative be deposited in any individual. The exercise of the supreme legislative power resides in an assembly called the Congress of the Union. The members of Congress are elected every two years by Mexican citizens, a member for every forty thousand inhabitants, or fraction exceeding twenty thousand, and he must be twenty-five years old. These can not be held responsible for the expression of their opinions while in the discharge of their duties.

The President must be a native, thirty-five years

of age, not an ecclesiastic, and a resident at the time of his election. The Chief Justice, in certain events, may act as President. Term of President, four years.

The Judicial power is vested in the Supreme, Circuit and District Courts.

Those powers that are not expressly conceded by the constitution to the federal functionaries are understood to be reserved to the States.

These are some of the main provisions of the Mexican Constitution, an enumeration of others would needlessly encumber this volume. But from the foregoing we have a clear insight into the principles which underlie their government. A striking similarity will be noticed between their constitution and that of the United States. It is a popular, representative government, in theory at least, but in practice and futherance of the fundamental ideas, much remaining to be learned—much for the better may come in the process of time from the education of the masses, and I must say I believe this most important subject is receiving the attention and all the aid the government, in its present condition, can afford. Elections, in many sections of the country, are travesties upon an expression of the popular will, as the names of the candidates to be voted for are *sent down from above* " the powers that be," and the form of the election simply registers the edict which has gone forth from another.

But this thing is not limited to Mexico; abuses of the popular franchise notoriously exist in other republican countries. It is a very difficult thing to obviate such results, and I know of nothing which will so soon tend in the right direction as increased intelligence and public virtue. Mexico is on the right road, with a recognition of the natural rights of her people, and those secured by certain constitutional safeguards, so that the subjects are not only unhindered, but encouraged to proceed in the right course to the fulfillment of her destiny as a nation. The wisdom of her legislation ought to be able, and I doubt not will do so, to develop her magnificent internal resources, so that in a few years no fairer field will be seen on the Western Hemisphere for happy homes, and happy millions.

Her statesmen, too, should display enough prudence and political foresight to avoid the breakers which come from international complications, while national dignity should not be sacrificed; yet, at no time should a mistaken or false assumption of this, jeopardize the public peace. Nations must discountenance precipitancy, and, like individuals, learn the more that spirit of forbearance which seldom misjudges, and seldom fails in its well-directed efforts to reach a reconciliation. Here is the danger of Mexico, with her immense frontiers bordering on a more powerful republic for many hundred miles, while on either side lives a restless, adventurous body, ready too often, upon unsubstantial grounds, to provoke hostilities, and precipitate a revolution. Many of them are only too anxious to become actors in such exciting scenes, caring nothing for the national honor and safety, but influenced solely by selfish considerations. The perpetual attrition between borderers, sooner or later, will eventuate in outbreaks, and to quell these, and avoid their repetition, will require conservative and consummate statesmanship. The establishment of an international board of arbitration to adjudicate and settle such affairs would go far towards relieving such matters of the grave character they now sometimes present. These tribunals would take jurisdiction of such cases at once and proceed to their settlement in a quiet, speedy and effective manner, the national relations in the meantime remaining unstrained. This appears to be one of the most feasible modes of solving this question, and I think, should receive the sanction of the respective governments. Were it known that such a tribunal would take immediate cognizance of such matters, and as speedily adjust them as practicable, I think it would tend to allay the inflamed condition of the public mind, and resolve these things more into matters of local than national importance from the commencement.

But Mexico is far from seeking any misunderstandings, knowing and feeling, as she does, her inferior strength, and that any conflict must ultimate to her detriment both in life and treasure. The experience of the last war is yet too fresh in the minds of her people, wherein she lost so much valuable territory, to desire the maintenance of her rights or the vindication of her national honor at the cannon's mouth. She would achieve by diplomacy what she might lose by war. But neither her public men, nor the temper of her masses, desire other than to follow the peaceful pursuits of life, much less to provoke to collision a more powerful rival at her door. She has now entered upon an industrial era, and is giving her best energies to the development of the infinite resources of the country, believing "that peace hath her victories no less renowned than war." It has been a land of revolutionary storms, men rose and fell, one regime succeeding another, to be in its turn followed by another of brief duration; changes were so frequent that instituted reforms failed of fulfillment and left the public interest paralyzed from such violent proceedings. Disorganization, to some extent, was everywhere; and, to some extent, every department of government felt its blighting effects. But permanent reforms come slowly, and so they come in this country, but now having come, every indication would seem to point to the fact that henceforth her march is forward, and her mission one of good to her people. Her matters of interior concern will doubtless be improved as time passes, and experience shows the necessity of reformation, and the difficulties now attending the management of these will find a solution in a higher intelligence and a more enlightened domestic policy. Mexico is not at all wanting in men of ability, men, in fact, of great capabilities. These, too, are not limited to any one walk in life, but are found in all of its different vocations. But there are few of this class in comparison with the great number of those who are debased in ignorance and unguided and unrestrained by moral influences. Measures reaching and raising the ignorant masses must be inaugurated and carried out before, as a nation, she can rightfully aspire to the first rank in the family of nations. The policy of her present administration, as well as that of the more recent ones, has looked to the betterment of the great body of her people. The great importance of this matter is seen and advocated by her more advanced speakers and writers, and new steps are being taken by each succeeding administration, to urge on the good work already commenced. But you can not raise a whole people in a single decade from the debasement of centuries. They can not, by a mere legislative enactment, be *plucked out* of such a condition, but they must *grow out of it*, and growth implies time, more or less. Surround them with the most favorable conditions which the law can guaranty them, and then let them, under proper instructions, work out their own social and political salvation. This is what may be and should be done, and, when done, they have their own destiny in their own hands. I believe this is the course now being adopted in this country, and in a few years its fruits will be seen to bless and gladden its people. Her immigration laws are liberal, and this infusion of other elements in the body politic will greatly redound to her welfare. She needs other blood to be infused into her veins to wake her from her long lethargy, the sleep of centuries—no nation needs it more, with probably the exception of the mother country, Spain. To vitalize and lift up the masses from the century-trodden roads is no easy task, but must be the labor of many men for many years addressed to such work. The skies of Mexico are manifestly brightening.

CHAPTER XLIX.

CHARACTER OF THE MOUNTAINEERS. — MISSIONARIES.

But these indications for the better appear not so much here as in other sections of the Republic. The hardy mountaineer does not move abreast with the spirit of the age. Isolated as he is, he is not brought in contact with the masses elsewhere moving forward to better and higher conditions in life. The fact is, he has an aversion to novelties, to change, even though they be for the better, and would prefer to live in his solitary surroundings undisturbed, uninvaded by advancing lines of a more enlightened civilization. Many years ago I had read and heard much of the many virtues of these dwellers in the mountains until I had come to invest them with preternatural excellencies. Nor do I now mean to say that, in some localities, they do not possess many sturdy virtues, but I do mean to say that in these mountains the entertainment of such an idea is altogether a false conception of their character. Living in such places, and with such natural surroundings, is favorable to the growth and development of a spirit of independence, and tends to give brusqueness and ruggedness to character. But then the advantages of cultivation are often lost, and the refinements and elegancies of life unknown. Coarseness blunts the finer sensibilities, and, too often, daily habits manifest shocking immoralities. So, from long observance, I have been forced to change the opinion formerly held as to the superabundant virtues of mountain people. Those who may differ with me should hold in obeyance an expression of their opinion until they shall have visited these scenes and mingled for a season with the uncultivated natives. If then, however, they should still persist in an opposite opinion, I will give them up as lost, and abandon them to the consequences of their own perverted judgments. Neither salt nor saltpetre would save them.

But as to their characteristics, I have hetofore sufficiently written, and now leave them with the hope that they may yet, in some good way, under some good providence, emerge from night into day. But it is a difficult task to convert the dwellers of the sixteenth into citizens of the nineteenth century, with all its light, its civil and religious freedom.

By this time an inquiry may have risen in the minds of some as to the outlook for missionaries in this field. Truly, in one sense, the harvest is ripe, but the reapers are few; but I am not prepared to say that, were the reapers more, the gathered harvest would be greater. The great missionary to India, Judson, I believe, preached many years without a single convert, and when asked what were the prospects, he replied, "As bright as the promises of God." I think it probable that had this been the field of his operations, he would have met with the same success, and when similarly questioned could have made the same beautiful reply. It will take a long time to overthrow faith in the saints, and the reception given here to the image-breaker would be the warmest of his life. I do not believe any visible results would attend missionary efforts here at an early day. The education, the habits ingrained into a second nature must be changed, and this can not be accomplished suddenly, by violence, but must be the outcome of an enlightened process through lessons imparted, precepts implanted through long periods of time. I would not leave the impression that it is a hopeless undertaking, but one of most difficult accomplishment. Impossibilities are unknown to God, to whom nations may be born in a day; but to human view, unaided by faith's telescope, there is a dreary moral waste stretching beyond the confines of human vision. To me it seems an uninviting field to the Protestant evangelist.

Protestants have missions and some churches in other portions of Mexico, but so far, I have never seen a Protestant minister, or a native Protestant in the mountains. Centuries ago the Jesuits established a line of missions throughout the country, extending far up into what is known as the State of California. At that date the Spanish language was spoken from Cape Horn to Washington Territory. These Jesuits thus obtained a foothold at an early period in the country, and down to the present time their influence remains unbroken. The Indians of this country were assiduously looked after, and these, too, by the Jesuit shepherds were gathered into the fold, and became then, and are now, communicants of the Catholic Church. They know nothing else; they and their fathers, and all those before them were indoctrinated in the same faith, and their lives are a veritable illustration of the line,

"Just as the twig is bent the tree is inclined."

I think it would take much time before the missionary could get a hearing, a much longer time before he could hope to exert any salutary influence upon the lives of the people. Here ignorance and bigotry live in close companionship, and differences of opinion receive but little toleration. The spirit of intolerance is the spirit of inquisition, which, happily for the world, is now viewed with the horror its cruelties were calculated to awaken. As we have seen, this intolerant spirit receives no governmental sanction; but the framers of the Constitution, catching the spirit of liberty, have wisely incorporated a provision in the fundamental laws guarantying religious freedom to all. Probably to President Juarez, more than to any other, is due the separation of church from State, and for which he has never been forgiven by the church party. However, his name brightens in history as the years fly, and his country's true lovers now in heart almost canonize his name. While here to the incoming of Protestants, there could be no legal objections, yet, practically speaking, they would, in the effort of propagandism, find many molestations. At all events, such are the views I now entertain upon this subject, based upon a knowledge of these people for many years.

CHAPTER L.

HOW AMERICANS ARE TREATED.—BUSINESS METHODS.

The inquiry is sometimes made, how are Americans received and treated in Mexico? In view of the numbers coming into this Republic, the question is not only a natural, but a pertinent one. Before the law equality is recognized, and all receive a cordial welcome, who come actuated by proper motives. The Mexican has his proper pride, his peculiarities of customs and habits as other people have, and to criticize these severely meets with his disfavor. Those who do so from absent-mindedness or ignorance of the amenities of life receive the ill-will of the population. I have sometimes thought that they submitted more patiently to animadversions upon their country and people than we have a right to expect. There are many Americans who seem to take pleasure in indulging in the bitterest denunciations of this country and their citizens, and in their presence. These same persons would not tolerate for a moment such language when uttered by a foreigner against the United

States. But this class of Americans, for the most part, are not worthy representatives of their country, but, by reason of such imprudence, the whole American race is brought into disrepute. These men, too, are overbearing in their dispositions, and in their conduct towards the Mexicans, whose enmity they incur, and whose forgiveness they never obtain. The Mexican seldom forgets an injury, but " nurses his wrath and keeps it warm " until an opportunity comes when vengeance is taken. Years may pass, but malice lives through them all, until he strikes his offenders down. So, for whatever differences there may be between the races in this country, I am not so sure but that in a majority of the cases the antagonism may have sprung from improper conduct upon the part of the intemperate Americans. At least it is not probable that they were wholly faultless. Too often, I am sure, they have provoked difficulties, which might have been avoided by a better demeanor. The legislation of the country offers to the foreigner encouraging inducements, bids him come, and bids him welcome to the rights and immunities of citizenship. And, if he come and demean himself as a law-abiding person, attend strictly to his own business and keep himself clear from partisanship, he will meet with kindness and a cordial welcome. The manner in which one deports himself will almost invariably indicate the treatment he will receive. As he gives, so he receives. This is so abroad; it is none the less so here. In a word, if a man will behave himself here as he should do everywhere, I believe he will seldom have occasion to complain of his treatment. I think myself that most of the complaints are indulged in by those who themselves have forgotten some of the common proprieties of life. If a man will bear himself as a gentleman, my conclusion is that he will seldom receive ungentlemanly treatment. Too often it is the case that Americans, coming to this country, throw off all restraints and give rein to excessive indecencies and immoralities, offending the better portion of the public, and irretrievably injuring themselves. They become drunken and besotted, often involved in difficulties, defy the peace and the authorities, to the shame of themselves and the scandal of their nation. Sooner or later they are landed in jail, and come forth with bitter recollections of the Mexican prison and people. These are the characters, generally speaking, who talk so much, and talk so badly as to the manner in which they have been received in Mexican communities.

The foregoing remarks have reference to the treatment given by the better and not the rougher element of Mexican society. The latter, in some numbers, will be found everywhere, but generally in the minority; when in excess in some exceptional localities, these then are, for the most part, in the mountain districts. And, as to these I have already given some pen sketches, their ways and doings, general conduct, and modes of life. Hence, of these things to speak more at length would be an unnecessary repetition. But it is observable even among these rough and disorderly elements, a proper personal deportment goes far towards disarming opposition, and conciliating a predisposed animosity. Among the ignorant prejudices are very strong, and nothing so rapidly weakens and destroys these as a quiet, consistent and gentlemanly demeanor. Kindness, justice, firmness, seldom fail to win their way, overcome intervening obstructions and achieve the purpose in view. Patience, too, must not be overlooked when brought into contact with such people, for its exercise will check hasty action, and further you in the prosecution of your object. While, for the foregoing reasons, I do not think one coming here will or need be mistreated, yet, I do not say I can recommend it to Americans as a desirable place to live. While the climate is salubrious, unexcelled, yet it will be found difficult for Americans readily and pleasantly to accommodate themselves to the new order of things. The habits and customs of the population are so different from his own that, unless he adopts them, he will feel somewhat discordant. And to live in perfect harmony there must be at least a partial conformity to the usages of society. And to do this he feels as if his life is a kind of a compromise, doing and saying things with disapproval of both judgment and conscience. The truth is, to live here is often to live with alternatives before you. You must accept the one course or the other, neither of which you would voluntarily adopt. So it is really a question of compromise, whether to do this or that, neither of which receives your sanction, yet, of necessity, compelled to act. It is an unpleasant predicament, but one from which you can not easily escape. Their modes of doing business are entirely different from those to which you have been accustomed, and this is embarrassing and obstructive. But to get along with them in negotiations, their ways you must learn, and, however much you may dislike them, you will find yourself compelled, measurably, to adopt them. To your surroundings you are compelled to accommodate yourself, or your business transactions will end in failures. It is not every one who can so bend himself to his changed relations, as to win favor and success. Their business modes to an American will appear narrow, close, intensely selfish, unmarked in the main by that liberal spirit which is indicative of comprehensiveness and business sagacity. The business, too, for the most part, is small in quantity and quality, and conducted on the most approved Shylock principles. These things, to those trained in different schools, are not only distasteful but repugnant, and it will take much time to become reconciled to such systems.

CHAPTER LI.

MARRYING IN THE COUNTRY.

Here I may remark upon a social phenomenon; it is that the majority of Americans who have been for a great many years in the country are seldom worth anything, either in purse or moral value. Somehow or other, they seem to have lost their moral force and drifted along with the Mexican tide to a status of indefinable worthlessness. I do not say all, but a majority, unfavorably impressed by those around them, have, in the race of life, fallen by the wayside into a state of financial and moral bankruptcy. The temptations were too many and too freqnent to go along with the rabble, and with weakened power of resistance they went below. The majority who live in this country for ten or fifteen years become pretty thouroughly Mexcianized, imbued with their tastes, and follow their habits. Unless they did, I can hardly see how one can remain so long in the country with any degree of satisfaction, with his early education and the remembrance of home habits and institutions, living as before intimated, in the mean time, a life of perpetual compromise. Should one marry in the country then he is fixed beyond escape, and probably the sooner he strikes his American colors in terms of unconditional capitulation, the sooner he will find harmony in the domestic circle, and business thrift beyond it. The husband can not change the *wife and all her relations;* these will be found too many for him, and discretion here, too, being the better part of valor, he must yield a compliance to "the powers that be." He can not then resist the fates; to do so would only be to rush upon the bucklers of his own destruction. If children are born, the ties are strengthened that bind him to his adopted land, and henceforth, while having the recollections of an American, he is a Mexican in fact, and in law. When married, he will be fortunate indeed if his wife's numerous relatives do not quarter themselves upon him, eating up his substance and poisoning his peace. For, like bees, they will come in swarms, but, unlike bees, they will make no honey for themselves. They will willingly and unseasonably, live with the American "*compadres,*" but will never be more than drones in the hive. So, should one, captivated by the charms of some black-eyed Senorita, desire to contract the matrimonial alliance, I would suggest, look long and well to the prospects of the future, ere he entangles himself for life in the meshes of wedlock. While doubtless there are some who marry happily, yet my observation has led me to conclude that, by far, the greater number from having so married, have skeletons at their feasts. If married early, then the probabilities for happiness are increased, as the husband material can be more readily bent in conformity to existing usages, than the toughened timber of bachelorhood. For yield he must to the inevitable, and to this he must make up his mind sooner or later, and become incorporated as a *passable* member of the social and political body. At first he may kick, but his refractory nature, under the influences continually pressing upon him, will eventually dissolve into a sweet submission to the firm supremacy which will henceforth guide his conduct and shape his life. Now, as to marrying in the country, one must make up his own mind, after casting the horoscope of the future, remembering what is one man's meat is another man's poison, and that now, as formally, the Latin proverb has force, " *nil disputandum de gustibus.*" I must again remind my readers that these remarks are limited to the circle of my immediate observation, and not to the territory beyond it, and with which I have but a partial acquaintance. I do this that my language may not be misconstrued into that of general application, when I desire its limitation to these mountainous regions.

In speaking of the business modes being objectionable to Americans, I omitted to refer to one especial feature of these which can not be overlooked. In all trades and commercial transactions you must ever be on the alert; here the want of vigilance will entail invariable losses. There is scarcely such a thing as trusting to the principle of the contracting parties, but the question is more narrowly weighed whether the interest or a selfish policy will not impel the party to a fulfilment of his obligations. He will meet them, and that promptly, if he sees it is to his interest to do so; but the reverse will be equally true when the conditions are changed. While extensive credits are given, yet there is a leverage held by the creditor in some way, and the fulcrum on which it rests is not exclusively the one of *principle*. An analysis will show that their punctuality and faithfulness in meeting their paper, proceeds from self-interest, and not from principle of the debtor. They watch each other with eyes of a hawk in all their transactions, and esteem it a triumph to overreach their customers and rivals. There are the fewest number who, in a trade, will not cheat you to your face, and rob you behind your back. They will not, unwatched, trust each other, and seem unfamiliar with fair and honorable dealing. Americans they look upon as legitimate prey for the vultures of their countrymen, and let no occasion pass, leaving no plumage unplucked. Your negotiations with such a people must all be with your eyes open and at arm's length. Unless this rule is strictly observed you will awake from your reverie a wiser and sadder man. Now from this I do not mean to say that there are no Mexicans honest from principle, but this idea only I intend to convey, that I do not know them all, and will therefore charitably suppose that some do exist. It is said that an honest man is the noblest work of God; if there is a lingering uncertainty as to the truthfulness of this declaration, certainly it is all gone by a slight paraphrase of the statement when we read, " an honest *Mexican* is the noblest work of God," at all events this is a most pertinent exclamation when applied to a majority of them with whom I have had dealings through a series of years. Rarities often give values. There are many men who will not *steal*, who are yet dishonest, for they will take undue advantage of you upon the first opportunity. This is my idea of dishonesty, and it is a standard measure, which fits as if made for them, the large majority of the Mexican people I have known. I do not write in bitterness, for personally I have received much kind treatment, but my effort is solely to delineate them with faithfulness, as I have seen and found them. And this leads me here to say, while a guest in their houses you will have paid you most marked attention, but while a customer in their stores you are viewed as a victim to be fleeced. The one is courtesy and hospitality, the other business and iniquity. And with the Mexican, when the one begins, the other ends—their entire co-existence is seldom seen. These are some of the unpleasant things which one must endure when he becomes a resident in the country, and to them long familiarity abates but little of your aversion. Again, knowing them as you do—you might almost say their inner lives—and then to see them, on stated occasions, parading their religious fervor, inspires a feeling like that we have for the broad, phylactery-wearing Pharisee. And somehow or other it does appear that the more notorious the known villain, the bigger will be the image of his patron saint suspended from his gallows-deserving neck. And these fellows you meet on every hand, men of the most abandoned characters, and the worst lives, and some of whom, for less than one dollar, would ply the assassin's vocation and make widowhood and orphanage. With such men you may, at times, be thrown into an unwilling association. Upon the other hand, I must say that, in their entertainments and social life, they observe those attentions and practice well those sweet civilties which make us almost forget for the time their outside conduct and dealings. Their formal politeness is excessive, and their repeated attentions wearisome. Of course much of this is the veriest sham, meaning nothing farther than a mere stereotyped conventionalism, and the observance of a traditional etiquette. How much of heart there is in it one need not inquire or say, but for the time, with suavity and grace, they smooth out wrinkles from the face of care, and, in winning ways and pleasant words, beguile the tedium of the hours. By way of parenthesis I might have remarked, that the latter part of the foregoing sentence has more particular reference to the *female* portion of the community. Probably this fact is sufficiently patent, and my word of explanation altogether unnecessary, but I certainly mean no reflection upon the preceptive faculty of my readers by making the fact stated emphatically conspicuous. The ladies, in every particular, are less unattractive than ‚the men, with less positive guile, and more positive friendship. While the men jealously view the Americans as rivals at the shrine of Beauty, the priestess there is disposed to look upon them without a rival, and to bless them with her encouraging benedictions. She is not at all averse to a matrimonial proposition, and, ambitious of a higher rank, aspires to be the presiding genius over some American's home. The American, generally speaking, has more money and brains than his Mexican rival, and the Senorita, like ‚her sisters across the border, sees no objection to these things, but in them many reasons for the faith and love that are within her. Hence an American husband is a praiseworthy ambition, and she thinks he will treat her better anyway than her own countrymen.

CHAPTER LII.

CONQUEST.—HISTORICAL FACTS.—PUBLIC DEBT.—
ACQUIRING REAL ESTATE.

We now allude to some important events in the history of Mexico. The Conquest under Cortez took place in 1521. He found the country ruled by native princes, at that time a splendid empire. Their rulers were Indians, and from whom have descended some of her most illustrious citizens.

The Republic was declared independent in February, 1821; it became an empire under Iturbide in the following year, and by Santa Anna was proclaimed a Republic in December, 1822. The abdication of Iturbide took place in March, 1823. Many have been the changes since that period, but to-day finds the government more stable and with brighter prospects for the future than at any former period in its checkered history. Peace prevails throughout her borders, and the signs of prosperity are seen on every hand. A steady perseverance in the policy announced in late years will redound to the general good of her people, and in the course of a few years give her an enviable place the among the nations of the earth. Her present constitution was adopted in 1857.

The Republic contains twenty-seven States, one Territory and one Federal District. The Territory is that long peninsula upon the Pacific Coast, known as Lower California. It is arid, poor and sparsely inhabited, but lately I see that there is a probability that a railroad will likely traverse its length from north to south. It is said to be a fine fruit region, and to contain some fine mines. A large copper property is now being worked there which was sold about two years since to a French syndicate for one million dollars.

The city of Mexico is situated within the Federal District, and this corresponds in many particulars to the District of Columbia in the United States. These are the geographical divisions of the country, and the foregoing some of its most important historical events. Such facts are well worth recording and remembering, although not strictly within the line of my correspondence. They serve to excite an interest, and it may be to gratify a reasonable curiosity. It is well to note here that there are some restrictive laws against Americans acquiring real estate in the Republic, but I think this applies to lands being acquired in the border States, and not to those in the interior. There are different modes of acquiring land. This may be done by denouncement, inheritance, adjudication, purchase, donation, prescription, accession, in each case pursuing the laws of the country. Of the public lands one may acquire by denouncement twenty-five hundred hectares (about two and a half acres each), but this limit may be increased at the pleasure of the government. The cost varies according to the quality of the land, but only a few cents to the acre. Now all the *inhabitants* may acquire a portion of these public lands unless they happen to be citizens, native or naturalized, of the United States or other foreign power bordering on the Republic, in which event they can not do so. Moreover, I am of the opinion that no American citizen can acquire real estate in a border State from a Mexican citizen, unless he becomes a citizen of Mexico, *resides* and has his domicile in this country. At least such was the law some years since, and I am not apprised of the fact, if it be such, that the law has been changed so as to permit it. I think it well to make this statement in view of the number who are coming to this country from the United States. This policy of Mexico was evidently grounded upon the apprehension that foreigners holding real estate along the border would be a menace, if not an actual insecurity to the territorial integrity of the Republic. And for this reason I am persuaded that such a restrictive law has been passed and enforced. This might be obviated by treaty stipulation between the United States and Mexico. The former, in such a solemn compact agreeing to leave the territory of Mexico as it is, and to discountenance actively and promptly all schemes and expeditions looking to any dismemberment of the latter, and in return the latter repealing all such prohibitory laws and affording to American citizens, whether resident or non-resident, the amplest protection to their persons and property of every kind, and this wherever situated. This would quiet any latent restiveness, and beget a more genuine cordiality between the two nations. Our commercial relations would be greatly benefitted by such a frank avowal, and such liberal legislation. It would, too, dissipate that "manifest destiny" dream in which some of our statesmen indulge, but this would be followed by more substantial relations and with the practical blessings to both countries which would flow from the same. Let this dream of absorption go, let us in peace make better what we have. This should be our "manifest destiny." Of course each should have similar rights and privileges in the domain of the other. And then the basis of our intercourse would be equality and justice, and likely to endure for an indefinite period to the welfare of both parties.

Mexico owes about $150,000,000, and the bonds of her consolidated debt are now quoted at 23½. Consolidated debt, Sterling London quotation, 30¾.

This would seem very low in view of her ability to meet the low rate of interest upon them, not exceeding three per cent., and the willingness she has shown to pay the same since she last arranged her debt. The uncertainties of government heretofore have unsettled her securities, but this should be no longer a depressing circumstance to bear her bonds. The fear that a change of administration would weaken her securities has now been obviated by a provision of Congress, ratified lately by two-thirds of the States, permitting President Diaz to be elected for a second term, which could not have been done in the absence of such a law. The Mexican statesmen had forecast enough to anticipate this trouble, and promptly to meet it at the threshold, by enacting the necessary legislation. She is now struggling to meet her public obligations since the adjustment of her debt, and since that time has paid her interest punctually, and has commenced again the resumption of her subventions, suspended some years since in consequence of the wide financial distress prevailing at the time. The debt of Mexico, upon examination, will be found to be comparatively insignificant. The United States owe nearly fourteen hundred millions, or about $23 to each inhabitant. Each Frenchman is burdened with $124 of the public debt; each Englishman with $147; each Hollander with $115; each Italian with $80; each Belgian with

$75; each German with $39, but each Mexican, assuming that there are eleven million inhabitants, has only $13.73 of the public debt upon his shoulders! Now, in view of her immense resources, her magnificent possibilities in a word, this debt, under any kind of passable financiering, can be carried without oppressing her people. Especially is this so since, in some of the largest cities, there is no municipal indebtedness. The city of Mexico, with a population of more than four hundred thousand inhabitants, has no public debt, I am told. This may seem strange to my American readers, but in some way they have so administered the city affairs as to escape up to this time, that incubus denominated a "municipal bonded indebtedness." Recently, however, I see that some of the leading journals are now advocating the issuance of bonds and placing them upon the market to raise several million of dollars to carry forward to completion that long-neglected sanitary work, the drainage of the valley. For the city to-day is in a very unsanitary condition, the death rate being fearfully high, as it has no system of sewerage worthy of the name, and it is with this view they wished to expend as soon as practicable, the money sought to be raised by the issuance of bonds. I do not see why they should not be a fine investment, based upon the assessable value of the city, and this managed as heretofore by her most sagacious financiers.

But one word more: this city, as well as others, in the absence of any public indebtedness, presents certainly, an unusual phenomenon, and a striking contrast to American municipal corporations. But referring again to the general indebtednes of the country at large, while this is low per capita, yet upon the other hand, the poverty of the masses is just now so general, and the burden of taxation from all sources so heavy, that it is with difficulty they can meet these public obligations. It falls, as as stated in some former chapter, oppressively upon the poor, since the wealthier classes are, in their large landed estates, practically exempt from taxation. But in this matter no change will likely come until the people are better educated, have more knowledge of their legal rights, and more independence of action, and only vote for those representatives of their own selection, and have the manly courage on this question of suffrage to repudiate the dictation of others. There is scarcely a doubt but that the people have been greatly robbed in this, that the money taken from them in the way of taxation has been grossly squandered by the public functionaries, and millions of it in some instances, diverted from its legitimate channels, have gone to swell the plethoric purses of unfaithful officials. It is a matter of general notoriety that one distinguished official, during his public career, misappropriated many millions by retaining and converting the same to his individual uses. I have yet to learn that any punishment of any kind has been meted out to him for his "*taking irregularities*," probably from the fact that he is secure, entrenched behind his stolen wealth, and can now defy investigating committees and inquisitorial courts. But such things had gone on unrepressed for so long a time that the people had become discouraged, depressed, and felt that their contributions were not for the public good, but for individual emolument. And it has only been within the last few years that a change for the better has taken place, and this has been followed by a better public feeling at large. While official corruption is yet not unknown, still of late years commendable progress has been made in filling high positions with more efficient and worthier men. At least such seems to be the general verdict of the country, and I accept it as a truthful indication of the fact. I am not in possession of the data to give any accurate idea of the indebtedness of the States, or the form in which it exists. But judging from the burdens imposed upon the people, I am convinced that much mal-administration, if not corruption in office, exists, for assuredly the benefits derived by the public, are few in proportion to the public money expended. But the masses know but little of such matters. Their duty is to pay, and the officials, faithful to their trust, see that they do not neglect the discharge of this obligation. And here I may remark that the governors of some of the States, are manifesting much interest in the advancement of education, and in the development of the industries of their commonwealths. All these are healthful signs of progress and of the approach of a better era. Material development and educational progress mark the prosperity of a State.

CHAPTER LIII.

CASAS GRANDES.— LEGEND.— MEXICO, LAND OF WONDERS. — CITY OF CHIHUAHUA. — CATHEDRAL.

With the proper enforcement of law, giving the necessary guarantees to person and property, a long step forward will be taken by the State in its mission of usefulness and beneficence. Perhaps too much should not be expected in too short a time, for States, like all other organized existences, have their infancy, youth and age, and with capabilities corresponding to their changed conditions. The wide diffusion of knowledge through liberal systems of education, will, in the end, supplant error with truth, and wrong with right. Then, in due time, abuses will be rectified, and the people, having been enlightened by the experience of the past, will enter upon a new and unexampled career of material and political advancement. These statements, somewhat disconnected as a narrative of facts, I confess, I have thought might as appropriately be inserted here as in any other connection, and on which my readers may reflect with some pleasure —probably with some profit.

We will now return from the general excursion just taken, to some matters of interest within this State, Chihuahua. I ask that you now accompany me to some old ruins called the "Casas Grandes," situated near the northwestern frontier, and doubtless the relics of the Aztec people. The Casas Grandes, or "Great Houses," when translated, are located on the west bank of the Las Casas Grandes River, which empties into the river Conchas. These houses are the remains of immense structures built centuries ago, and now sinking into mouldering ruins. They occupy a space of eight hundred feet, from north to south, and two hundred and fifty from east to west. They were built of adobes, sun-dried brick, but much larger than those now generally in use among the Mexicans. The outer buildings were, it appears, not more than one story high, while those within were from three to six stories. On one side may be seen the ruins of a continuous fortification, while the eastern and western fronts are irregular with projecting walls. These appear to have been courtyards within the enclosure of different dimensions.

A beautiful legend is related by the Spanish historians of the journeyings of the Aztecs, some of whom, at an early period, migrated to that portion of the State and built the Casas Grandes, while others, going farther north, located in the Territory of Arizona. Antonio Garcia Cubas in his work relates the legend as follows :

"Huitziton, a person of great authority among the Aztecs, heard in the branches of a tree the trilling of a small bird, which, in its song, repeated the sound 'tihuc,' the literal meaning of which is, 'let us go.' Huitziton, being struck at this, and communicating his impression to another personage, called Tecpaltzin, they both induced the Aztecs to leave the country, interpreting the song as a mandate from divinity. Even to the present day, there is a bird known among the Mexicans by the name of 'Tihuntochan' (Let us go home). In 1160 they commenced their peregrination, and, passing by a large river, which historians concur in being the Colorado, and which discharges itself into the Gulf of California, they advanced towards the river Gila, after remaining some time at a place known to-day by the name of Casa Grande, not far from the shores of the river. From thence they continued their road, and again took up quarters at a place to the northwest of Chihuahua, now called, like the previous stopping-place, 'Las Casas Grandes,' and whose ruins show the vast proportions of the ancient building and fortress. Leaving behind them the wide 'Sierra de la Tarahumara' they afterwards went to Hueycolhuacan, now Culiacan, capital of the State of Sinaloa, and there remained for three years, during which time he made the statue of their god, Huitzilopochtli, which was to accompany them in their expedition. During their peregrination the tribe was divided into two factions, one faction settling on a sandy promontory called Tlaltelolco. The name of Mexico was given to the new city, in honor of their god, who was born of a virgin belonging to the family of Citli, and he was cradled in the heart of a magneay plant (metl); hence the name 'Mecitti,' afterward changed into 'Mexico.'"

Such is the legendary history of the origin of these famous ruins. They are all well worth the study of the antiquarian. Who were these people, what was their mission, for what purpose were these immense building constructed, and how did they live? Were there populous settlements near there, and if so, how did their inhabitants subsist, from the woods, or from the fruits of well-tilled fields? There are many inquiries suggested, and many curious speculations, as we think upon the subject. But so much is wrapped in obscurity that all our conclusions at last are uncertain, and resolve themselves into unprofitable speculations. The same mystery enfolds them as shrouds the origin and life of the cave-dwellers and mound-builders. But the ruins are there, magnificent in their desolation, attesting for their long-forgotten builders no little enterprise and fertility of resources. Doubtless their leaders were men of brains and daring, and, with lives consecrated to a purpose, perchance to some ambitious project, led their followers thither to its accomplishment, first through the conquest of the wilderness. But these, as before suggested, are mere idle surmisings, and we leave their fragmentary annals to the more entertaining search and study of the antiquarian. Nothing now written, reliable, survives their extinction, and their rise, progress, and decline, their virtues, vices and exploits have fallen alike into oblivion's tomb. In the vicinity of these Casas Grandes are said to be some good mines, and I believe a railroad is now projected to run to or near there, starting at Deming in New Mexico. If so, it will open up a fine field to the enterprise of the mining adventurer and capitalist, for, until recently, the Indians have held almost undisputed possession of these mountains against the incursion of all others. That portion of the State was visited this year by an earthquake, the shock of which was very violent and continued for many days. It destroyed some and injured other villages, and, in many respects, changed the entire aspect of nature. It is reported that mines, unknown before, were exposed to view, the watercourses were changed and other striking phenomena presented.

Mexico, in some particulars, is truly a land of wonders. Earthquakes and volcanoes in some parts are not infrequent; its valleys, under well-directed culture, will teem with abundant harvests, and its mountains continue for ages to give their precious contributions to the commerce of the world.

Let us now pass to the city of Chihuahua, the capital of the State, and make a few remarks touching the same for information of my readers. It is situated near the center of the State, on the Conchos River, about two hundred and thirty miles southwest from El Paso, and one thousand miles from the city of Mexico, and contains probably fifteen or eighteen thousand inhabitants. The streets are broad, well-paved, and cross each other at right angles. These, too, to the credit of the authorities, are kept well-swept and clean. All Mexican towns and cities have their public squares, called "plazas," and Chihuahua has several of these. The principal one, however, is near the center of the business portion of the city, and is handsomely ornamented with trees and flowering shrubs, and a fine fountain of pure water, conducted thither by an aqueduct from a stream several miles distant. Here, several evenings in the week, the public band discourses music to the thousands who assemble there. The plaza is immediately in front of the celebrated cathedral of which so much has been said and written. I, too, must say a few words descriptive of the same. Some have said it is one of the finest buildings in the world, but I am not enthusiastic enough to endorse any such exaggerated statement. It is a large building, constructed of brown stone, which seems to be of an inferior building quality, gothic in style, with dome and towers. The statues of the twelve apostles are placed in an appropriate position in front, of life size, seemingly sculptured from the commonest stone, and that, too, by apprentices at the business. I am sure Michael Angelo would condemn them as caricatures of his great art, and consign them and the authors to the oblivion they so richly merit. The cathedral, like other churches here, has no seats, and the worshipers must kneel or stand during their devotions upon the stone floor. And this floor, in many places, has been worn in holes and uneven places by the multitude of worshipers through long years since it was built. It is an open church, into which there is a living stream of humanity pouring and emerging during the hours of the day and a portion of the night. You never pass there unless the devotees are seen on bended knees in front of the altar, motionless as statues, saying their silent prayers. The women, in numbers, far exceed the men in their attendance. The fact is, my observation has led me to conclude that comparatively few men there are regular attendants at the services of the church. The cathedral is said to have cost eight hundred thousand dollars, and was built by the contribution of one real ($12\frac{1}{2}$ cts.), from each marc ($8), which was taken at that time from the Santa Eulalia Mine, situated but a short distance from the city. This, then, was in bonanza which seemed inexhaustible, and continued so for nine years. Sufficient data from the above is furnished to make the calculation easy as to the yield of the mine during that period. It is also said that a reserve fund of one hundred thousand dollars additional was set aside from the output during that time, having the same basis of apportionment as the cathedral building fund. But I caution my readers to discount all these big Mexican stories at usurious rates, and then they will be more likely to approximate the truth.

Formerly, between the cities of San Antonio, Santa Fe and St. Louis, a considerable trade was carried on. In this city, too, is said to have been confined the patriot Hidalgo in the Jesuit Convent of San Francisco, and who was executed there in 1811. A monument is there, reared in his memory, in the Plaza De Armas, commemorative of his patriotism.

CHAPTER LIV.

INSTITUTIONS OF CHIHUAHUA.—IRON MINE OF DURANGO.—EDUCATION.

A mint is located here which does a considerable business. There are four banks also, which are liberally patronized and have large capital stock. The buildings were formerly one story high, but of late years the architecture has become more imposing, having two and three stories and with a more elegant finish. The Mexican Central Railroad passes through this city from El Paso to the city of Mexico, and has effected a great many changes in the appearances of things since its coming. The sleepy old city was awakened from its long slumber by the passing cars, and for the time new life was infused into its drowsy inhabitants. A considerable number of Americans now reside there, pursuing different vocations and meeting with more or less success, according to their capacity, aptitude and attention to business. The city is lighted with coal oil, a contract for the same having been made with some shrewd American some years since. The water supply is good and abundant. A great many American vehicles are seen upon the streets; the duties upon carriages are so much upon each *wheel*, formerly, I think, thirty dollars. It is probable this has been modified so as to reduce it to only *twenty* dollars a wheel. This may appear rather a singular mode of levying duties, but not more so than was adopted some years since, when goods were hauled from the United States to the city, and they collected *five hundred dollars* upon each wagon load, the size of the wagon being immaterial, the small ones paying as much as the large ones. The hotels are not first-class, but endurable, as you expect to leave soon for other parts. The modern convenience, the street car, drawn by mules is seen upon the streets, but not so profitable to its owners or so popular as in other cities. There are two telegraph offices, one with an American, and the other with a Mexican operator. Messages from the United States will stop at the American office and will not be sent forward to any interior point by the Mexican line, unless there is an express agreement to that effect. In the absence of such an agreement, if the postage is paid, it will be sent to its destination by mail. They are now building a fine State house, but the progress is very slow, and the probabilities are that many years will transpire before its completion. The city, I believe, has a very good system of public schools. The Supreme Court sits here also.

With several of the judges I have the pleasure of a personal acquaintance, and found them intelligent and agreeable gentlemen. The city contains some twenty lawyers or more, Mexicans, but I feel convinced were an American to locate there who spoke the language, and was well qualified, he could get a fine practice in due course of time. There is a great deal of business done by the Americans in the State in the purchase of lands, mining and other enterprizes, and these desire to do business very naturally with those with whom they can converse and understand. The city, too, has its full complement of the medical profession, but an American physician who has resided there for ten or twelve years has the leading practice at this time, and has had it for some years. He is eminently qualified, not only as a practitioner, but as a surgeon, and has a most lucrative practice. There are also one or two American dentists who are doing well, but Americans, I believe it is conceded, excel all others in this profession. There are one or two flourishing mills, but so far as I know none for grinding corn, the "*metates*" (stones) of the antediluvian, still performing this service. The railways leading to different points are generally good and on which travel the lumbering wooden wheeled vehicles of old, as well as the modernized Concord coaches, carrying mail and passengers. The scenes presented remind us of those we saw in portions of the United States, more than a quarter of a century ago, but which have now "passed the way of all the earth." These are some of the features of the old city, said to have been built in the sixteenth century, and as we walk its streets, and view its belongings, we feel as if we had been transferred to some olden land, hoary with memories of the past.

These imperfect sketches from Mexico would be more so, were I now not to tell you something of the great iron mountain in Durango, adjoining this State. 1 know Bro. Jonathan has much of which he can boast, and in this, from long practice, has acquired a remarkable proficiency, but I doubt whether such a body of iron ore exists elsewhere in the world. Some claim it is an aerolite which had fallen on the plain, and disconnected from any ledge or deposit of ore. But then this, by some recent writer, is denied, and he gives the geological formation about and underneath it, and claims it is of volcanic origin. Ward, in his History of Mexico, says it is composed of iron ores of two distinct qualities, crystallized and magnetic, both equally rich, as these contain from sixty to seventy-five per cent. of pure iron. It is called the "Cerro de Mercado," and is 1,750 varas (33 inches each) in length from east to west, and 400 varas in width, and the height from the surface of the plain 234 varas, "which cuts, as it were, in the middle horizontally," making the result in cubic measurement, in veras, 60,000,000. From analysis of the pure iron it contains, the amount of ore it is estimated in the mass is more than 5,000,000,000 of quintals (100 lbs.), and from this, if the percentage of pure iron is only 50 per cent., although it assays 75 per cent., the whole body will produce 2,500,000,000 quintals of metallic iron, and then if this is estimated at $5 per hundred in Mexico, it would represent the sum of $12,500,000,000, or more, it is said, than the product of all the mines in Mexico since 1772 to 1880, which has been estimated at $4,000,000,000. But to give a more distinct idea of this enormous mass of iron, if the amount produced in England annually for the last 330 years has been 15,000,000 quintals, the whole amount during that time has been 4,950,000,000 of quintals, *or only a little over one-third* of the amount of pure iron contained in the " Cerro de Mercado," which is almost untouched, while thousands of tons are brought from England and the United States. Now nature never does a useless thing, but stores her supplies for human needs. Then the time will come when this immense treasure must be fashioned into forms to supply and meet human wants. But if it is not like " carrying coals to Newcastle " for this country to import iron, I am at a loss for a proper simile. This is a big iron story, but it is not "a fiction founded on fact," but a truth attested by many travelers, among them the illustrious Humboldt, who had some of its specimens analyzed. So it is not in gold and silver exclusively that Mexico excels, but in the most serviceable of all the metals, in iron, she can boast of the biggest single bonanza, I presume, in the world.

The figures above furnish interesting data by which to gauge this enormous pile of unworked iron. It would seem sufficient for thousands of forges for thousands of years to come. In the laboratory of nature it has been reserved until now, when at the bidding of men it must come forth from its long resting-place, and go out into the varied activities of life in its mission of usefulness.

It may interest my readers now to know something of other matters outside of these mountain ranges in this Republic; and probably information on no subject would be more cheerfully welcomed than upon that of education, which so vitally effects the well-being of the people and State. This is now obligatory in the majority of the States—penalties being inflicted for its non-observance, and rewards for its observance. Elementary education comprises: Reading, writing, Spanish grammar, arithmetic, tables of weights and measures, morality and good manners. And in the girl's schools, needle work and other useful arts. In some of the States, geography, national history and drawing are compulsory, and in schools not maintained by the government, geometry and algebra are taught, with elements of natural history, French language and ornamental drawing. There are between eight and ten thousand primary schools in the Republic. More than six hundred are supported by the State government and more than five thousand by municipal authorities. Scholars of both sexes attend these schools. In the Republic there are more than one hundred establishments of what are termed secondary and professional instruction. These include preparatory schools, civil colleges of jurisprudence, schools of medicine and pharmacy, schools for engineers, naval and commercial schools, academies of arts and sciences, agricultural schools, academies of fine arts, conservatories of music and oratory, military colleges, seminaries supported by the Catholic clergy, blind, deaf and dumb schools, and secondary schools for girls. In these latter mathematics, cosmography, geography, domestic medicine, history and chronology, book-keeping, domestic economy, and duties of women in society, natural, figured and ornamental drawing, manual labors, horticulture and gardening, music, the French and Italian languages are taught. I presume a young lady instructed in the foregoing might be said to be "highly accomplished." She ought to be a "sweet girl graduate." There are nearly four hundred thousand pupils. There are twenty public libraries, containing 236,000 volumes, and it is said that private libraries, containing from 1,000 to 8,000 volumes, are numerous. Some even have as many as 20,000 volumes. There are some fine museums in the Republic of antiquities and paintings. "In the Republic are 63 institutions dedicated to the cultivation of the arts and sciences, of which 29 are scientific, 21 literary, 20 artistical, and 3 of a mixed character."

The foregoing will give some conception of the educational facilities furnished the youth and citizens of the Republic. These show that the arts and sciences, the useful, as well as the ornamental branches of education are not wanting in enthusiastic students. The older portions of the Republic, as is natural to suppose, have more of the refinements of life and the elegances of culture than the mountainous districts. I believe this is so everywhere, the natural surroundings giving complexion to the character of the inhabitants. At least such is the theory of some, and many facts go to sustain it.

CHAPTER LV.

THE TRAMP.—LOCAL ATTACHMENTS.—PACKERS.
—INCIDENTS.

There is another character hitherto unalluded to, whose demerits merit mention. I now refer to that ubiquitous individual called the tramp. He is also indigenous to this section, though the exotic article is more frequently seen. How they subsist is a mystery, as the relay stations are here more widely separated, and yet they do, and seem to flourish like a " green bay tree," though under the most discouraging conditions. I learn, too, when he was not here " the memory of man runneth not to the contrary." An intelligent old gentleman who has been residing in the country for nearly half a century tells me that he was here coeval with his earliest recollection, frequent and active—that is, active in his way. This period long antedated the railroads in this country, and when wagons and pack-trains exclusively did the transportation business. He said they would often attach themselves to some wagon train and ask the privilege of remaining with it during the night, which was given upon the express condition that they would lie down and have themselves tied securely until morning. Knowing their traits so well, this measure was adopted in abundant caution to prevent theft, and probably murder. If they would not submit to this reasonable requirement, then they were ordered to leave the encampment. But inasmuch as the Indians were at that time very numerous and warlike, these vagrants generally permitted themselves to be tied for the safety of themselves and of their entertainers. Here he is on the tramp, tramp, from one point to another, without any well-defined object, save it be to gratify an abnormal desire of his nature, just to be wandering aimlessly hither and thither. He has a natural aversion to steady employment, and when his temporary earnings are exhausted, then he is ready, pressed by his necessities, if not his innate meanness, to inflict some injury or commit some crime. The genus here is certainly a bad one, but how he can be best utilized, or eliminated from society, is one of the knotty problems of the age. He is unquestionably a dangerous element—vigorous idleness always is—for the unoccupied are mischief-breeding and mischief-making. Charities expended upon such objects are charities misapplied, for it is a direct encouragment to laziness, and indirectly stimulates viciousness. But good people often give to them rather than to take the trouble to investigate their claims upon their bounty, and furthermore by so doing, they the sooner are freed from their annoying applications. Well conducted, organized charity is much better for society, both the givers and the receivers. It lessens imposition, and then becomes a true benefaction worthily bestowed. But I believe the most pestilent of these characters seen here are "not to the manor born," but importations from other countries, with broken fortunes and misspent lives. They are, as if they were resting under the curse of Cain, veritable wanderers upon the face of the earth. And with these gentry they prefer to wander rather than to work. In this floating body different nationalities are most unworthily represented. In point of numbers, I think the American is in the ascendant, due probably as much to his proximity as to his restless disposition. I don't believe anything good can come out of this walking Nazarene. When the habit is fixed, he becomes one of the incurables, and all efforts at reformation are generally futile. His course is onward and downward, but never upward. The tramp is ever changing localities, but never changing conditions. Vicissitudes come to his restless spirit, but these are marked by no improvement, and he lives on as he walks on, unchanged for the better. He meets his end at last, friendless and homeless, and by unfeeling strangers is dumped into his rude grave with a sigh of relief that their trouble, too, is over, as well as his. He dies as dieth the fool, leaving the world no better for his having lived in it. Such is his life, and such his death, and now no memory survives the one or the other.

Generally speaking, however, the Mexicans, not tramps, have strong local attachments. It matters not how uninviting his habitation, and how far he may wander, his heart and his thoughts will turn to that spot, the center of his affections. It may be nothing more than a mud hut built on the side of the mountain, or a framework of poles with thatched roof, it is all the same to him as if it were a castle or a palace. And while for want of these home conditions which, with us, make home the sphere of woman recognized and blessed, yet to him his home has an attractiveness as no other place, and a charm unbroken with the changes of the years. We would not call it home unless there were other attractions than with him, and these must "come from tender ties and sweeter associations." But so it is, reared in the most inaccessible places, with the most ungainly surroundings, he would not exchange these for the most favored spots, with sweep of plain, and fertile soil, with winding river, and mountain view. I have known persons raised in these canyons go out of them on trips to the city of Mexico or to San Francisco, and become almost homesick before the business of their trip had been concluded. It is said they sighed for their native *tortillas* and beans worse than did the Israelites in their exodus for the flesh-pots of Egypt. I heard of one wealthy Mexican, who took his family, consisting of his wife and some grown daughters, on quite an extended tour, visiting the principal cities of the United States and Europe, and upon their return, when they landed in the Mexican port, they expressed themselves as being overjoyed, for now they could once more *get something fit to eat!* To them the best hotels abroad could furnish nothing so palatable, so appetizing as *corn cakes and beans!* But I apprehend other things than their delicious bill of fare drew them homeward. But it is a fact the natives here seldom leave, and when they do, return from choice. There is to them an attraction, unseen by me, which roots them to the rocky soil. I repeat, they would not exchange their adobe hovels for a palace elsewhere, their unfenced canyon patches, not for alluvial lands on the deltas nor broad prairie acres. Naught they care for the busy world beyond. The quiet world about them fills up the measure of their joys and all ambitious ends.

Formerly I have had occasion to allude to the packers, the freight carriers in the mountains, but inasmuch as they are very important factors in the business economy of these parts, they merit more than a mere allusion. They are a rough class, brought up on the road, and living upon it nearly all the time, with their trains of mules and burros. Their home attractions are not very strong, as they seldom remain there for any considerable length of time. But packing, going and coming from distant points take up nearly all their time. One place suits them nearly as well as another, provided there is a sufficiency of water and pasturage for their animals. They travel from ten to twelve, and sometimes fifteen miles a day, camping early and starting late. They are familiar with all the camping places, and graduate their speed so as to reach them in due season. Like the remainder of his countrymen, he is in no hurry to leave his stopping-place or reach his destination. I have known them to be on the road for more than sixty days, leisurely pursuing their way, when, had they made seasonable time, they could have delivered their freight in less than one-third of that time. But since his birth he has never been in a hurry, nor will he be until his death. There are only two things, in the doing of which have I ever seen a Mexican manifest any haste, the one is taking a pack from a mule, and the other, taking—a drink! In doing the former he is stimulated to some activity, in the latter he is *precipitate!* They lead a rough life upon the road, with the coarsest, and often scanty food and scantier clothing, with no tents to shield them from the cold rains and colder winds, but when night comes, they fall upon the cold ground, often covered with sleet or snow, and, pillowing their heads upon the rocks, with the uncurtained stars above, catch visions, not of ascending and descending angels, but "*see sights*," such as Jacob never saw from consecrated Bethel.

The provoking slowless in the delivery of their cargoes has often reminded me of an incident which took place at a mining camp in the southeastern part of the State of Nevada some years since. A merchant living at the place had bought quite a stock of goods, and it was all important to him to get in his goods as soon as possible, as this class of goods was in great demand at the time. Wagons were at that time the only means of transportation to that point, and the Mormons had a monopoly of the carrying trade. After waiting a reasonable time for his goods, and not hearing anything from them, losing money every day by their non-arrival, he wrote in every direction to learn something of their whereabouts. Still not hearing anything for a good while farther, he ventured to address a note to the Mormon Bishop, and " in due course of mail" that clerical official responded in substance as follows: "Your letter was duly received, making inquiry, etc.; in reply to which I have the pleasure to write, upon diligent investigation, I find that Bro. John Smith has your goods out at his house; they are *perfectly safe, under a good shelter,* and as soon as he "*lays by*" *and gathers his crop, he will forward them to you without delay!* I might add that Bro. Smith having had sealed unto him, recently, his *seventh* wife, he could not well leave his family at this time. At last account Bro. Smith and wife were doing well. *The goods are all right.*" The expectant merchant in the case cited had the promise of the high church dignitary that his goods *would come,* but here the coming of the Mexican freighter is unfortified by any such assurance, and the faith in the promise of his coming is childlike in its simplicity. Often they will reach camp, and if a favored locality, will remain there until they fatten their stock, and then continue their journey until they find a better place, or from some eccentric freak or sheer caprice, go on to their destination! There is no rule by which you can measure him, no standard now known by which you can gauge his in-comings and out-goings. In his methods of business, he defies the ordinary rules of calculation, and makes his own whims the elastic rules which govern his business affairs. Now and then, too, in his travels, he sees some mule with top-heavy cargo losing the center of gravity, from some misstep or other mischance, go tumbling hundreds of feet below to certain destruction. He gathers the unbroken pieces, loads them on another animal, goes on his way, not rejoicing, but accepts the catastrophe as one of the "flings of outrageous fortune." From twenty to fifty generally make up a train, preceded often by a boy with some old horse, with or without a bell, which they will follow from day to day, through thick and thin. In meeting these trains of mules upon the narrow mountain paths, you must give the way, for their law of the road is to take it all, and unless you do this with much promptitude, you are liable to be dragged from your animal by their projecting bundles. This danger is not inconsiderable, and it can only be averted by observing the caution already expressed. Of course such people never accumulate anything; the rolling stone gathers no moss. They literally live hard, and die poor. I presume they fill their place, an humble one, it is true, in the business operations of the country, and the country could not well afford to do without them. It takes, we hear it often said, a great many people to make a world, and these must have different tastes, adaptations and capacities. I suppose in filling his sphere, the packer, too, has found his business level which suits him better than anything else, and for this reason contributes to the aggregate of the general good. The word *toughness* does not fitly express their moral status, but some other as yet uninvented term may the better describe this condition. While this is so, he is not wholly bad, but now and then gleams of good-heartedness and generosity shine forth from his rugged nature like sunbeams dancing with the shadows upon his mountain home.

CHAPTER LVI.

CARGADORES.—EL BURRO.

There is another class of laborers in this country worthy of mention, called *cargadores*, literally burden-carriers. But these are found at the shipping ports, and their business is to take from the lighters the goods, boxes, bales, bundles; in fact, all kinds of freight, to the shore at the wharf. To do this, it is often necessary for them to wade to a considerable distance out into the bay, and to a considerable depth also, to receive their cargoes. It is simply remarkable how much one of these men can carry, not infrequently more than five hundred pounds. They have been brought up to it from their youth, and certain muscles have become so developed, and such a dexterity has been acquired by long practice in the handling of such things, that their feats of strength and endurance are almost amazing. Those men, too, have their " unions." It was some years since, I think, in the city of Mazatlan or Guymas, when it was sought to introduce some labor-saving appliance to transfer this freight to the shore, thus superseding the labor of these men; they rose in a body and demolished their business rival. Since then they have not sought its re-introduction, and cargadores "hold the bay," and monopolize the business. Any machinery coming in conflict with their interest is regarded by them as their deadly enemy, to which they will give no quarter. Somehow it appears that the Mexicans can pack more than anybody else, whether large or small. Often I have seen boys carrying loads which far exceeded their own weight, for I have learned the fact by actually weighing the burden and then the boy. From the time they are five years old they commence packing burdens and continue it through life, acquiring much strength and skill in their handling. It is interesting to watch these cargadores managing huge boxes and barrels and great misshapen pieces of freight, how it calls into play their educated muscles, and with what apparent ease they perform their herculean tasks. These, too, are a certain species of middle men between the seller and the buyer, to whom a certain tribute must be paid.

Speaking of these burden-bearers reminds me of a half-promise I made, some pages back, to speak more at length of the burro, for, as a carrier of freights, his services are so well recognized that he has sometimes been denominated the "Mountain Schooner." And he is as much entitled to such a distinctive honor as the dromedary to being called "the ship of the desert." I presume these seen here are the unimproved breed, small, wiry, and tough. But small as they are, weighing only a few hundred pounds, I have seen one pack four or five hundred pounds of broken rock for a considerable distance down a rough mountain path, picking his way as cautiously to avoid accidents, as if in the conscious discharge of a high duty. He has no racing qualities, but when made, his feet were set and his speed was gauged to a certain grade, and there is nothing on earth can break this regulation. No threats or entreaties, no kind of influence can make him step one step more, or one step quicker, so as to break the law of his life. He has no blind side upon which you can approach, and with human flattery and sweet beguilement to so cajole him as to cause him to vary one iota from his life mission. His eyes are wide-awake, mild in their expression, but firm in their resolve, and he will neither be led nor driven by his keepers from his burro desires and purposes. Here he is not only an exemplary, but a most useful member of society, and without him here, I am sure the wheels of progress would cease to roll. He is often abused, at times shamefully treated, and yet no word of rebellion escapes his patient lips. He is worked hard, and when his driver is exhausted in his efforts to move him, then he is turned loose and told to go until the morning, and find something to eat wherever he can, in order to bear his master's burdens again to-morrow. Released from his thongs and shackles, he saunters forth, with his scars and sores and bruises, to nibble the dry grass and leaves, and finish, perchance, with a desert of old, greasy rags and scraps of leather and paper. He has no compunctious throbbing as to whose forage he eats, as this with him is wholly a matter of taste and not of conscience. From such a repast of the night he is ready again for the punishments of to-morrow. He deserves a better fate, but truly here have his lines fallen in evil places. His hardihood is most astonishing, doing the heaviest drudgery and subsisting almost on thin air and nothing. While pacific in his disposition, seldom attempting violence with his rear extremities, yet he is dogmatic in his views of things, in fact, so much so that some of his critics have thought his firmness of opinion had degenerated into stubbornness of will. If this imputation were true, " 'tis a pity 'tis true," yet it could hardly be otherwise, when his father and mother were somewhat noted for this unamiable quality before him. I might have remarked that his digestive functions are wonderful. I would not say he could not, with impunity, banquet upon a pile of old scrap tin, and enjoy the feast too, especially if he were permitted undisturbed to approach and appropriate it by stealth, for, like members of the human race, especially his master, he enjoys forbidden fruit the most. For you know bad boys say stolen watermelons eat the best, and in the make up of the burro there is a good deal of the bad boy. Whether his slowness is constitutional, or derived from long association with the Mexican, is one of those questions to the solution of which I invite the lovers of " fancy stock," and the curious students of ethnology. Treat him well and he is faithful, treat him ill and he is faithful still, philosophically expecting more roughness of treatment than roughness of forage.

It is not improbable, driven by one of the young Noahs, he packed his own provisions into the big vessel, and, after the falling of the water, when the " Ark rested on Ararat," he had forage to spare, and came forth from his long rest as fat and as sportive as a thoroughbred Kentucky bluegrass filly. In his whole history it is the only restful vacation he ever had ; he did n't disturb the other animals, and for once the other animals did n't disturb him.

His valuable life is seldom prolonged. From severe usage, or because " death loves a shining mark," in a few years, the burro historian chronicles, the transmigration of his spirit, and his stout bones, glittering in the sunshine and the moonbeams, uncovered and uncared for, rest with the rocks of the valley. After life's jerks and bangs and bruises, he sleeps well with his fathers. The twilight of antiquity knew him, he has lived through all the succeeding ages, and is destined to survive till "the last syllable of recorded time." *Viva, viva el burro!*

His flesh is much relished by the Indian epicure. Upon the burro ham, or other choice, jucy parts, he feasts with almost as much genuine satisfaction as upon his favorite dish, the savory, fat prairie dog, for the eating of which he would return a blow for any interruption, though this were even made by his own mother!

CHAPTER LVII.

SUGGESTIONS AS TO REFORMS.

Mexico has but little danger to anticipate from her more southern neighbors, Gautemala, Costa Rica, San Salvador, and Honduras. So long as she maintains her non-intervention policy, but little trouble will come from said States. While she might not be averse to their union with her all-Spanish speaking people, yet I am not aware that she is ambitious of extending her territorial domain. Certainly not, if such an extension would involve a sanguinary conflict. But to the north she must look for her probable dangers. And it is to be hoped that the wisdom of wise men may overrule the folly of foolish ones, and that the flags of the two lands may float side by side in peace. Peace from without assured, Mexico can address her energies to her domestic concerns, the upbuilding of her industries, and the uplifting of her people; the true functions of government. To do this effectually, many abuses must be corrected, new measures introduced, reforms set on foot. These things can be done, but their consummation necessitates time. The body of the people must be educated not only in the cities, the centers of population, but in the rural districts as well. No government is stable built on an ignorant rabble. The education must go to such an extent that they may be able to see and appreciate their rights and privileges, and the blessings of good government. It must rise higher than the influence of the demagogue, and be stronger than the selfishness of the partisan. This education, however acquired, whether enforced by the government or not, must pervade the masses as a leaven, and then it will lift them up to a higher and truer conception of government, and of their own manhood. While today she is not wanting in educational enterprises, yet they are insufficient in numbers and character to meet the public requirements. In the extension of these educational facilities, she is making, of late years, most commendable progress; yet in this particular so much remains to be done that her efforts already made are rather undervalued. Upon this subject her leading men are abreast of the age, and are strong advocates of compulsory education, and recent manifestations in the several States bespeak, at no distant period, its general acceptance. The more intelligent the constituency, the better the representatives. Then, the more enlightened the people, the better will be the representative government. The election farces of to-day, when the ballots bespeak not the will of the voter, but of another, will be followed by a better elective system, where the ballot will register his own choice, and proclaim the will of a freeman. The people must be educated to a higher self-respect, to view themselves as more important factors in the affairs of government. They must break their reverence for the manipulating politician, the political mountebank, and give growth to their own consequence as members of society and citizens of the State. Until this is done, we can expect no permanent change for the better; but they will be driven forward like dumb cattle, unthinkingly and unresistingly, to the shambles. But a mere intellectual education is not sufficient, without some moral enlargement. Intellect, without moral growth, is only half education; but intellect with morals is education complete. Thus equipped, one carries within himself the highest constituents of citizenship. In this is Mexico sadly in need: the improvement of her public morals. Many of her public men are intellectually strong, but morally weak, and, of course, wanting in that moral force which inspires confidence and carries conviction. But it may be said this defect obtains elsewhere; true, but this does not make it less conspicuous here. Mere intellect, unswayed by moral forces, is a potent element of danger; but controlled by these, it is a divine instrumentality.

Something, too, should be done to lessen the gambling mania, such a widespread evil, and one which effects so seriously the earnings of the poorer classes. From this their time and thoughts should be turned, and given employment in other channels more profitable to themselves and to the commonwealth. You can hardly hope to extirpate such an evil; but its curse may be diminished by a repression of its universal, flagrant conspicuousness. Certainly, it should not only not receive the countenance of the authorities, but be by them and the law discouraged in every possible manner. At present the case is far otherwise; the highest and the lowest, State, government and municipal officers, jostle each other for space at the gaming tables. When certain practices are unmixed evils, leading, in the end, to profligacy and ruin, it then becomes the duty of the governing power to strike them down with a strong arm, for the salvation of the public. I have already pointed out the malignity of this vice in the country, and it is unncessary again to rehearse its evil effects. Its influence is so demoralizing, that those affected by it are rendered in a short time unfit for the discharge of the proper duties which they owe to themselves, their families and society. The nuisance should be drawfed in its proportions, if not abated, by the most stringent, penal legislation.

The evil of drunkeness, too, should be suppressed; its victims, men and boys, in some way should be rescued from the clutches of such a monster. If it continues ungoverned for many years, the harvest of evil will be as broad as the land. If there are now restrictive laws, they fail to restrict, and the evil grows apace with the times. But here, again, in this matter, something must be done to check its progress and save the people. Between drinking and gambling, the daily earnings of the working classes go to the ruin of home and the impoverishment of its members. If this serpent continues its course unmolested, unchecked by law, with its fangs unbroken, and its poison undrawn, this will become a nation of drunkards and soon ripe for extinction. So much misspent time, and so much of labor's products misapplied, weaken the body politic no less than the individuals themselves. It was never designed that man should throw himself away and become the slave of a consuming appetite. He was born for a better destiny, and, if need be, the State should see that he attains it.

Again, wise laws are the needs of a country; but these are useless unless enforced. This country has some fine laws, conceived by practical legislators, to meet public necessities, and yet in many sections they are inoperative by reason of their non-enforcement. This is strikingly true in reference to the criminal laws. For some reason or other they have neither spirit nor life—they are dead. The truth is, the fault of the age is not so much a want of knowledge, as a want of common honesty. Men—officials—know generally what they should do; but are dishonest in the failure to discharge their duties to the public. They will make a bargain with themselves, or, what is worse, it may be with some other person, and if they find they will make more by not doing, than doing, their duty, then they will dishonestly fail to discharge it. "They know the right, and yet the wrong pursue." Good officials should fill these most important positions. If they can not be obtained in the immediate vicinity, as is often the case, then they should be selected elsewhere and commissioned to that particular locality. As it is, the officials are wanting in every necessary qualification in many places, intellectually, idiots, and morally, felons. No country can survive such an unwise administration of its laws. These must be duly enforced, whether right or wrong; if wrong, the more stringently enforced, the sooner repealed.

CHAPTER LVIII.

GENERAL REFLECTIONS.

We have now reached in our ramblings a point at which we may properly pause and indulge in some general reflections. And, in doing so, if we give expression to ideas already advanced, it will be with the view of emphasizing their importance. We have, in a somewhat discursive way, treated of a variety of topics as they suggested themselves, without much reference to order or connectedness. We spoke of the revolutions through which the country had passed, and how, by these convulsions, everything was unsettled. Law and order during their prevalence were practically in abeyance. Life and property had an uncertain tenure, whether one or the other body of the revolutionists prevailed for the time. The industries of the country were completely prostrated by these political disturbances, and the great mass of the people remained in a condition of deep poverty, ignorance and wretchedness. In fine, but little advancement of any kind was made in any department of life. It could scarcely have been otherwise where there was so little authority, and so much lawlessness. But happily, in the course of time, a new order of things came into existence, and, by the courage, patriotism and statesmanship of a few men, the skies so long overcast became bright with the stars of hope, " old things passed away," and the prophecy of a better future was heard on every hand. This was only a few years since, and to-day Mexico begins to realize throughout her borders the fruition from her bettered condition. For centuries, it may be affirmed, she has not had such general tranquillity as in the last decade, nor has she made such material progress as during the last period. Her statesmen and her people, or at least the best informed of them, now seem alive to the importance of continuing in the good course so auspiciously begun. But it is manifestly true that this can only be done by the maintainance of peace within and without her territorial limits. The central government must keep itself sufficiently strong to stifle in their incipiency any uprisings instigated by disappointed demagogues and ambitious leaders. Some of these yet remain in the country, ready as marplots to seize upon any opportunity promising any chance to disturb the established order of things. As her lines of communication are far better than ever before, she can more readily throw her troops to any given point to quell any insurrectionary movements. Heretofore, these revolutions and counter revolutions have been fatal to her credit abroad, for loans could not be negotiated in the money centers, for capitalists could see no promise of repayment from a government in power to-day, and which to-morrow might be overthrown. The governments changed as flowed the ebb and tide of changing fortune. Money seeks a stable order of things, faith, too, in the honor and ability of the promisor. For these reasons Mexico could not pay what she had borrowed, and of course could not borrow more; her revenues, such as they were, were applied and misapplied to her home obligations instead of her foreign debts. In consequence of such a condition of things, many public works were unbuilt, and other matters of public importance unprosecuted. Her internal dissensions reacted in a fatal manner upon her public credit and stopped her in the path of national progress. But now her credit, I am glad to say, is becoming re-established in the exchanges of this and the old world. I learn, within a very recent time, she has, through her financial agents, negotiated a loan in Europe of more than fifty millions of dollars. With this, it is her purpose to retire a portion of her English debt, her floating home debt bearing interest, and then apply the residue to some needed public works. The rate of interest is not more than six per cent. Confidence is of slow growth, money is sensitive, and a suspicion of confidence is fatal to investments. But the ability to make the loan just stated indicates clearly the confidence abroad in the stability of the government, and in the wise and faithful application of its revenues. Such a loan would give her much immediate relief, too, for in order to meet some of her most pressing obligations she has been compelled for this purpose to hypothecate her custom home receipts in advance. Hereafter this will be obviated by this economic negotiation.

And this restored confidence will grow with the growth and strength of Mexico. As she evinces a disposition and ability to meet her obligations, her credit will steadily advance in the monetary markets. And there is now no reason why she should not, in a few years, be able to command all the money she may desire. A foreign war or internecine strife are the only things which I can now see that might retard her future career. The importance of the maintenance of peace at home and having friendly relations abroad, can not be over-estimated. At this juncture, from a domestic or foreign war, however great her recuperative power, she would not recover for many long years to come. Above all things she needs peace, and must have it. More and more must come into prominence the pursuits of peace rather than the profession of arms. Every encouragement must be given to the husbandman and manufacturers, to the products of the soil, and the varied products of machinery. This will give employment to her people and bring in its train thrift and contentment. Hundreds of thousands of acres are now idle, untouched by the magical plough-share, but upon cultivation ready to recompense the ploughman with abundant yields. Fruits of almost infinite variety and description grow and are harvested at the gatherers' pleasure. These are some of the peaceful industries which make the homes of tenants happy. But one blast of war would change the face of fortune, and the plow would stand in its furrow and the wheels and spindles would cease to hum their music. The curse of war long outlives its duration, its blighting consequences beyond the reach of human computation. No, Mexico must keep herself from such a calamity, and give her people one good chance in the race of national life. The world is moving, and she should and will move with it, if only unhindered by some such incalculable misfortune as war. But I now think her danger is more to be apprehended from foreign than domestic strife. It may, and then may not, come in years.

As already said, she has an immense frontier, extending for many hundreds of miles, touching on the north and east the possessions of the United States. It will require the most consummate prudence, conservatism and no little statesmanship to prevent the friction engendered by conflicting interest, and the injuries inflicted by one side upon the other from sooner or later kindling the fires of open hostility. Closer commercial relations may avert such a catastrophe, and that these may have such a beneficent result is an argument in the interest of humanity, no less than is self-interest, why they should be established. Commerce is peace, non-interchange is estrangement. Let these commercial ties be made so strong that their disruption would mean untold losses to the parties, and then peace would have commerce as her most eloquent advocate. Again, let not the representatives of the respective governments be too hasty in their deliberations or conclusions, uninflunced by the clamors of partisans, and upon the presentations of grievances, give to them a prompt, but the fullest and fairest investigation. But to this matter, as already indicated, I believe, for the speedy adjustment of such complaints an international arbitration board, with carefully defined powers, would be more satisfactory. Such an organization, composed of prudent, just and wise members, would readily detect the causes of irritation and quickly apply the needed measures to remedy the evil by the infliction of punishment or the award of damages. Such complaints would not then linger for years in the archives of the State department, until the aggrieved had exhausted his patience, his time and his money in the futile attempts to get a final hearing. The expeditiousness of such a tribunal would be in the interest of justice, justice to both parties, and especially would it be in the furtherance of peace. Having heretofore adverted to this matter, I only do so again, at this time, to impress its importance upon the public mind, with a view of its ultimate adoption. As matters are at present, there is almost a practical denial of justice to the complainant, however meritorious his petition. Assuming it to be a valid claim, then, when shall he receive payment? is the question; "it may be in years, it may be not at all. Life is too active, and time is too fleeting to continue longer such unreasonable delays. The times demand quicker dispositions and more active measures.

CHAPTER LIX.

GENERAL REFLECTIONS—CONCLUDED.

Another thing: the enormous burdens now imposed upon importations and the products of the country, in the way of taxation in one form or other, must be greatly modified. The schedules of tariffs should be remodeled, imposing new imports, modifying and abolishing old ones to meet the public expenditures. Prohibitory tariffs bring death, and not life. I know this is a profound, economic study, and changed conditions require corresponding changes. What may be wise in one State, at one time, may be unwise in the same State at another time, or in different States. Each in its wisdom must judge of its financial needs and adopt the best measures to meet the same. But mere local benefits should never be permitted to override the general good. The advantages to the majority should be kept steadily in view, although in doing so local inconveniences and injuries may ensue. Lower taxation induces greater consumption, stimulates labor, and encourages trade. As decreased postage increased correspondence and postal receipts, to decrease taxation in many instances will increase importation and the public revenues. But in what class of cases these changes should be made, is a question to be resolved by the financiers of the country upon the most careful study and searching investigation. I entertain not a doubt that great changes may be made in the existing tariffs, and these to the improvement of the public exchequer. Every government must live upon its revenues derived from different sources. But these may be imposed in such a way, or upon such articles, as to impede the progress of the country, either crippling or permanently disabling it. The inter-State duties —that is, one State imposing duties upon articles coming into it from another State—is not only a flagrant violation of constitutional law, but a policy deserving the severest reprobation, and is ruinous in the extreme. The federal government should assert its power in this particular, and see that its organic law is obeyed. Longer now to permit its violation unchallenged, is to incur the disrespect of its most loyal citizens. Its lines of transportation should be extended, and its means of intercommunication greatly multiplied, opening up remote sections and giving increased facilities to the traveler and trade. The undeveloped wealth of the country can not now be foretold. Its agriculture in one sense is in its infancy, and many of its forests of precious woods untouched by the woodman's axe. Its mining regions, though worked for centuries, are yet unexhausted, and new developments are being made, and new bonanzas unearthed, rivaling those in the olden time of historic fame. All these things need new modes of work and handling, new and quicker ways of shipment. The mines of the Western United States are but the fringe, the outskirts of the immense mineral body which Mexico holds within her dominion. For time to come her mines must continue to furnish her principal articles of export. And just as new and improved methods are adopted for the extraction of these treasures will this industry farther grow in importance. Her sugar interest must grow in importance, too, but for years to come, by reason, among other things, of the scarcity of labor, it will remain of secondary value. I do not believe she will ever be a large exporter of sugar to the United States, certainly not for many years. Sorghum and beet sugar are now rapidly coming to the front, and as little as we may now dream, these may supersede in a few years to no inconsiderable extent the foreign product. Again, improved machinery for working the sugar-cane, new processes, the "diffusion" for instance, increases to the maximum the extraction, and adds amazingly to the aggregate product. It is said that the sugar-cane of Cuba contains about eighteen per cent. of saccharine matter, but the Cuban planter is only able to extract with his methods about seven per cent. The American cane contains twelve per cent. of saccharine matter, and by what is known as the "diffusion process," recently introduced, more than eleven per cent. of this is extracted. I think the ratio of extraction in Mexico is nearly the same as in Cuba. There is assuredly no immediate danger from Mexican sugar in the United States coming in serious conflict with the "infant industry" there.

Her coffee plantations, rightly handled and encouraged, will return ample profits to their proprietors. Those merit, if any industry does, the paternal care of the government. There is an immense area of territory adapted to its cultivation, and which, in the course of time, will be utilized for that purpose. The consumption of coffee is on the increase, and its production and proper stimulus will correspond to the demand. In the raising of this, she will find formidable rivals in some of her nearest neighbors, to say nothing of the immense output from the empire of Brazil.

But there is another thing which demands a change. The cumbrous copper money now in use should be retired, and this replaced by pieces of the finer metals as a circulating medium. Particularly would this be desirable for the purposes of small change. For larger transactions, the bills of her banks, bottomed on an unquestioned solid basis, might be used. Already some of her banking institutions do an immense business and enjoy the full confidence of the commercial public. There are others, I can say, whose notes are not received with so much favor, but in their circulation are subject to heavy discounts, and especially is this the case when found some distance from home. The National Bank of Mexico, located in the city, has a capital of more than thirty millions of dollars and transacts an enormous business. Mexico, in many localities, presents a fine field for banking operations. Capital, directed by integrity, enterprise, and business sagacity, in many of the larger cities would now pay splendid dividends. The advantages to the country, to be derived from good banking institutions, are coming to be appreciated more and more by enlightened nations. Probably it may not be generally known, but the city of Buenos Ayres, the capital of the Argentine Republic, South America, has a banking house with a capital of $37,000,000, circulation of $22,000,000, deposits of $56,000,000, and loans and discounts of $67,000,000. It is said the deposits in all the banks there amount to $64 per capita against $49 in the United States. It is unnecesary to make further reference to this matter, but we may indulge the hope that Mexico will, in a short time, so regulate her fiscal affairs, her currency, as to redound to her permanent good.

There is one other matter most noticeable to the student of Mexican affairs, seen here on every hand. I now refer to the priest-ridden character of the people. Priest-craft, it matters not under what banner of *denominationalism* it marches, should be resisted most firmly. Here it happens to be the Catholic hierarchy. The people in their religious life seem to have no thought, no mind, no will of their own, but all these are sunk in those of the priest. Independence is lost and manhood is surrendered. They consult the will of the priest, and not that of their Maker, for guides of conduct and rules of life. Servitude is their condition, and the priest is their master. For themselves they dare not think, or if they do, they dare not speak their thoughts. His power stifles their thoughts and seals their lips. He speaks, and they hear; he commands, and they obey. This obedience is full and prompt, for it is given to him who, they believe, holds the keys to the kingdom, who can shut and no man open; who can open and no man can shut. In his keeping they unreservedly entrust their eternal destiny—believe when they sleep on earth they will wake with him in heaven. They neither think, nor care to think, but simply to believe he holds their passports to the better world. With such a power, he moulds them as the pliant clay in his hands, and fashions them to his sovereign will. Here he has no rebellious subjects; their souls are not their own, and he is free to shape their lives as to him, not to them, seems best. His followers are, if we may so term them, a kind of human nonentities, existing in the sense of breathing, and yet not living in the sense of being free, moral agents. For their shortcomings, faults and crimes, he takes their confessions and expunges from the record the penalty for their sins. All the women here believe in these things with an unshaken faith, and the few men who do not, do n't believe in anything.

This is the pitiable religious condition in which we here find human beings; in this respect, probably here no better now than a century ago. The world has gone forward, but they have not gone forward with the world. Priest-craft still forges their shackles, and they still wear them, as it forged them, and they wore them in the long-ago. Changes everywhere have come in the march of time and the spread of civilization, but no changes here. The enlightened spirit of the age has here, as yet, failed to illumine the spiritual vision of these people. Their priest-worship and idolatry of saints bespeak their slavish debasement, which no language of mine can fitly portray. All ages and classes are affected by this priestly influence. If this were more frequently than at present directed in other channels, in the inculcation of right and honesty, in the denunciation of wrong, and villainy, and crime, and in the enforcement of the duties of good citizenship, with me it would lose much of its odium. If these surpliced dignitaries would only take half the pains and trouble to teach the youth their duties to society—doing right, being honest, and keeping innocent—that they take to impress them with their holy importance, and to teach them certain formulas, cross-making and genuflections, then the land would be freer from its hordes of robbers and assassins. With such an unlimited influence in this way much good might be accomplished. Better far that it should be used as a prevention of evil, than after its commission as a pardoning power. Too often the offender, after the pardon of his moral guilt by the priest—if then for his legal guilt society seeks his punishment—he thinks society regards him as its enemy, and he in turn becomes the open enemy of society. No, this is not the age for the continuance, much less the cultivation of such superstitious slavishness, and it should be buried with the follies of the past. A new era has dawned upon the world, and a better faith with a better reason, and a better practice, should guide to the heavenly haven life's mariners.

The spirit of investigation is abroad, the spirit of inquiry is awakened as never before, old errors must crumble into ruins, and Truth, born from above, must emerge into light, glorious in its developments, and as radiantly beautiful as the feet of them that bring the glad tidings of salvation. This Truth may have slumbered for centuries in the past, but in the centuries of the future, in the good providence of its Almighty Author, its saving manifestations as never before will be witnessed, and its conquests extended until at last the varied tribes, tongues and peoples of earth shall be gathered into the family of God. Let the unfettered truth have its free course.

CHAPTER LX.

CONCLUSION — LOVE OF THE OLD FLAG WHEN SEEN FROM A FOREIGN LAND.

I find I have already extended these general reflections beyond my anticipation, and, lest I be wearisome, I will now bring them to a close. But I will say that the foregoing are some of the more important matters, in my conception, deserving the earnest consideration of the Mexican people. It is probable these have received the attention of her thinking population; but as yet, for reasons which, when fully known, may be satisfactory, they remain in their present condition, subject to the criticism, and often animadversions of observant foreigners. I know it is easy to criticise the administration of others, even when those criticised may concur in the justness of the criticism, but from insuperable circumstances unknown to the critic, the line of policy already inaugurated must be pursued. The critic in the given case furnishes no new information, and by his obtrusive suggestions renders no practical aid to him who is, for the time, in management. The value of our observations must rest upon a basis as broad as the knowledge of the *entire* facts. So, while my observations are gratuitous, though founded upon an experience here of some years, I trust the friendly spirit in which they are offered will relieve them from any offensiveness.

And now, to my readers I will say, we have been journeying together for a considerable time; but the period now approaches when the " best of friends must part." We have visited the mountains of the Sierra Madre, and seen them in their loneliness, their ruggedness and beauty. The mountain streams have passed us, as they went flashing, in light and beauty, shouting to the sea. With awe-inspired souls we have looked upon those awful gorges, rents in nature's face, that tell of primeval throes, made in those early creative periods described by the Biblical writer as the mornings and evenings of the first days. We have seen some of the ruins of a long-lost, forgotten people. We have gone into the houses of the mountaineer, and familiarized ourselves with their characters, their habits and modes of life. We have looked into the different modes of government, to some extent examined their practical operations, their defects and excellencies. We have marked with pleasure the evidence of national progress, and indulged in prophecies of future greatness. We have ventured to point to some reefs ahead, to be shunned by the steersman of State, some lurking dangers in the sea of the future. And, if at times, in the discussion of characters, my language may have seemed severe, it was severe only because it was true. My words were not barbed with bitterness, but only winged with truth. The varities of climate have been marked by the diversities of products corresponding to the different altitudes. In some respects, we have found this a "goodly land," not exactly flowing in milk and honey, and with clustering grapes, like those of Eschol, but, as yet, more "goodly" in promise than fruition. We have found her a young Republic, struggling with the problems of self-government, and, I believe, honestly striving to "put off the old and put on the new," in order to elevate and better her people. She is our little sister, and, as she walks side by side and hand in ours, turns up her smiling face for some returning smile, some words of comfort, cheer and counsel. But to return; we have spoken of her great resources, her mountains of minerals, whose surface is explored, but whose depths are yet untouched. And as we passed, matters of internal polity have not been overlooked. That vital question, taxation in its different forms, has received some discussion. With much pleasure we have noted the question of education exciting an interest almost everywhere. We have seen educational institutions, increasing under the fostering care of the States and general government, both in numbers and efficiency. But there are many more things, to which we can not now refer, but to which we made hasty reference as we passed along. I hope our companionionship has been pleasant, unmarred by a single word or incident. To me it has been a labor of love to guide you in these wilds, to point out scenes such as elsewhere do not exist; to talk of men and things unlike those we have seen in other parts. It is grateful to my heart to think that with some these pages may have chased some cares away, and filled up the hours with some pleasant thoughts. To know that they had made one care, one trouble, one wrinkle less, would double my delight. As often ship acquaintances to a distant port part with keen regrets, never to see each other more, so it is with a feeling not unmixed with sadness we near our journey's close. As this is my first, perhaps my last literary excursion, I would not leave you here in the heart of the Sierra Madre, but we will make our adieus, retrace our steps to the frontier, cross over the river, and disband. However much our pleasure may here have been, on our return, the stars and stripes, when first seen from a foreign land, will thrill our hearts with a deeper joy than they ever inspired before. The moistened eye, the quivering lip, will speak the deep emotions of the heart. Once more the sight of that flag will cause the words of Drake to spring from the memory to the lips, and we all exclaim:

"When Freedom from her mountain height
Unfurled her standard to the air,
She took the azure robe of night
And set its stars of glory there."

Then its stars, seen from its streaming folds, will awake the patriotic minstrelsy of the heart. That flag is mine, and yours, and behind it is a power slumbering in the arms and wills of sixty millions of freemen. At the tocsin of war its embattled defenders would leap forth in full armor, as leaped Minerva in full panoply from the brain of Jove. Its eagles with unwearied wing can fly farther than those of Rome ever did.

Home at last, for in the shadow of that banner is every American's home. Gaze not, with longing eyes, across the Rio Grande. Build up and beautify the waste places of your own country. Make two spears of grass to grow where but one grew before. As already urged, build up the waste places with the useful arts and industries. And the waste lands, these beautify with flowering shrubs and vines, or, by an applied knowledge of agricultural chemistry and improved systems of tillage, convert them into waving grain fields. Inculcate a lofty patriotism and the true principles of popular government, carry them out, and its manifold blessings in ever increasing showers will fall upon our happy millions.

And now, to conclude, I will say, as said the Judean Roman governor, upon that occasion, the most momentous in the history of our race, "What I have written, I have written;" but to these words I must add, with a farewell bow, and a misgiving unaffected, "*would it were worthier.*"

www.ingramcontent.com/pod-product-compliance
Lightning Source LLC
Chambersburg PA
CBHW020526300426
44111CB00008B/554